W9-BMU-498

Praise for *Taking the Lead on Adolescent Literacy*

"The Literacy Project is a systemic process that guarantees all students access to superior instructional strategies."

—Kathleen P. Norton, Principal
Arvada High School
Jefferson County, CO

"Following the process outlined in this book allowed our literacy team to personalize the project to our school and needs. Our team presented our project to our staff in August and our teachers have implemented it faithfully. Our students know the slogan and are excited about the project. The literacy team has kept the excitement high for the year.

This literacy project changed the culture and focus of our school in less than a year."

—Trip Sargent, Principal
North Arvada Middle School
Jefferson County, CO

"I have seen numerous educational initiatives come and go in my forty some years working with schools, but nothing has been as important, relevant, or long lasting as adolescent literacy. Schools, with principals and teachers who have stayed the course with embedded literacy strategies across the curriculum, with a focus on literacy rich culture and structures in their buildings, with students using literacy strategies on their own, and with staff and students reading and sharing, are the schools that have made significant gains in their educational achievement."

—Betty A. Jordan, Director
Washington County Consortium
Machias, ME

"Judith Irvin and her team have created a valuable resource and guidebook for school districts serious about improving the literacy achievement of their students. This volume expands and deepens the other contributions they have provided, especially Taking Action on Literacy Leadership. *As a professional literacy educator actively involved in partnerships with schools and districts working to improve literacy, I read each chapter from a very concrete perspective: how did these suggestions and the lists of concerns and issues reflect my experiences and were the suggestions and model for change ones I could embrace? In each chapter I found honest descriptions of the tough issues faced by schools trying to focus on literacy across the content areas. More important, the chapters are full of guidelines and practical suggestions for dealing with the challenges. The implementation maps and the rubrics that help school literacy teams diagnose, establish goals, monitor implementation, and sustain the changes they want are particularly valuable resources. This team knows that change requires a systems approach with all levels of school and community involved over an extended time frame. I heartily recommend this as a very useful tool for schools wanting to implement a schoolwide commitment to literacy."*

—Donna Ogle, National-Louis University
Chicago, IL

"Wow! This book gives school and district leaders and teams the what, why, and how to do the rocket science work of getting every student to read and write at grade level or above. Principals and literacy teams no longer need to be stuck in the 'We don't know what to do next' world of frustration."

—Bess Scott, Director of Elementary Education
Lincoln Public Schools, NE

"The connections regarding best practice research from multiple fields—differentiation, professional development, curriculum mapping, 21st-century literacy, assessment, and instructional strategies—are critical and very well done. These connections are made in a professional,

understandable way with theories and classroom applications articulated across grade levels and in many formats: scoring guides, prose, questions, vignettes, case studies, and graphics."

—Darlene Castelli, Literacy Coach/Reading Specialist
Clayton High School, MO

"The most beneficial aspect of the literacy action planning process was providing training and asking for input from teachers from the very beginning. Literacy Support Team Members were able to reflect on the unique and specific strengths and needs of their buildings and utilize this information to develop a practical implementation plan. The time spent working together on the Literacy Action Plan helped to build community and foster a sense of ownership in the change process. Rather than being "acted upon" with a top-down initiative, staff members were an integral part of enacting change within their own learning environments and for their own students. This was very powerful and a primary reason that all four secondary schools were able to launch the initiative so successfully."

—Lisa White, District ELA Coordinator
Plymouth Public Schools
Plymouth, MA

"This rich resource walks middle and high school literacy leaders through a comprehensive process for conceptualizing, initiating, and, most important, sustaining a schoolwide literacy learning program. The authors clearly know teachers and schools, and their reality-tested tools will prove invaluable in guiding and supporting middle and high school literacy leaders."

—Doug Buehl, Author, *Classroom Strategies for Interactive Learning*

"Most school administrators know in concept that they need to have a Literacy Leadership Team, but what exactly would such a team do? Plan a book fair or a parent spaghetti night? Organize a contest for the most books read? Publish a 'word of the day?' These may all be worthy activities, but are these things that will help our students become stronger in their ability to access content knowledge through text? As educators living in this world of high-stakes accountability, we need a way to focus our activities to be sure that our hard work is well spent. The literacy action planning process developed by Dr. Judith Irvin and her colleagues has helped several schools in our district realistically assess their strengths and opportunities for improvement and develop concrete action plans for schoolwide literacy improvement."

—Connie Kolosey, Supervisor of Secondary Reading
Pinellas County, FL

"The Five-Stage Literacy Leadership Process in the book provided my principals and teachers with an easy-to-follow, research-based guide to develop a successful Literacy Program within their school."

—Jerryelyn L. Jones, Chief Area Officer, Area 24
Chicago Public Schools, Chicago, IL

FOR GRADES 4–12

Taking the Lead on Adolescent Literacy

ACTION STEPS FOR SCHOOLWIDE SUCCESS

Judith Irvin
Julie Meltzer
Nancy Dean
Martha Jan Mickler

Foreword by
ANDRÉS HENRÍQUEZ

A Joint Publication

Copyright © 2010 by Judith L. Irvin

All rights reserved. When forms and sample documents are included, their use is authorized only by educators, local school sites, and/or noncommercial or nonprofit entities that have purchased the book. Except for that usage, no part of this book may be reproduced or utilized in any form or by any means, electronic or mechanical, including photocopying, recording, or by any information storage and retrieval system, without permission in writing from the publisher.

For information:

Corwin
A SAGE Company
2455 Teller Road
Thousand Oaks, California 91320
(800) 233-9936
Fax: (800) 417-2466
www.corwin.com

SAGE India Pvt. Ltd.
B 1/I 1 Mohan Cooperative
Industrial Area
Mathura Road, New Delhi 110 044
India

SAGE Ltd.
1 Oliver's Yard
55 City Road
London EC1Y 1SP
United Kingdom

SAGE Asia-Pacific Pte. Ltd.
33 Pekin Street #02-01
Far East Square
Singapore 048763

Printed in the United States of America

Library of Congress Cataloging-in-Publication Data

Taking the lead on adolescent literacy : action steps for schoolwide success/Judith L. Irvin [et al.]; foreword by Andrés Henríquez.
"A joint publication with the International Reading Association"
p. cm.
Includes bibliographical references and index.
ISBN 978-1-4129-7980-1 (pbk.)
1. Language arts (Secondary) 2. Literacy programs. 3. School improvement programs. I. Irvin, Judith L., 1947- II. Title.

LB1631.T239 2010
428.4071'2—dc22 2009051374

This book is printed on acid-free paper.

10 11 12 13 14 10 9 8 7 6 5 4 3 2

Acquisitions Editor: Carol Chambers Collins
Associate Editor: Megan Bedell
Editorial Assistants: Sarah Bartlett, Allison Scott
Production Editor: Libby Larson
Copy Editor: Jeannette K. McCoy
Typesetter: C&M Digitals (P) Ltd.
Proofreader: Charlotte J. Waisner
Indexer: Ellen Slavitz
Cover and Graphic Designer: Michael Dubowe

Contents

Foreword

The publication of *Taking the Lead on Adolescent Literacy* marks an exciting moment for schools, students, and educational leaders across the country. It reflects a change in our understanding of literacy, and makes available the results of years of work to understand and bring attention to the needs of upper elementary, middle, and high school students. These adolescent learners have been overlooked far too long in the necessary, yet incomplete, efforts to improve schools and student learning.

When Carnegie Corporation's Advancing Literacy initiative was launched in 2003 the educational community and the country at large had awakened anew to the underlying crisis of literacy achievement in our schools. In 2001, The National Academy of Science release, *Preventing Reading Difficulties in Young Children,* along with the *Report of the National Reading Panel,* shaped the design of early-elementary literacy initiatives made possible by Title I funds, especially Reading First and Early Reading First. Additional funds provided much-needed resources for research in the area of early reading. While there were certainly controversies about the implementation of the government programs, the investment in reading was welcomed by many.

At the same time, educators' interest in the less-explored issue of adolescent literacy was on the rise. Two important publications helped catalyze this attention. The International Reading Association's excellent paper, *Adolescent Literacy: A Position Statement,* raised awareness and provided a primer for understanding adolescents' struggle with reading. The RAND Reading Study Group's report, *Reading for Understanding,* underscored the literacy skills needed for comprehension of complex text. These reports were released just as philanthropic dollars were being heavily invested in high school reform and at the same time that the Foundations realized that incoming ninth graders—as many as 70 percent according to the Nation's Report Card—were significantly behind in reading skills.

Carnegie Corporation of New York seized the moment, building upon its legacy of improving and expanding educational attainment with the launch of the Advancing Literacy Initiative. The goal was to ensure that middle and high school students received the attention they deserved and to address what the Corporation's president, Vartan Gregorian, had identified as a:

> challenging disconnect in our educational system, namely, that what is expected in academic achievement for middle and high school students has significantly increased, [yet] the way in which students are taught to read, comprehend, and write about subject matter has not kept pace with the demands of schooling (Carnegie Council on Advancing Adolescent Literacy, 2010, p viii.)

As the program officer leading this work, it became clear to me that not only was it essential to develop knowledge and practices around adolescent literacy, it was also essential to address the twin needs of developing public support and finding ways to engineer schools so that adolescent literacy would be a priority. We saw early on that leadership would be a key component in bringing critical mass and sustainability to adolescent literacy improvements over time. In fact, in the first report of the Advancing Literacy Program, *Reading Next: A Vision for Action and Research in Middle and High School Literacy* (Biancarosa & Snow, 2004) "leadership" was one of the 15 critical elements included.

To bring the work of adolescent literacy to scale, to make strides in increased academic achievement, high school graduation rates, and college attainment, we need to engage school leaders—especially principals—in this Herculean effort. But how? How do school leaders strategically plan for schoolwide change? How do school literacy leaders create a vision for literacy-rich schools? How can the use of data establish a foundation for focusing on literacy?

Taking the Lead on Adolescent Literacy: Action Steps for Schoolwide Success effectively tackles and answers these compelling questions. This thorough and practical guide is designed to help school and district leaders create and execute a successful plan for adolescent literacy. Judith Irvin and her colleagues present the knowledge, expertise, and mix of strategies needed for school and district leaders to develop a comprehensive plan, support teachers to improve instruction, use data, build leadership capacity, and allocate resources. These basic principles will put schools on track to an improved, sustained culture of literacy and student performance.

Now is exactly the right time for *Taking the Lead on Adolescent Literacy:* the data are available, the need is understood, and effective practices have been identified. The wealth of knowledge in this book paves the way for educational leaders to transform the educational outcomes and lives of their adolescent students.

This book will give you confidence, direction, and the necessary tools to enhance your own leadership, decision-making, and vision for your school. Good luck!

—Andrés Henríquez
Program Officer, National Program
Carnegie Corporation of New York

Acknowledgments

Corwin gratefully acknowledges the contributions of the following reviewers:

Molly Burger, Principal
Middleton Middle School
Middleton, ID

Darlene Castelli, Literacy Coach/Reading Specialist
Clayton High School
Clayton, MO

Joan Eggert, Reading Specialist, Grades 5–8
Indian Mound Middle School
McFarland, WI

Bess Scott, Director of Elementary Education
Lincoln Public Schools
Lincoln, NE

Bill Sommers, High School Principal
Chaska Public School
Austin, TX

About the Authors

Judith Irvin, PhD, is a professor at Florida State University in Tallahassee, Florida, and the executive director of the National Literacy Project, a nonprofit organization dedicated to improving middle and high school literacy. Her repertoire includes chairing the research committee for the National Middle School Association for six years and serving on the Commission on Adolescent Literacy of the International Reading Association. She has written and edited numerous books, chapters, and articles on adolescent literacy—most notably *Reading and the High School Student: Strategies to Enhance Literacy* (with Douglas Buehl and Ronald Klemp, 2007), *Strategies for Enhancing Literacy and Learning in Middle School Content Area Classrooms* (with Douglas Buehl and Barbara Radcliffe, 2007) and *Teaching Middle School Reading* (with James Rycik, 2005).

Judith recently completed two books as a result of a project funded by Carnegie Corporation of New York: *Taking Action on Adolescent Literacy: An Implementation Guide for School Leaders* (with Julie Meltzer and Melinda Dukes, Association for Supervision and Curriculum Development, 2007) and *Meeting the Challenge of Adolescent Literacy: Practical Ideas for Literacy Leaders* (with Julie Meltzer, Martha Jan Mickler, Melvina Phillips, and Nancy Dean, 2009). She is a speaker and consultant to school systems and professional organizations throughout the nation. Judith spent eight years as a middle and high school social studies and reading teacher.

Julie Meltzer, PhD, is Senior Advisor for Research, Strategy, and Design at Public Consulting Group's Center for Resource Management (PCG-CRM) in Portsmouth, New Hampshire. She is responsible for the design of consulting services related to 21st Century Teaching and Learning, Response to Intervention (RtI), and Literacy and Learning. As director of the Adolescent Literacy Project at the LAB at Brown University, she developed the Adolescent Literacy Support Framework showcased on the Knowledge Loom Web site and was on the development team for the Council of Chief State School Officers' (CCSSO) *Adolescent Literacy Toolkit*. A sought-after keynote speaker, author, reviewer, conference presenter, and workshop leader, she seeks to empower educators to apply promising research-based practices to support the literacy development and learning needs of students. Julie is a coauthor of *Meeting the Challenge of Adolescent Literacy: Practical Ideas for Literacy Leaders* (with Judith Irvin, Martha Jan Mickler, Melvina Phillips, and Nancy Dean, 2009), and *Taking Action on Adolescent Literacy: An Implementation Guide for School Leaders* (with Judith Irvin and Melinda Dukes, 2007). She is also the author of *Adolescent Literacy Resources: Linking Research and Practice* (2002), and articles that have appeared in *Educational Leadership, Phi Delta Kappan, Principal Leadership, In Perspective,* and other educational publications. She brings substantive experience as a teacher, teacher educator, and leadership coach to her work in the areas of systemic school improvement, capacity building, and design of professional development services and materials. Julie and her colleagues work with schools and districts throughout the country.

Nancy Dean, EdS, is Professor Emerita at the P.K. Yonge Developmental Research School, University of Florida, Gainesville, Florida. During her 39 years in education, she has taught middle and high school English, special education, reading, debate, social studies, English for speakers of other languages, and Advanced Placement English. She is also an experienced literacy coach and curriculum specialist.

Committed to school literacy reform and meaningful professional development, she has worked extensively with teachers and school leaders in urban and rural schools throughout the United States. She is an associate director of the National Literacy Project and a lead presenter for that organization. In addition, she is a national consultant in secondary literacy and literacy leadership and director of *Leadership Through Reading*, a cross-age tutoring program.

Nancy is the author of *Voice Lessons: Classroom Activities to Teach Diction, Detail, Imagery, Syntax, and Tone* (2000); *Discovering Voice: Voice Lessons for Middle and High School* (2006); and the *Writing Intervention Kit for High School* (2008). She is also coauthor (with Candace Harper) of *Succeeding in Reading: A Complete Cross-Age Tutoring Program* (2006), and *Meeting the Challenge in Adolescent Literacy: Practical Ideas for Literacy Leaders* (with Judith Irvin, Julie Meltzer, Martha Jan Mickler, and Melvina Phillips, 2009).

Martha Jan Mickler, PhD, is currently a private consultant specializing in adolescent literacy. She works with administrators and teachers in classroom and seminar settings with the focus on developing literacy leadership and helping teachers integrate literacy within academic and fine arts content areas. She has held a variety of leadership positions in education, including Supervisor of Secondary Reading (Pinellas County, Florida); Principal, Fairyland Elementary School (Walker County, Georgia); Supervisor of English and World Languages and Director of Teaching and Learning (Chattanooga Public Schools, Tennessee); and Director of Music Therapy (New Jersey Neuropsychiatric Institute, Princeton, New Jersey). She was also a resource teacher at Fairyland School and a piano instructor and performing artist for Cadek Conservatory (Chattanooga, Tennessee).

Martha Jan has been active in many professional organizations, including the National Council of Teachers, serving as President of the Tennessee Council of Teachers from 1997 to 1999. She serves on the Editorial Review Board for the *Journal of Adolescent and Adult Literacy* and has coauthored a book on literacy leadership: *Meeting the Challenge of Adolescent Literacy: Practical Ideas for School Leaders* (with Judith Irvin, Julie Meltzer, Melvina Phillips, and Nancy Dean, 2009). Her published articles have appeared in many periodicals, including the *Journal of Special Education*, *Classroom Leadership*, *Spelling Progress Quarterly*, and *Computers, Reading, and Language Arts*.

The hard work and dedication of many teacher leaders and literacy teams throughout the country were indispensable in the conceptualization and actualization of this book. Their voices, struggles, and triumphs echo through every chapter. This book is more than a "thank you." It is recognition of the power of education to change lives. It is to these hard-working and passionate administrators and teachers that this book is dedicated.

Judith Irvin
Julie Meltzer
Nancy Dean
Martha Jan Mickler

PART I

The Model, Process, and Rubrics

Rationale for a Schoolwide Focus on Literacy

School leaders like you are charged with improving student achievement and increasing graduation rates. This, as you know, is a daunting task. As students move through the grades, the task of providing high-quality education at all levels requires multifaceted and systemic decision making that often makes it hard to know where to start and, once started, how to stay on course.

However, we know that schools that specifically embark on a journey to improve literacy and learning have a better chance of graduating greater numbers of students who are active learners, proficient readers, and fluent writers. These schools are willing to prioritize literacy as a central mission of the school and to organize for action around this central theme. And in school after school, it is working. Higher numbers of graduates, more engagement with school by students and teachers, and higher test scores attest to the promise of this route.

During the past ten years, we have observed school leaders who know a great deal about what works in the essential areas of systemic school reform, teacher professional development, leadership coaching, and use of data. The key, however, is to put this body of knowledge to work as part of a schoolwide literacy improvement effort that will directly impact student literacy and achievement. Our work with school leaders throughout the country has shown us how a sustained focus on literacy can be used as a lever for school improvement. The literacy leadership process described in *Taking the Lead on Adolescent Literacy* will support you and your colleagues as you work to ensure students are prepared to meet their future as readers, writers, and thinkers.

WHY FOCUS ON LITERACY?

In multiple studies and policy reports, literacy (or the lack of literacy) has been closely linked to dropout rates, discipline issues, grades, employability, success in higher education, civic participation, and 21st-century skills. Indeed, literacy is essential for success in almost every area of life. Literacy is far more than the ability to read and write basic text. Rather, literacy is the ability to read, write, speak, listen, and think in order to learn, communicate, and make meaning of increasingly complex print and online texts. Literacy and content learning are deeply intertwined. If one struggles as a reader or writer, it is nearly impossible to succeed academically.

Whether your school is large or small, in an urban, suburban, or rural setting, your students will benefit from ongoing instruction and practice that enable them to meet the literacy demands of college, career, and good citizenship. As you think about students in your school, you know that some are performing considerably below grade level. Others, however, may be reading and writing on grade level but continue to struggle with the ever increasingly complex texts they are expected to comprehend and respond to. Some students may excel in the areas of reading and writing and, as a result, need more rigor and challenge to avoid boredom and academic apathy. Others may be unable to transfer literacy skills across all content areas or read strategically, analytically, or fluently when confronted with advanced texts. In all of these instances, it is critical that as a school leader you are able to plan, implement, and troubleshoot a literacy improvement effort that meets the literacy needs of all students in your school.

Ensuring that all students develop high levels of literacy requires schools to make a concerted, coordinated effort to improve students' proficiency as readers, writers, and critical and creative thinkers. This, in turn, makes possible increased student achievement, which leads to higher graduation rates. Our premise is simple—and is borne out by numerous examples: a systemic literacy improvement effort can be a powerful lever for school improvement. This systemic approach to improving literacy in Grades 4 through 12 involves the following synergistic actions:

- The development and communication of a compelling vision
- Ongoing collaboration between administrators and teachers
- Unflinching, data-based assessment
- The setting of clear, measurable goals that address important issues related to curriculum, instruction, assessment, and school culture
- The development of a quality literacy action plan
- Active implementation of the plan
- Monitoring of progress toward stated goals

These tasks are challenging and complex. But they are doable. Accomplishing these tasks through a focused, collaborative process can produce dramatic results for improved student literacy and learning.

Support Provided by This Book and the Literacy Leadership Process

This book includes field-tested and practical tools, approaches, rubrics, resources, and strategies that school and district leaders across the country have found helpful as they design, implement, and monitor a literacy initiative. Whether you are a building level administrator, a district or school literacy coach, a superintendent, supervisor, coordinator, or literacy team leader, this book will give you and your colleagues a process to enact systemic improvement of students' abilities as readers, writers, and thinkers. As you read this section of the book, you may be thinking the following:

- *Where do we start? I've already got more than I can handle. We do not have a literacy team, and I am not sure what the team would do if we had one.*
- *Another new initiative? We already have a school improvement plan. Our goal this year is dropout prevention and raising test scores. How does this conversation about literacy connect to these goals?*
- *Literacy is not my job. The English Department takes care of this.*

You and your colleagues can use this book to guide you through a five-stage, continuous improvement process. The process builds on best practices outlined in the research-and-practice literature as well as the successful literacy improvement efforts of many schools across the country. Using this literacy leadership process, you can work collaboratively with other teacher leaders and administrators to develop a literacy action plan and implement, monitor, and evaluate its success.

As with all effective action planning processes, the literacy leadership process described in this book is cyclical, beginning by assessing, implementing, and monitoring, and ending by reassessing, reviewing, and adjusting for the following year. What makes this process more than a general action planning template is the specificity of the materials. Everything in this process is designed to support the design and implementation of an effective literacy action plan in upper elementary, middle, and high schools.

Relationship of the Literacy Leadership Process to the *Taking Action Literacy Leadership Model*

The literacy leadership process is based on the *Taking Action Literacy Leadership Model* that was developed through a project funded by the Carnegie Corporation of New York. The model was designed to answer the question "What do literacy leaders need to do to successfully improve student literacy and learning in Grades 4 through 12?" The model is based on multiple data sources, including strategies that successful principals use to improve student literacy in their schools, the research and practice literature, feedback from educational leaders throughout the country, and reviews by a national advisory board. The model is fully described in *Taking Action on Adolescent Literacy: An Implementation Guide for School Leaders* (Irvin, Meltzer, & Dukes, 2007). The model incorporates two synergistic components: goal areas (represented in the graphic by a center circle surrounded by two concentric bands) and action points (represented in the graphic by a five-point star).

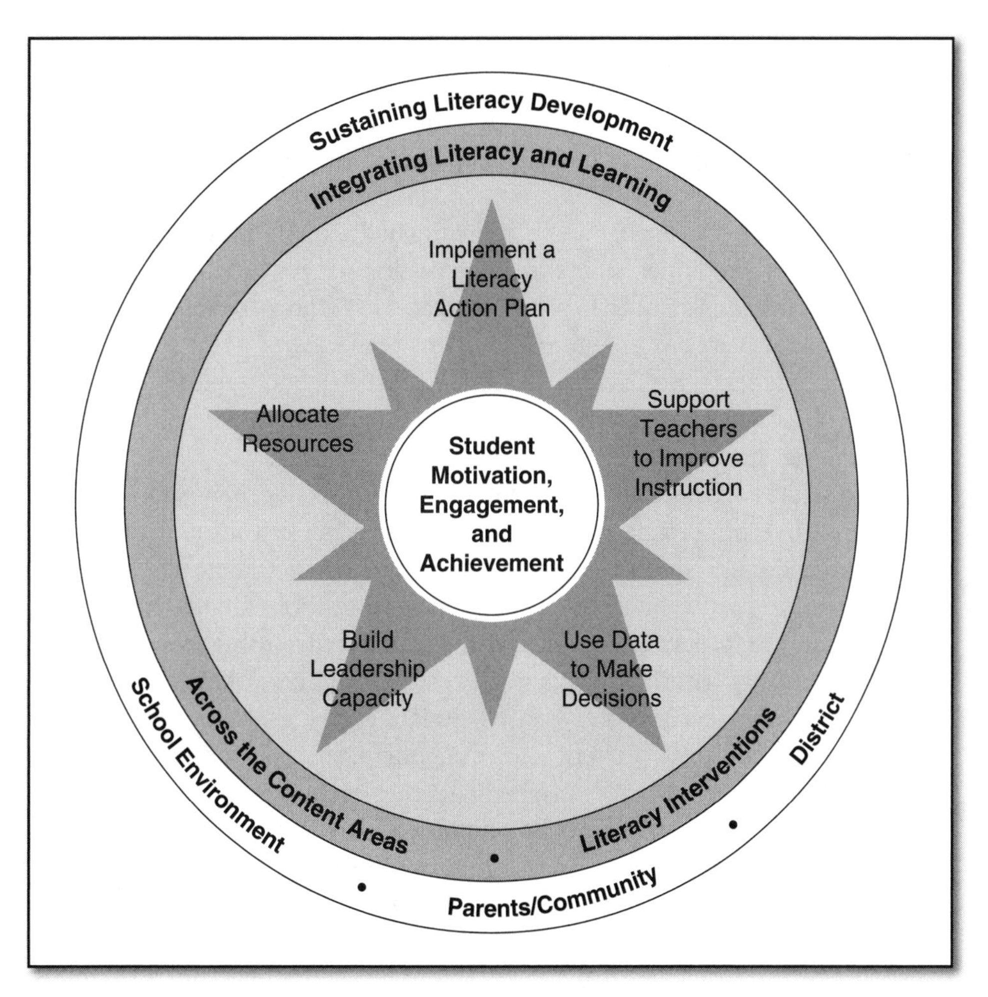

Taking Action Literacy Leadership Model

Understanding the components of the *Taking Action Literacy Leadership Model* helps a literacy team understand the larger picture of school change that leads to a sustainable literacy improvement effort. The set of six literacy action rubrics that are the centerpiece of the literacy leadership process are aligned with this model.

Goal Areas of the Model

The goal areas of the model correspond to the three critical outcomes of a schoolwide literacy improvement effort. At the center of the literacy initiative is *Student Motivation, Engagement, and Achievement.* When students are motivated and engaged to read and write in school, they can improve their abilities as readers, writers, and thinkers. Improved achievement follows, both in content knowledge and in literacy and learning skills. The second goal area is *Integrating Literacy and Learning,* which focuses on the school's instructional offerings and has two components: *Literacy Across the Content Areas* and *Literacy Interventions. Literacy Across the Content Areas* includes the content-focused courses that students take as they move through the grades (e.g., math, science, social studies, English/language arts, art, music, and foreign language). Students grow as readers and writers when they learn to apply literacy skills (such as activating prior knowledge, summarizing, questioning, and sequencing) to complex content area text. *Literacy Interventions* targets those students whose performance is significantly below their grade placement level. Literacy interventions can be offered in many formats, including an academic literacy class, an English language learners (ELL) teacher team teaching with an English/language arts teacher, or before and after school tutoring sessions. Whatever the format, literacy interventions are intended to provide targeted assistance to under-performing students so that they become more proficient readers and writers. Addressing the literacy and learning needs of all students in a school typically requires a focus on both components (content area and intervention) of *Integrating Literacy and Learning* to meet students' literacy and learning needs.

The goal area represented by the outer band, *Sustaining Literacy Development,* represents three important components necessary to sustain and promote a school-based literacy improvement initiative. First, it is critical to establish a *Literacy-Rich School Environment.* This includes a school climate that actively communicates to students that they are important contributing members of the school community through displays of current student work in hallways and classrooms, evidence of literacy-related student activities, and celebrations of progress. The school environment is also, of course, positively or adversely influenced by the policies, structures, schedule, and practices of the school. When these policies and structures focus on supporting all students to grow as readers, writers, and thinkers, a literacy-rich culture can be developed and maintained.

Parents and Community Members can also provide critical resources for student literacy development. When schools work collaboratively to invite and access the support and opportunities provided by their families and through the community, students get the message that they and their futures are seen as a valuable asset worth investing in.

Finally, *District Support* can mitigate the many roadblocks and pitfalls that often accompany fledgling initiatives. Districts can broker resources across schools, establish literacy improvement as a priority across the district, and facilitate school-based efforts. District leaders can provide schools with resources to support teachers as they embark on a new instructional model where a strict focus on content delivery shifts to an expectation that teachers provide literacy-embedded content instruction. District leadership can also provide direct support to instructional leaders through professional development and to school-based literacy leadership teams as they carry out their literacy action plans.

Action Points of the Model

The five action points located in the center of the model describe the actions that literacy leaders need to take to initiate and sustain a literacy improvement effort successfully: (1) implement a plan, (2) support teachers to improve instruction, (3) use data, (4) build leadership capacity, and (5) allocate resources. These action points are not necessarily sequential. However, our experience with schools has shown us that designing and implementing an effective literacy action plan is critical to achieving results. Without a solid plan, the good intentions of teachers and leaders may evolve into random activities that lack cohesion and purpose. But developing and implementing a plan to improve literacy can be complicated and time-consuming. Further, many plans get developed that do not ever get implemented. The quality of the plan only matters if it is put into action to improve students' literacy and learning. A guided process for developing and implementing an effective literacy plan is, therefore, the central topic of this book.

Literacy leaders take many different approaches to initiating and sustaining literacy improvement. Some begin with professional development and supporting teachers to improve instruction, some begin with collecting and examining the data, some begin by establishing a literacy team and building leadership capacity, and some begin by locating resources to support the effort. Sooner or later, we found that a successful literacy improvement initiative requires all five of these actions.

These actions correspond to the five action points on the graphic of the *Taking Action Literacy Leadership Model.* You will learn more about these action points in Chapter 4 (Stage 4) when the team uses the action points to troubleshoot issues and challenges that can accompany the plan's implementation. The action points are highlighted again in Chapters 6 and 7 where they are used to show action steps that school and district leaders can take to ensure adequate support of school-based literacy improvement efforts.

A second book, *Meeting the Challenge of Adolescent Literacy: Practical Ideas for Literacy Leaders* (Irvin, Meltzer, Mickler, Phillips, & Dean, 2009), is also aligned to the *Taking Action Literacy Leadership Model.* This book was written to assist literacy leaders as they address common challenges and barriers to literacy improvement from an issues-based perspective. Using the action points of the *Taking Action Literacy Leadership Model,* the book provides ideas and approaches that literacy leaders can use to address sixteen critical issues. The tools included in *Meeting the Challenge of Adolescent Literacy* may be particularly useful to you during the implementation stage of the action planning process (Chapter 4, Stage 4). Resource E at the back of this book contains a matrix showing resources from the first two books, *Taking Action on Adolescent Literacy* and *Meeting the Challenge of Adolescent Literacy,* and how the resources correspond to the five stages of the literacy leadership process.

HOW THE LITERACY LEADERSHIP PROCESS WAS DEVELOPED

The four authors of this book have spent many years working in schools and districts helping educators develop, implement, and monitor schoolwide literacy action plans. In our work with literacy leadership teams, we have noticed that well-meaning team members often want a quick solution to their literacy challenges. As a result, administrators or teacher leaders tend to identify a need and then procure a new program or add an additional course to meet that need. This fragmented approach, while well intended, often becomes narrow in focus and fails to put in place the structures and policies that make meaningful changes sustainable.

Over the past decade, we have developed a process that helps literacy leaders build a comprehensive, sustainable literacy improvement effort. This literacy leadership process is based on six literacy action rubrics that are aligned to the goal areas of the *Taking Action Literacy Leadership Model.* These rubrics have been field-tested over the past several years with school-based literacy teams in several states across the United States.

The next section of this book, Introduction to the Literacy Action Rubrics, introduces you to the first five literacy action rubrics that are school-based (the sixth rubric describes the district's role in supporting school-based literacy improvement efforts and is discussed in detail in Chapter 7). The components of each rubric are summarized so you can get an overview of the elements that are critical to a schoolwide literacy improvement effort. Descriptions of what these components look like in action at the upper elementary, middle, and high school levels can be found in Resource C. Literacy leadership teams that are charged with developing and implementing a literacy improvement plan will use the literacy action rubrics in both Stage 2 (Chapter 2) and Stage 5 (Chapter 5) of the literacy leadership process. Team members will find it helpful to refer back to the rubrics frequently to identify further needs, troubleshoot implementation, monitor progress, and refine action steps. School and district administrators can use the literacy action rubrics to come quickly up to speed with what needs to be addressed as part of a systemic focus on improving literacy. District administrators can use Literacy Action Rubric 6 to develop a districtwide literacy action plan that supports ongoing, school-based literacy improvement efforts.

THE FIVE-STAGE LITERACY LEADERSHIP PROCESS

You may have read school improvement plans that are well written and speak to the many needs of a school. We have found, however, that many improvement plans fail to specifically target literacy improvement as central to the school's mission even when literacy has been identified as an area that needs to be addressed. We find that many improvement plans also prescribe changes unrelated to the specific strengths and needs of the school or that the changes that are planned, while well-meaning, will not lead to the desired increases in student achievement. We suspect that in many cases those charged with improving student literacy and learning are not certain which steps would be most helpful to take.

The literacy leadership process outlined in this book is quite different from prescriptive approaches. We do not define your school's literacy needs, nor do we dictate which components your school literacy plan should include. Instead, the literacy leadership team assesses the literacy strengths and needs of the school using the literacy action rubrics that focus the team's attention on important components of literacy improvement. As the team proceeds through the five-stage process to develop and implement a customized plan, they address the needs of students and build on the existing capacity of the school. The five stages of the continuous improvement process described in this book represent the cyclical nature of assessment, planning, implementation, monitoring, review, and revision.

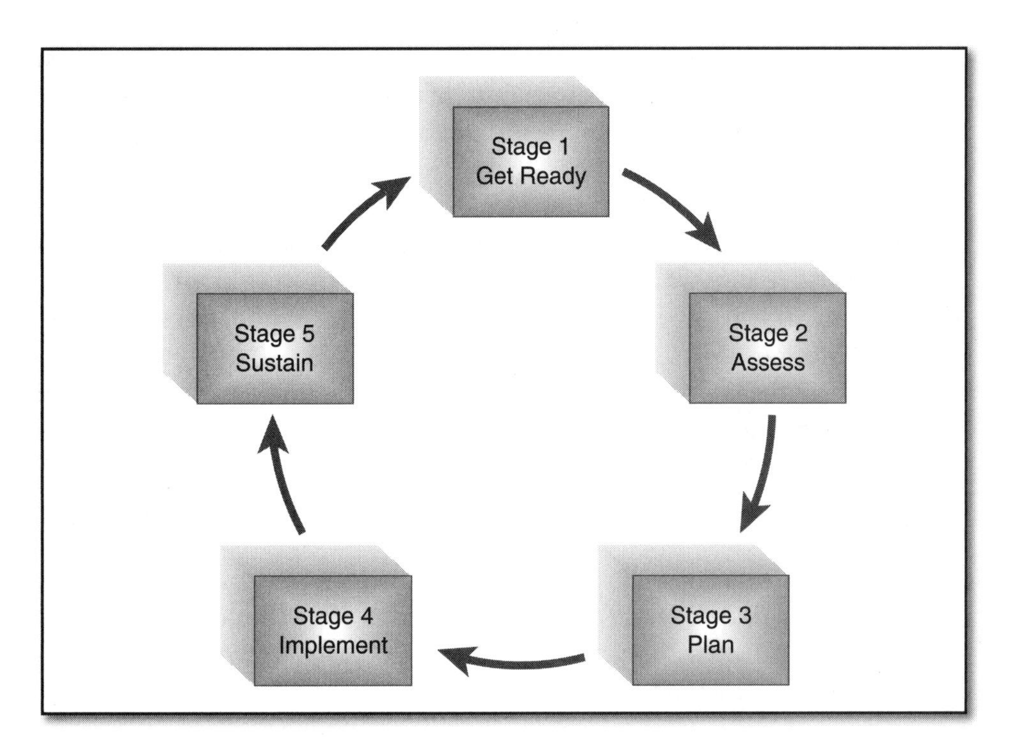

The Literacy Leadership Process

In Stage 1, you and your colleagues build the literacy leadership team and establish the need for a literacy improvement effort. You create, reestablish, or affirm the literacy leadership team and build a data-driven vision for a culture of literacy that will inspire the entire school to join forces in the literacy improvement initiative.

In Stage 2, the literacy team identifies the strengths of your school, examines your school data, uses the literacy action rubrics to assess your school's capacity to support systemic literacy development, and converts the self-assessment into measurable literacy action goals. This step-by-step process will help you and the other members of your literacy leadership team determine the scope of your literacy improvement effort and establish appropriate literacy action goals for your school.

In Stage 3, the literacy team develops implementation maps for each of the literacy action goals using the literacy action rubrics as a guide. We provide you with an implementation map development protocol so that you have a step-by-step process for developing your more formal literacy action plan. We also provide you with a sample implementation map to give you an idea of how action planning links to the goal areas and literacy action rubrics of the *Taking Action Literacy Leadership Model.* We suggest ways of soliciting feedback on your goals and your action plan from the entire school community and a process for finalizing your plan.

In Stage 4, you begin implementing your literacy action plan. The book provides support as you monitor and troubleshoot the implementation of the plan and assess the progress you have made toward your goals during the year. Since your plan has been designed by your literacy leadership team based on data and the team's collective understanding of your school, chances are it will not end up on a shelf gathering dust. Just to make sure, however, we provide you with processes and tools to keep your plan's action steps front and center in the minds (and actions) of teachers and staff. We suggest strategies that the team can use to organize for action and generate more active participation in the initiative by students, teachers, and administrators. We provide you with strategies to troubleshoot implementation when the data suggest that progress is slow toward one or more of the action goals. We also remind you of the importance of celebrating progress, and we provide some ideas on how you might involve the school community in these celebrations.

In Stage 5, the literacy leadership team reviews summative data as outlined by the literacy action plan to determine if the goals have been met. Based on the data, the team decides whether to keep a specific goal and revise the action steps as needed, discard the goal, select a new goal, or perhaps to move to another goal area from the *Taking Action Literacy Leadership Model.* You will revisit the literacy action rubrics and will complete new implementation maps for new and revised goals. In this stage, we also provide strategies for evaluating the efficacy of the team and for sustaining momentum as you move forward with the literacy initiative into the next school year.

HOW TO USE THE LITERACY LEADERSHIP PROCESS

Taking the Lead on Adolescent Literacy is designed as a comprehensive support for developing, implementing, and monitoring a literacy action plan for your school. If you are at the very beginning of this effort, you will probably want to follow each of the steps sequentially. If you already have a literacy plan, you may wish to scan Stage 1 and see if you want to conduct any of these activities before moving on to Stages 2 and 3. If you proceed to Stage 2, you may wish to choose one or two rubrics, conduct a schoolwide assessment, and use this information to revise, refine, or update your current literacy improvement goals. If your school has been engaged in a literacy improvement effort for two to four years, you might scan the information in Stages 1, 2, and 3 to determine if you want to engage in any of these activities but may wish to focus your efforts on Stages 4 and 5.

We have field-tested the components of the process extensively to be sure that the process is both efficient and effective in supporting literacy improvement. Although you may begin at different stages of the process, it is essential that you carefully consider where to begin and what to include. Often, the omission of steps in the process will make more work in the long run. For example, taking the time to build consensus on important issues and sharing ownership of the literacy action plan facilitates implementation and ensures that there is greater participation by members of the school community.

Good luck! We hope *Taking the Lead on Adolescent Literacy* will provide the ongoing guidance you need to establish or sustain a robust literacy improvement effort in your school or district.

Introduction to the Literacy Action Rubrics

The six literacy action rubrics are at the center of the literacy leadership process described in this book. The purpose of each literacy action rubric is to make the elements of an effective schoolwide literacy improvement initiative clear and concrete. The rubrics can be used to assess levels of implementation based on a range of criteria rather than a single numerical score. Using the rubrics, literacy team members can determine qualitative differences in levels of implementation of the components that support the success of a schoolwide literacy initiative. The rubrics can be used

- by a literacy leadership team, teaching team, department, or professional learning community to understand the core components of a schoolwide literacy initiative and to develop a common language and common vision of what an effective literacy improvement effort would look like (see Chapter 1);
- to conduct a needs assessment, identifying areas of current strength and weakness and supporting the development of improvement goals (see Chapter 2);
- to develop action steps associated with each literacy action goal, specifying areas where work is needed (see Chapter 3);
- by a literacy leadership team to troubleshoot implementation and measure progress toward stated goals (see Chapter 4);
- by a literacy leadership team to update goals and revise the implementation maps and literacy action plan for the following year (see Chapter 5);
- by school administrators to develop literacy walk-through focus areas, to discuss literacy goals with teachers, and to develop a mentoring program for new teachers (see Chapter 6); and
- by district administrators to conduct a needs assessment across schools and/or support school-based teams to engage in the literacy leadership process. District administrators can also use Literacy Action Rubric 6, the District Rubric, to conduct a district needs assessment, to determine how to best support school-based literacy efforts and to develop a districtwide literacy action plan (see Chapter 7).

The literacy action rubrics focus the conversation on what teachers and leaders can (and should) do to support students to improve their reading, writing, and thinking. Individual teachers can, and often do, provide rich literacy and learning experiences for students. In the absence of a schoolwide literacy improvement effort, however, literacy support for students can be haphazard and often results in uneven access to literacy instruction and guided practice. Whether or not students receive improvement-related content literacy instruction is often determined by factors such as the preferences and pedagogy of individual teachers, the types of reading and writing students will do as a part of each class, grading and assessment practices, types and availability of interventions, and the design of the master schedule.

When viewed as an interrelated set of variables, the literacy action rubrics describe what is necessary to put in place if we truly want to improve student literacy and learning. The rubrics highlight the schoolwide practices that teachers and administrators can use to activate their collective power to make a difference for the students they serve. The indicators on each rubric describe specific, concrete ways that educators serving students in Grades 4 through 12 can provide this support effectively and systemically.

The core components of each rubric are based in the research and practice literature about what best supports improved student literacy development. The literacy action rubrics were field-tested over a three-year period with school-based literacy teams in several states. Teams used the rubrics in multiple ways and provided input on where the components and indicators needed to be clearer. Each rubric was further reviewed for practicality, usability, and consistency. This iterative revision cycle has produced a set of tools that educators can use confidently to guide their work as they implement literacy improvement efforts in their schools.

DESCRIPTION OF THE RUBRICS

The six literacy action rubrics are aligned to the three goal areas of the *Taking Action Literacy Leadership Model*. For each rubric, we used the conceptual base of the leadership model to design a scoring guide focused on implementation of that goal area. The three goal areas and six rubrics are as follows:

1. Student Motivation, Engagement, and Achievement (Rubric 1)
2. Integrating Literacy and Learning
   - Literacy Across the Content Areas (Rubric 2)
   - Literacy Interventions (Rubric 3)
3. Sustaining Literacy Development
   - Literacy-Rich School Environment, Policies, and Culture (Rubric 4)
   - Parent and Community Involvement (Rubric 5)
   - District Support of School-Based Literacy Improvement Efforts (Rubric 6; this rubric is discussed in Chapter 7)

All of the literacy action rubrics have a consistent format and text structure. Each rubric has a *desired outcome* statement, which clearly describes what the school community would be doing if the goal area was being adequately addressed. Each rubric is then broken down into *components.* Within each component are *indicators* that precisely describe each aspect of the component. Each indicator within a component is described at four *levels of implementation:*

Level 1: *Little or no evidence* of implementation

Level 2: Evidence of *emerging* implementation

Level 3: Evidence of *consistent* implementation

Level 4: Evidence of *exemplary* implementation

Level 4, *exemplary implementation,* is the ultimate goal, describing optimal literacy support and development. This level represents what an upper elementary, middle, or high school that successfully focuses on literacy improvement looks, acts, and feels like. Solid, consistent implementation at Level 3 should result in improvement of student literacy and learning. Levels 1 and 2 indicate areas of concern and a need for concentrated effort to meet the desired outcomes of improved student literacy and learning.

As in the *Taking Action Literacy Leadership Model* itself, the components of the six rubrics overlap and are synergistic. That is, actions planned to address one component will typically impact others. In fact, one criterion for inclusion of a component is its likelihood to support literacy development on multiple levels. You will notice that in some cases individual components are repeated on more than one rubric. Teams can be sure that, no matter which goals they focus upon, essential elements of an effective literacy action plan will be addressed.

In the rest of this section, you will find a brief description of each of the five literacy action rubrics that focus on *school level implementation* followed by a list of the rubric's components and indicators. The complete rubrics are provided at the end of this chapter. The following summary of the rubrics is helpful before you decide which of the rubrics you will use to develop or revise your literacy action plan. However, we suggest that you examine the rubrics themselves carefully in order to understand the components at each level of implementation. Resource C provides examples of what each component of each rubric "looks like" at Level 4 implementation in the upper elementary, middle, and high school levels. Depending on the literacy team's individual and collective level of expertise, you may want to refer to Resource C as you review each rubric, clarifying and discussing relevant terms and building a conceptual understanding of each of the goal areas of the *Taking Action Literacy Leadership Model.*

Rubric 1: Student Motivation, Engagement, and Achievement

The *Student Motivation, Engagement, and Achievement* rubric describes five classroom practices that motivate students to engage in reading, writing, and learning—connections to other life experiences, choice, collaboration, use of technology, and goal setting. In addition, the rubric addresses specific contextual support for improving student motivation, engagement, and achievement in school, such as teacher expectations, literacy instruction, feedback and grading practices, and recognition of student work. In the table that follows, you will find a chart of the components of Rubric 1 and a summary of the indicators, focused on the essential aspects of quality implementation.

Rubric 1: Student Motivation, Engagement, and Achievement	
Desired Outcome: Students actively engage in reading, writing, and thinking to improve learning outcomes.	
Component	**Summary of the Indicators**
A. Relevance	• Connections between learning and other life experiences • Meaningful assignments
B. Choice	• Options of how to learn • Options of what to read and write • Options of how to demonstrate learning
C. Collaborative learning	• Student collaboration • Pair and small group work with clear roles, tasks, and expectations
D. Use of technology	• Use of technology for research, communication, and collaboration • Use of technology to research, write, and present
E. Goal setting	• Use of goals to improve students' performance as readers, writers, and learners
F. Teacher expectations	• Communicated belief that all students will succeed academically • Use of modeling and guided practice opportunities to help students meet high expectations
G. Classroom instruction	• Focus on reading, writing, and vocabulary instruction across the curriculum • Use of classroom routines to involve students actively in reading, writing, and learning • Use of instructional strategies to strengthen content learning while supporting literacy development • Student's independent use of literacy support strategies
H. Feedback and grading practices	• Specific feedback on student performance • Use of rubrics and models • Student-centered grading practices
I. Recognition of student work	• Prominent display of student work • Public recognition of academic achievement

Rubric 2: Literacy Across the Content Areas

The *Literacy Across the Content Areas* rubric describes six components to enhance instruction in the content areas. Four of these—classroom instruction, differentiation, assignments, and research and use of text—are related to individual teacher practice. Two of these components—curriculum alignment and feedback and grading policies—are more reliant on departmental, grade-level, or school-level policies. All six directly impact the likelihood of students' active involvement with reading, writing, and vocabulary development as an integral part of content area teaching and learning. A systemic approach to implementing these components would mean that implementation is an expectation in all classrooms and supported through teacher professional development, monitoring, and policies and procedures, becoming part of the very culture of the school. In the table that follows, you will find a chart of the components of Rubric 2 and a summary of the indicators, focused on the essential aspects of quality implementation.

Rubric 2: Literacy Across the Content Areas **Desired Outcome:** Teachers consistently integrate high quality reading, writing, and vocabulary instruction to improve all students' literacy development and content learning.	
Component	**Summary of the Indicators**
A. Classroom instruction	• Content area reading, writing, and vocabulary instruction are emphasized • Teachers use classroom routines to involve students in reading, writing, and learning • Teachers use strategies to strengthen content learning and literacy development • Teachers encourage students to use literacy support strategies
B. Curriculum alignment	• Content area courses include the development of specified literacy skills • Literacy development and content build by grade level • Rigorous content and strong literacy support
C. Differentiation	• Use of flexible grouping • Use of different materials for different interests and skill levels • Use of strategies to support learning needs
D. Feedback and grading practices	• Specific feedback on student performance • Use of rubrics and models • Student-centered grading practices
E. Assignments	• Meaningful purpose • High order thinking • Students work collaboratively • Varied ways to demonstrate learning • Use of technology
F. Research and use of text	• Use of a variety of text • Regular research with synthesis of multiple sources • Opportunities to present findings

Rubric 3: Literacy Interventions

The *Literacy Interventions* rubric describes the components of a successful literacy intervention program that supplements quality content literacy instruction in the classroom to address the needs of struggling readers and writers. The five components of the rubric describe the requisite teacher knowledge and skills to accelerate the progress of struggling readers and writers and the systemic support needed to implement an exemplary intervention program. These include the use of data to inform placement and instruction, fidelity of intervention implementation, differentiated literacy support, appropriate staffing, and teacher collaboration. In the table that follows, you will find a chart of the components of Rubric 3 and a summary of the indicators, focused on the essential aspects of quality implementation.

Rubric 3: Literacy Interventions	
Desired Outcome: Appropriate and adequate literacy interventions exist to support struggling readers and writers to attain and maintain grade level achievement within the context of a schoolwide literacy improvement effort.	
Component	**Summary of the Indicators**
A. Reading assessment	• Availability of data to determine students' reading levels • Availability of additional testing to determine needs of struggling readers • Reading assessment data collected multiple times
B. Use of data	• Use of multiple types of data for student placement • Use of progress monitoring • Use of data to inform instruction
C. Types of interventions	• Multiple types and formats of interventions • Use of placement and exit procedures • Differentiated literacy support in the content areas
D. Staffing	• Qualified intervention teachers • ELL and special education teachers have background in literacy • Availability of a reading specialist to work with content and intervention teachers
E. Implementation of interventions	• Fidelity of implementation • Instruction matched to student needs • Materials and technology support instruction
F. Teacher collaboration	• Content area and intervention teacher collaboration

Rubric 4: Literacy-Rich School Environment, Policies, and Culture

The *Literacy-Rich School Environment, Policies, and Culture* rubric describes the eight components essential to creating a literacy-rich environment and the structures, support, schedule, and policies needed to fully implement a culture focused on literacy improvement. The interrelated components of this rubric include a clear vision for improved literacy, high teacher expectations, time dedicated to literacy, recognition and display of student work, active teacher involvement, a master schedule that supports literacy, literacy-related clubs and activities, and an active library media center. The table that follows is a chart of the components of Rubric 4 and a summary of the indicators focused on the essential aspects of quality implementation.

Rubric 4: Literacy-Rich School Environment, Policies, and Culture

Desired Outcome: The school's culture, environment, policies, and support structures focus on improving literacy and learning.

Component	Summary of the Indicators
A. Vision	• Articulated, shared vision for improved literacy • Evidence of a focus on literacy in classrooms • Resources indicate support for literacy
B. Teacher expectations	• Communicated belief that all students can succeed academically • Use of modeling and guided practice opportunities to help students meet high expectations
C. Time to read	• Multiple opportunities to read, write, and discuss content
D. Recognition of student work	• Prominent display of student work • Public recognition of of meeting individual and collective literacy goals
E. Teacher participation	• Participation in literacy professional development • Sharing of resources and strategies • Use of data to improve instruction
F. Master schedule	• Time for literacy interventions • Common planning time to work on literacy and learning • Time for literacy-related professional development
G. Clubs and activities	• Literacy-related clubs and extra-curricular activities • Authentic literacy experiences
H. Library media center	• Consistent use of the library media center • Variety of relevant books and other materials, including leveled print materials • Certified, qualified personnel with background in literacy • Media and technology center as a resource for teachers and students

Rubric 5: Parent and Community Involvement

The *Parent and Community Involvement* rubric describes family and community support for literacy activities at the school and how this support can enhance the school's literacy program. This rubric focuses on the benefits gained when the school collaboratively works with families and community members to support the success of literacy improvement efforts through regular two-way communication and sponsorship of literacy-related activities. The rubric also notes the importance of student ownership of the literacy initiative and student participation in sharing their progress as readers, writers, and learners in Grades 4 through 12. The table that follows is a chart of the components of Rubric 5 and a summary of the indicators focused on the essential aspects of quality implementation.

Rubric 5: Parent and Community Involvement	
Desired Outcome: Families and community members work closely with school leaders to actively support the school's focus on literacy development.	
Component	**Summary of the Indicators**
A. Involvement	• Family support for literacy • Family and community participation in literacy activities • Community support for literacy experiences outside of school
B. Communication	• Regular communication with all stakeholders • Native language outreach for ELL families • Public forums to disseminate information about the literacy initiative
C. Collaborative support	• Teacher-family collaboration about literacy progress • Provision of literacy-support resources to families • Student involvement in communicating literacy progress

Rubrics 1 through 5 focus on school implementation and the next section describes how you and your colleagues can use these literacy action rubrics to support your work of improving literacy and learning. Rubric 6 is the district rubric and is discussed further in Chapter 7.

USING THE LITERACY ACTION RUBRICS

Once you understand the structure and content of the literacy action rubrics, you are ready to use them to improve your school's literacy efforts. We wrote the components and indicators to be as jargon free as possible. However, some general education terms used in the rubrics, such as *differentiation* or *curriculum alignment,* have a specific meaning when applied to literacy instruction. You may wish to discuss these terms and build a common language with your colleagues about effective literacy practice and support using Resource C (Examples) and Resource F (Glossary).

As described in the beginning of this chapter, you can use the literacy action rubrics for many purposes. First, as you have probably already discovered, you can use the rubrics to learn about literacy. You can examine the indicators, the components and levels of implementation, and the examples of the components in action to deepen your understanding of the concepts and best practices of a literacy initiative.

We have also found that the rubrics can help teachers, administrators, and students create a vision for and collaboratively define what a literacy-rich school looks and feels like as suggested in Chapter 1. Educators often have a hard time implementing what they cannot collectively visualize. In Chapter 2, your team will read about how to use the literacy action rubrics to assess your school and develop literacy action goals. Literacy leadership team members can select which rubrics to focus upon and individually assess the school on each component of the selected rubrics. Then, the team will reach consensus on high need areas and write literacy action goals based on the language of the rubrics.

In Chapter 3, the team uses the rubrics to create the literacy action plan. Using the language of the rubrics and returning to the rubrics for guidance and understanding, the team constructs implementation maps to address all of the team's literacy action goals. Each implementation map specifies the action steps, timelines, key people, and measures of success needed to achieve each literacy action goal. In this chapter, we provide a process and protocols you can use to develop a practical, school-specific literacy action plan based on the components of the rubrics that are most critical for you to address.

In Chapter 4, we explain how to use the rubrics to implement and monitor your school's progress toward goals. Returning to the rubrics as you check your progress toward completion of the action steps of your plan will help you stay focused and keep on track. In addition, you can continue to deepen your understanding of literacy through examining the rubrics and reviewing Resource C (Examples) and Resource F (Glossary) as you implement your literacy action plan.

In Chapter 5, we explain how to sustain your literacy initiative by revising and updating the literacy action plan, guided by the literacy action rubrics. The team uses the rubrics to revise and update the literacy action plan. Team members revisit the rubrics and go through the school assessment and consensus building process again, using the comparative data to revise your literacy action plan.

As you can see, the literacy action rubrics anchor a seamless process from assessment through goal setting to action planning. The rubrics serve as a roadmap to ensure that your efforts are focused and purposeful and aligned with what many others have found to be powerful actions to take to increase student motivation, engagement, and achievement, the ultimate goal of an adolescent literacy initiative.

We suggest that you take some time to familiarize yourself with each rubric, reviewing carefully the components and focus points. We believe that you will find it valuable to return to the rubrics to focus your discussions and planning wherever you are in your school's journey toward literacy improvement.

THE LITERACY ACTION RUBRICS

Literacy Action Rubric 1: Student Motivation, Engagement, and Achievement

Desired Outcome	Components	Level 1 *Little or No Evidence of Implementation*	Level 2 *Evidence of Emerging Implementation*	Level 3 *Evidence of Consistent Implementation*	Level 4 *Evidence of Exemplary Implementation*
Students actively engage in reading, writing, and thinking to improve learning outcomes.	**A Relevance**	Students seldom see connections between content being studied and their life experiences or other real life applications.	Students sometimes make connections between the content they are learning and their life experiences or other real life applications.	Students often make connections between what they are learning and their life experiences or other real life applications.	Students consistently make connections between what is being learned and their life experiences or other real life applications.
		Reading and writing assignments seldom have a purpose that is meaningful to students or an audience beyond the teacher.	Reading and writing assignments sometimes have a purpose that is meaningful to students or an audience beyond the teacher.	Reading and writing assignments often have a purpose that is meaningful to students and/or an audience beyond the teacher.	Reading and writing assignments typically have a purpose that is meaningful to students and/or an audience beyond the teacher.
	B Choice	Students seldom have a choice about how to complete an assignment.	Students sometimes have choice about how to complete an assignment.	Students often have choice about how to complete an assignment.	Students consistently and routinely have a variety of choices in how to complete an assignment.
		Students seldom have choice about what they read, write, or investigate.	Students sometimes have choice about what they read, write, or investigate.	Students often have choice about what to read, write, or investigate.	Students consistently and routinely have choice relative to what to read, write, or investigate.
		Students seldom have choice about how they can demonstrate learning from a set of structured or guided options.	Students sometimes have choice about how they can demonstrate learning from a set of structured or guided options.	Students often have choice about how they can demonstrate learning from a set of structured or guided options.	Students consistently and routinely have a choice about how to demonstrate learning from a set of structured or guided options.
	C Collaborative Learning	Students rarely work collaboratively to read, write, or investigate.	Students sometimes work in pairs or small groups on projects.	Students often read, write, and/or investigate in pairs or small group, and are individually responsible for their learning.	Students routinely read, write, and/or investigate in pairs or small groups, and are individually responsible for their learning.
		Pairs or small group assignments rarely have a clear purpose, tasks, roles, and expectations.	Pairs or small group assignments sometimes have clear purpose, but lack clarity about tasks, roles, and expectations.	Pairs or small group assignments often have clear purpose, tasks, roles, and expectations.	Pairs or small group assignments routinely have clear purpose, tasks, roles, and expectations.

Desired Outcome	Components	Level 1 ***Little or No Evidence of Implementation***	Level 2 ***Evidence of Emerging Implementation***	Level 3 ***Evidence of Consistent Implementation***	Level 4 ***Evidence of Exemplary Implementation***
	D **Use of Technology**	Few students regularly use technology to research, collect, and analyze data and communicate and collaborate with others.	Some students regularly use technology to research and evaluate content, collect, and analyze data and communicate and collaborate with others.	Most students regularly use technology to research and evaluate content, collect, and analyze data and communicate and collaborate with others.	All students routinely use technology to research and evaluate content, collect, and analyze data and communicate and collaborate with others.
		Few students regularly use technology to research, write, and present.	Some students regularly use technology to research, write, and present.	Most students regularly use technology to research, write, and present.	All students routinely use technology to research, write, and present.
	E **Goal Setting**	Few students are supported in setting and working toward goals to improve their performance as readers, writers, and learners.	Some students are supported in setting and working toward goals to improve their performance as readers, writers, and learners.	Most students are supported in setting and working toward goals to improve their performance as readers, writers, and learners.	All students are supported in setting and working toward goals to improve their performance as readers, writers, and learners.
	F **Teacher Expectations**	Teachers hold and communicate the expectation that few students will succeed academically.	Teachers hold and communicate the expectation that some students will succeed academically.	Teachers hold and communicate the expectation that most students will succeed academically.	Teachers hold and communicate the expectation that all students will succeed academically.
		Few teachers provide modeling and guided practice opportunities to help students meet high expectations.	Some teachers occasionally provide modeling and guided practice opportunities to help students meet high expectations.	Many teachers often provide modeling and guided practice opportunities to help students meet high expectations.	Almost all teachers consistently provide modeling and guided practice opportunities to help students meet high expectations.

(Continued)

(Continued)

Desired Outcome	Components	Level 1 *Little or No Evidence of Implementation*	Level 2 *Evidence of Emerging Implementation*	Level 3 *Evidence of Consistent Implementation*	Level 4 *Evidence of Exemplary Implementation*
	G Classroom Instruction	Content area reading and writing instruction and vocabulary development are a strong focus in only a few classes on a given day.	Content area reading and writing instruction and vocabulary development are a strong focus in some classes on a given day.	Content area reading and writing instruction and vocabulary development are a strong focus in most classes on a given day.	Content area reading and writing instruction and vocabulary development are a strong focus in almost all classes on a given day.
		Few teachers use classroom routines to involve students actively in reading, writing, and learning,	Some teachers use classroom routines to involve students actively in reading, writing, and learning.	Most teachers consistently use classroom routines to involve students actively in reading, writing, and learning.	Almost all teachers consistently use classroom routines to involve students actively in reading, writing, and learning.
		Few teachers select, teach, model, and use instructional strategies to strengthen content learning while supporting literacy development.	Some teachers select, teach, model, and use instructional strategies to strengthen content learning while supporting literacy development.	Most teachers select, teach, model, and use instructional strategies to strengthen content learning while supporting literacy development.	Almost all teachers select, teach, model, and use instructional strategies to strengthen content learning while supporting literacy development.
		Few teachers encourage students to select and use literacy support strategies that match the content area demands and the task at hand.	Some teachers encourage students to select and use literacy support strategies that match the content area demands and the task at hand.	Many teachers encourage students to select and use literacy support strategies that match the content area demands and the task at hand.	Most teachers encourage students to select and use literacy support strategies that match the content area demands and the task at hand.

Desired Outcome	Components	**Level 1** *Little or No Evidence of Implementation*	**Level 2** *Evidence of Emerging Implementation*	**Level 3** *Evidence of Consistent Implementation*	**Level 4** *Evidence of Exemplary Implementation*
	H Feedback and Grading Practices	Teachers seldom give specific feedback on student performance.	Teachers sometimes give specific feedback on student performance.	Teachers usually give specific feedback on student performance.	Teachers routinely give specific feedback on student performance.
		Rubrics and models are seldom used to communicate expectations for quality work.	Rubrics and models are sometimes used to communicate expectations for quality work.	Rubrics and models are typically used to communicate expectations for quality work.	Rubrics and models are routinely used to communicate expectations for quality work.
		Few teachers use grading practices that support redoing, revising, and make up of work.	Some teachers use grading practices that support redoing, revising, and make up of work.	Many teachers use grading practices that support redoing, revising, and make up of work.	Almost all teachers use grading practices that support the redoing, revising, and make up of work.
	I Recognition of Student Work	Current student work is prominently displayed in only a few classrooms or areas of the school, if at all.	Current student work is prominently displayed in some classrooms and some areas of the school.	Current student work is prominently displayed in most classrooms and many areas of the school and provides some evidence that students are valued as developing writers, thinkers, researchers, and presenters.	Current student work is prominently displayed in all classrooms and throughout the school and provides ample evidence that students are valued as developing writers, thinkers, researchers, and presenters.
		Progress toward individual and collective literacy goals is seldom announced, if at all.	Progress toward individual and collective literacy goals is sometimes announced and celebrated publicly.	Progress toward individual and collective literacy goals is often announced and celebrated publicly.	Progress toward individual and collective literacy goals is always announced and celebrated publicly.

Copyright © 2010 by Judith L. Irvin. All rights reserved. Reprinted from *Taking the Lead on Adolescent Literacy: Action Steps for Schoolwide Success,* by Judith Irvin, Julie Meltzer, Nancy Dean, and Martha Jan Mickler. Thousand Oaks, CA: Corwin, www.corwin.com. Reproduction authorized only for the local school site or nonprofit organization that has purchased this book.

Literacy Action Rubric 2: Literacy Across the Content Areas

Desired Outcome	Components	Level 1 *Little or No Evidence of Implementation*	Level 2 *Evidence of Emerging Implementation*	Level 3 *Evidence of Consistent Implementation*	Level 4 *Evidence of Exemplary Implementation*
Teachers consistently integrate high quality reading, writing, and vocabulary instruction to improve all students' literacy development and content learning.	A Classroom Instruction	Content area reading and writing instruction and vocabulary development are strongly emphasized in only a few classes on a given day.	Content area reading and writing instruction and vocabulary development are strongly emphasized in some classes on a given day.	Content area reading and writing instruction and vocabulary development are strongly emphasized in most classes on a given day.	Content area reading and writing instruction and vocabulary development are strongly emphasized in almost all classes on a given day.
		Few teachers use classroom routines to involve students actively in reading, writing, and learning.	Some teachers use classroom routines to involve students actively in reading, writing, and learning.	Most teachers consistently use classroom routines to involve students actively in reading, writing, and learning.	Almost all teachers consistently use classroom routines to involve students actively in reading, writing, and learning.
		Few teachers select, teach, model, and use instructional strategies to strengthen content learning while supporting literacy development.	Some teachers select, teach, model, and use instructional strategies to strengthen content learning while supporting literacy development.	Most teachers select, teach, model, and use instructional strategies to strengthen content learning while supporting literacy development.	Almost all teachers select, teach, model, and use instructional strategies to strengthen content learning while supporting literacy development.
		Few teachers encourage students to select and use literacy support strategies that match the content area demands and the task at hand.	Some teachers encourage students to select and use literacy support strategies that match the content area demands and the task at hand.	Many teachers encourage students to select and use literacy support strategies that match the content area demands and the task at hand.	Most teachers encourage students to select and use literacy support strategies that match the content area demands and the task at hand.
	B Curriculum Alignment	Few content area courses include the development of specified literacy habits and skills, types of text, and amounts of reading and writing.	Some content area courses include the development of specified literacy habits and skills, types of text, and amounts of reading and writing.	Most content area courses include the development of specified literacy habits and skills, types of text, and amounts of reading and writing.	All content area courses include the development of specified literacy habits and skills, types of text, and amounts of reading and writing.
		Course content and literacy development does not build by grade level.	In some departments, course content and literacy development builds by grade level.	In most departments, course content and literacy development builds by grade level.	In all departments, course content and literacy development builds by grade level.
		Only a few students have access to rigorous course content and strong literacy	Only some students have access to rigorous course content and	Most students have access to rigorous course content and strong literacy	All students have access to rigorous course content and strong literacy

Desired Outcome	Components	Level 1 *Little or No Evidence of Implementation*	Level 2 *Evidence of Emerging Implementation*	Level 3 *Evidence of Consistent Implementation*	Level 4 *Evidence of Exemplary Implementation*
	C Differentiation	Few teachers use flexible grouping to meet the literacy needs of students.	Some teachers use flexible grouping to meet the literacy needs of students.	Many teachers use flexible grouping to meet the literacy needs of students.	Almost all teachers use flexible grouping to meet the literacy needs of students.
		Teachers seldom use instructional materials that are aligned with varying reading levels and/or student interests.	Teachers sometimes use instructional materials that are aligned with varying reading levels and/or student interests.	Teachers often use instructional materials that are aligned with varying reading levels and/or student interests.	Teachers routinely use instructional materials that are aligned with varying reading levels and/or student interests.
		Teachers seldom provide students with specific strategies to use if they experience difficulty with an assignment.	Teachers sometimes provide students with specific strategies to use if they experience difficulty with an assignment.	Teachers often provide students with specific strategies to use if they experience difficulty with an assignment.	Teachers routinely provide students with specific strategies to use if they experience difficulty with an assignment.
	D Feedback and Grading Practices	Teachers seldom give specific and timely feedback on student performance.	Teachers sometimes give specific and timely feedback on student performance.	Teachers usually give specific and timely feedback on student performance.	Teachers routinely give specific and timely feedback on student performance.
		Rubrics and models are seldom used to communicate expectations for quality work.	Rubrics and models are sometimes used to communicate expectations for quality work.	Rubrics and models are typically used to communicate expectations for quality work.	Rubrics and models are routinely used to communicate expectations for quality work.
		Few teachers use grading practices that support redoing, revising, and making up of work.	Some teachers use grading practices that support redoing, revising, and making up of work.	Many teachers use grading practices that support redoing, revising, and making up of work.	Almost all teachers use grading practices that support the redoing, revising, and making up of work.

(Continued)

(Continued)

Desired Outcome	Components	Level 1 *Little or No Evidence of Implementation*	Level 2 *Evidence of Emerging Implementation*	Level 3 *Evidence of Consistent Implementation*	Level 4 *Evidence of Exemplary Implementation*
	E Assignments	Reading and writing assignments seldom have a purpose that is meaningful to students or acknowledge an audience beyond the teacher.	Reading and writing assignments sometimes have a purpose that is meaningful to students or acknowledge an audience beyond the teacher.	Reading and writing assignments often have a purpose that is meaningful to students and/or acknowledge an audience beyond the teacher.	Reading and writing assignments typically have a purpose that is meaningful to students and/or acknowledge an audience beyond the teacher.
		Assignments seldom require higher order critical thinking about content.	Assignments sometimes require higher order critical thinking about content.	Assignments typically require higher order critical thinking about content.	Assignments always require higher order critical thinking about content.
		Assignments seldom require students to work collaboratively when reading, writing, or investigating.	Assignments sometimes require students to work collaboratively when reading, writing, or investigating.	Assignments often require students to work collaboratively when reading, writing, or investigating.	Assignments almost always require students to work collaboratively when reading, writing, or investigating.
		Assignments seldom include choice about what students read, write, or investigate.	Assignments sometimes include choice about what students read, write, or investigate.	Assignments often include choice about what students read, write, or investigate.	Assignments routinely include choice about what students read, write, or investigate.
		Few assignments require students to use technology to research, write, or present.	Some assignments require students to use technology to research, write, or present.	Many assignments require students to use technology to research, write, or present.	Most assignments require students to use technology to research, write, or present.

Desired Outcome	Components	Level 1 *Little or No Evidence of Implementation*	Level 2 *Evidence of Emerging Implementation*	Level 3 *Evidence of Consistent Implementation*	Level 4 *Evidence of Exemplary Implementation*
	F Research and Use of Text	Few teachers regularly use a variety of print and electronic texts as sources of content information in addition to textbooks.	Some teachers regularly use a variety of print and electronic texts as sources of content information in addition to textbooks.	Many teachers regularly use a variety of print and electronic texts as sources of content information in addition to textbooks.	Almost all teachers regularly use a variety of print and electronic texts as sources of content information in addition to textbooks.
		Few students routinely conduct research and draw conclusions based on critical evaluation and synthesis of multiple sources.	Some students routinely conduct research and draw conclusions based on critical evaluation and synthesis of multiple sources.	Many students routinely conduct research and draw conclusions based on critical evaluation and synthesis of multiple sources.	All students routinely conduct research and draw conclusions based on critical evaluation and synthesis of multiple sources.
		Few students have multiple opportunities each year to present their findings in various formats.	Some students have multiple opportunities each year to present their findings in various formats.	Most students have multiple opportunities each year to present their findings in various formats.	All students have multiple opportunities each year to present their findings in various formats.

Copyright © 2010 by Judith L. Irvin. All rights reserved. Reprinted from *Taking the Lead on Adolescent Literacy: Action Steps for Schoolwide Success*, by Judith Irvin, Julie Meltzer, Nancy Dean, and Martha Jan Mickler. Thousand Oaks, CA: Corwin, www.corwin.com. Reproduction authorized only for the local school site or nonprofit organization that has purchased this book.

Literacy Action Rubric 3: Literacy Interventions

Desired Outcome	Components	Level 1 *Little or No Evidence of Implementation*	Level 2 *Evidence of Emerging Implementation*	Level 3 *Evidence of Consistent Implementation*	Level 4 *Evidence of Exemplary Implementation*
Appropriate and adequate literacy interventions exist to support struggling readers and writers to attain and maintain grade level achievement within the context of a schoolwide literacy improvement effort.	**A** **Reading Assessment**	Limited assessment data are available about student reading achievement with some grade levels having no available information at all.	Some teachers and administrators have ready access to current assessment data to determine the reading needs of some students.	Some teachers and administrators have access to current assessment data to determine the reading needs of all students.	All teachers and administrators have ready access to current assessment data to determine the reading needs of all students.
		No further assessment protocol exists for students who are two or more years behind in reading.	Some students with scores indicating they are two or more years behind are further tested to determine their specific literacy needs.	All students with scores indicating they are two or more years behind are further tested to determine their specific literacy needs.	All students with scores indicating they are two or more years behind are further tested to determine their specific literacy needs, and their growth as readers and writers is monitored.
		Reading assessment data are collected but seldom used for intervention planning.	Reading assessment data are collected and used occasionally for intervention planning.	Reading assessment data are collected and used a minimum of two times per year for intervention planning.	Reading assessment data are collected and used a minimum of three times per year for intervention planning.

Desired Outcome	Components	Level 1 *Little or No Evidence of Implementation*	Level 2 *Evidence of Emerging Implementation*	Level 3 *Evidence of Consistent Implementation*	Level 4 *Evidence of Exemplary Implementation*
	B Use of Data	Data are not used to assign struggling students to interventions.	Only one source of data is used to assign struggling students to interventions.	At least two sources of data are used to assign struggling students to interventions.	Multiple types of data, including diagnostic data, are used to assign struggling students to interventions.
		Few intervention classes include regular progress monitoring.	Some intervention classes include regular progress monitoring.	Most intervention classes include regular progress monitoring.	All intervention classes include regular progress monitoring.
		Data are seldom used to guide instruction.	Data are sometimes used to guide instruction.	Data are often used to guide instruction.	Data are routinely used to guide instruction.
	C Types of Interventions	No specific interventions for students scoring below grade level in reading are provided except to special education students or English language learners (ELL).	Few intervention options beyond their English/language arts classes are provided for students who score below grade level in reading.	Several intervention options (e.g., additional classes, tutoring, technology support, strong content literacy support, summer academy) are provided for students who score below grade level in reading.	Multiple types of interventions (e.g., additional classes, tutoring, technology support, strong content literacy support, summer academy) are provided for students who score below grade level in reading.
		Placement procedures and exit criteria for intervention options are not in place.	Placement procedures and exit criteria for intervention options are in place but seldom applied.	Placement procedures and exit criteria for intervention options are in place and often applied.	Placement procedures and exit criteria for all intervention options are in place and consistently applied.
		Struggling readers and writers seldom experience differentiated literacy instruction in their content area classes.	Struggling readers and writers sometimes experience differentiated literacy instruction in their content area classes.	Struggling readers and writers often experience differentiated literacy instruction in their content area classes.	Struggling readers and writers consistently experience differentiated literacy instruction in their content area classes.

(Continued)

(Continued)

Desired Outcome	Components	Level 1 *Little or No Evidence of Implementation*	Level 2 *Evidence of Emerging Implementation*	Level 3 *Evidence of Consistent Implementation*	Level 4 *Evidence of Exemplary Implementation*
	D Staffing	If offered, interventions may be staffed by personnel with little or no training in how to meet the needs of struggling readers.	Some interventions are staffed by teachers with a background in reading.	Most intervention classes are staffed by qualified teachers with a background in reading.	All intervention classes are staffed by qualified teachers with a strong background in reading.
		Few teachers of English language learners and special education teachers have a strong background in reading.	Some teachers of English language learners and special education teachers have a strong background in reading.	Most teachers of English language learners and special education teachers have a strong background in reading.	All teachers of English language learners and special education teachers have a strong background in reading.
		A certified reading specialist is not available to consult with content and intervention teachers.	A certified reading specialist seldom consults with content and intervention teachers.	A certified reading specialist sometimes consults with content and intervention teachers.	A certified reading specialist consults regularly with content and intervention teachers.
	E Implementation of Interventions	If offered, intervention programs are generally not implemented as intended.	Some intervention programs are implemented as intended.	Most intervention programs are implemented as intended.	All intervention programs are implemented as intended.
		Instructional approaches are not matched to student needs.	Instructional approaches are sometimes matched to student needs.	Instructional approaches are usually matched to student needs.	Instructional approaches are always matched to student needs.
		Appropriate materials and technology to support quality instruction are not typically available to intervention teachers.	Appropriate materials and technology to support quality instruction are sometimes used by intervention teachers.	Appropriate materials and technology to support quality instruction are often used by intervention teachers.	Appropriate materials and technology to support quality instruction are consistently used by intervention teachers.
	F Teacher Collaboration	Content area and intervention teachers generally do not meet to coordinate assignments and to discuss student needs, use of literacy support strategies, and vocabulary development.	Few content area and intervention teachers regularly meet to coordinate assignments and to discuss student needs, use of literacy support strategies, and vocabulary development.	Some content area and intervention teachers meet regularly to coordinate assignments and to discuss student needs, use of literacy support strategies, and vocabulary development.	Most content area and intervention teachers meet regularly to coordinate assignments and to discuss student needs, use of literacy support strategies, and vocabulary development.

Literacy Action Rubric 4: Literacy-Rich School Environment, Policies, and Culture

Desired Outcome	Components	Level 1 *Little or No Evidence of Implementation*	Level 2 *Evidence of Emerging Implementation*	Level 3 *Evidence of Consistent Implementation*	Level 4 *Evidence of Exemplary Implementation*
A schoolwide culture, environment, set of policies, and support structures that focus on sustained literacy improvement is evident.	**A** **Vision**	A shared vision for improved literacy does not exist, and literacy development is not discussed as part of the school's mission and focus.	A shared vision for improved literacy exists and is occasionally referenced; literacy improvement is sometimes talked about as one of the school's initiatives.	A shared vision for improved literacy is articulated in writing, is publicly displayed, and literacy improvement is talked about as a major focus of the school.	A shared vision for improved literacy is articulated in writing, publicly displayed, and teachers, administrators, and students talk about how they are working toward the school's literacy goals.
		Evidence of a focus on literacy improvement can be found in a few classrooms.	Evidence of a focus on literacy improvement can be found in some classrooms.	Strong evidence of a focus on literacy improvement can be found in many classrooms.	Strong evidence of a focus on literacy improvement can be found in almost all classrooms.
		Resources provided by the district and school do not indicate that literacy improvement is a focus in the school.	Resources provided by the district and school primarily target only students scoring below grade level in reading.	Resources provided by the district and school indicate support for the literacy improvement for all students.	Resources provided by the district, school, and community indicate strong, support for the literacy improvement for all students.
	B **Teacher Expectations**	Teachers hold and communicate the expectation that few students will succeed academically.	Teachers hold and communicate the expectation that some students will succeed academically.	Teachers hold and communicate the expectation that most students will succeed academically.	Teachers hold and communicate the expectation that all students will succeed academically.
		Few teachers provide modeling and guided practice opportunities to help students meet high expectations.	Some teachers occasionally provide modeling and guided practice opportunities to help students meet high expectations.	Many teachers often provide modeling and guided practice opportunities to help students meet high expectations.	Almost all teachers consistently provide modeling and guided practice opportunities to help students meet high expectations.
	C **Time to Read and Write**	Few students read, write, and actively discuss content multiple times during the school day.	Some students read, write, and actively discuss content multiple times during the school day.	Most students read, write, and actively discuss content multiple times during the school day.	All students read, write, and actively discuss content multiple times during the school day.

(Continued)

(Continued)

Desired Outcome	Components	Level 1 *Little or No Evidence of Implementation*	Level 2 *Evidence of Emerging Implementation*	Level 3 *Evidence of Consistent Implementation*	Level 4 *Evidence of Exemplary Implementation*
	D Recognition of Student Work	Current student work is prominently displayed in only a few classrooms and areas of the school, if at all.	Current student work is prominently displayed in some classroom and areas of the school.	Current student work is prominently displayed in most classrooms and many areas of the school and provides some evidence that students are valued as developing writers, thinkers, researchers, and presenters.	Current student work is prominently displayed in all classrooms and throughout the school and provides ample evidence that students are valued as developing writers, thinkers, researchers, and presenters.
		Progress toward individual and collective literacy goals is seldom announced, if at all.	Progress toward individual and collective literacy goals is sometimes announced and celebrated publicly.	Progress toward individual and collective literacy goals is often announced and celebrated publicly.	Progress toward individual and collective literacy goals is always announced and celebrated publicly.
	E Teacher Participation	Few teachers actively participate in multiple opportunities for literacy professional development.	Some teachers actively participate in multiple opportunities for literacy professional development.	Most teachers actively participate in multiple opportunities for literacy professional development.	All teachers actively participate in multiple opportunities for literacy professional development.
		Few teachers actively seek and share resources and strategies to improve students' literacy and learning.	Some teachers actively seek and share resources and strategies to improve students' literacy and learning.	Many teachers actively seek and share resources and strategies to improve students' literacy and learning.	Almost all teachers actively seek and share resources and strategies to improve students' literacy and learning.
		Few teachers consult regularly with literacy coaches, peer coaches, and/or literacy specialists to examine data and/or to improve classroom instruction.	Some teachers consult regularly with literacy coaches, peer coaches, and/or literacy specialists to examine data and/or to improve classroom instruction.	Many teachers consult regularly with literacy coaches, peer coaches, and/or literacy specialists to examine data and/or to improve classroom instruction.	Almost all teachers consult regularly with literacy coaches, peer coaches, and/or literacy specialists to examine data and/or to improve classroom instruction.

Desired Outcome	Components	Level 1 *Little or No Evidence of Implementation*	Level 2 *Evidence of Emerging Implementation*	Level 3 *Evidence of Consistent Implementation*	Level 4 *Evidence of Exemplary Implementation*
	F **Master Schedule**	The master schedule provides time for literacy interventions for only a few students who need additional support.	The master schedule provides time for literacy interventions for some students who need additional support.	The master schedule provides time for literacy interventions for most students who need additional support.	The master schedule provides time for literacy interventions for all students who need additional support.
		Common planning time is not scheduled for teachers to work on improving student literacy and learning.	Occasional common planning time for teachers is scheduled and sometimes used for teachers to work on improving student literacy and learning.	Adequate common planning time for teachers is scheduled and expected to be used for teachers to work on improving student literacy and learning.	Adequate common planning time for teachers is scheduled and routinely used for teachers to work on improving student literacy and learning.
		Few teachers participate in professional development focused on improving literacy and learning.	Most teachers participate in professional development focused on improving literacy and learning at least twice a year.	Every teacher participates in professional development focused on improving literacy and learning at least four times a year.	Every teacher and administrator participates in professional development focused on improving literacy and learning at least one time per month.
	G **Clubs and Activities**	Some clubs and extracurricular activities are available for students but few, if any, have a literacy focus.	Literacy-related clubs (e.g., debate, poetry, drama) and extracurricular activities (e.g., newspaper, yearbook) are available and accessed by a few students.	Literacy-related clubs (e.g., debate, poetry, drama) and extracurricular activities (e.g., newspaper, yearbook) are available and accessed by some students.	Literacy-related clubs (e.g., debate, poetry, drama) and extracurricular activities (e.g., newspaper, yearbook) are available and accessed by many students.
		Few students participate in authentic literacy experiences (e.g., grade level or community reads, reading to nursing home residents, writing letters to veterans, or making books on tape for younger students).	Some students participate in authentic literacy experiences (e.g., grade level or community reads, reading to nursing home residents, writing letters to veterans, or making books on tape for younger students).	Many students participate in authentic literacy experiences (e.g., grade level or community reads, reading to nursing home residents, writing letters to veterans, or making books on tape for younger students).	Almost all students participate in authentic literacy experiences (e.g., grade level or community reads, reading to nursing home residents, writing letters to veterans, or making books on tape for younger students).

(Continued)

(Continued)

Desired Outcome	Components	**Level 1** *Little or No Evidence of Implementation*	**Level 2** *Evidence of Emerging Implementation*	**Level 3** *Evidence of Consistent Implementation*	**Level 4** *Evidence of Exemplary Implementation*
	H Library Media Center	The center may be inadequately staffed, under resourced, or difficult to access; using the center is not a priority for most teachers.	Some students and teachers make use of the library media center; a few classes require use of the library media center as a resource.	Many students and teachers make use of the library media center; some classes require use of the library media center as a resource.	Almost all students and teachers make use of the library media center; most classes require use of the library media center as a resource.
		None of the library collection of print materials provides information about reading levels.	Some of the collection of print materials provides reading level information to support differentiated instruction and independent reading.	Much of the collection of print materials provides reading level information to support differentiated instruction and independent reading.	Almost all of the collection of print materials provides reading level information to support differentiated instruction and independent reading.
		The library media center is not adequately staffed.	The library media center is adequately staffed but core personnel are not certified.	The library media center is staffed by professionally certified personnel.	The library media center is staffed by professionally certified personnel who have a background in literacy.
		The library media center does not sponsor literacy activities and is not connected to the literacy improvement effort.	The library media center sponsors a few literacy activities but is not strongly connected to the literacy improvement effort.	The library media center sponsors some literacy activities and actively supports the literacy improvement effort.	The library media center sponsors a variety of literacy activities and is an essential resource for the literacy improvement effort.

Copyright © 2010 by Judith L. Irvin. All rights reserved. Reprinted from *Taking the Lead on Adolescent Literacy: Action Steps for Schoolwide Success,* by Judith Irvin, Julie Meltzer, Nancy Dean, and Martha Jan Mickler. Thousand Oaks, CA: Corwin, www.corwin.com. Reproduction authorized only for the local school site or nonprofit organization that has purchased this book.

Literacy Action Rubric 5: Parent and Community Involvement

Desired Outcome	Components	Level 1 *Little or No Evidence of Implementation*	Level 2 *Evidence of Emerging Implementation*	Level 3 *Evidence of Consistent Implementation*	Level 4 *Evidence of Exemplary Implementation*
Families and community members work closely with school leaders to actively support the school's focus on literacy development.	A Involvement	Few families actively support the school's focus on literacy development.	Some families actively support the school's focus on literacy development.	Many families actively support the school's focus on literacy development.	Most families actively support the school's focus on literacy development.
		Family members and community leaders generally do not serve on committees, volunteer, or participate in school-based literacy events.	Family members and community leaders seldom serve on committees or volunteer, and occasionally participate in school-based literacy events.	Family members and community leaders sometimes serve on committees or volunteer, and often participate in school-based literacy events.	Family members and community leaders regularly serve on committees or volunteer, and always participate in school-based literacy events.
		Community members generally do not support student engagement in literacy-rich experiences in civic, business, and organizational settings.	Community members support a few students' engagement in literacy-rich experiences in civic, business, and organizational settings.	Community members support some students' engagement in literacy-rich experiences in civic, business, and organizational settings.	Community members support many students' engagement in literacy-rich experiences in civic, business, and organizational settings.
	B Communication	Little communication exists between the school and parents and community members about literacy activities.	The school communicates with parents through occasional newsletters and updates to the school Web site about literacy activities.	The school communicates with parents through regular newsletters and updates to the school Web site about literacy activities.	The school communicates with all stakeholders through regular newsletters, frequent updates to the school Web site, and through the local newspaper about literacy activities.
		Communication with non-English speaking family members seldom includes native language outreach about literacy activities (e.g., newsletters, videotapes, and Web sites).	Communication with non-English speaking family members includes occasional native language outreach about literacy activities (e.g., newsletters, videotapes, and Web sites).	Communication with non-English speaking family members includes regular native language outreach about literacy activities (e.g., newsletters, videotapes, and Web sites).	Communication with non-English speaking family members includes multiple forms of native language outreach about literacy activities (e.g., newsletters, videotapes, and Web sites).

(Continued)

(Continued)

Desired Outcome	Components	Level 1 *Little or No Evidence of Implementation*	Level 2 *Evidence of Emerging Implementation*	Level 3 *Evidence of Consistent Implementation*	Level 4 *Evidence of Exemplary Implementation*
		The school does not inform families and community members about the progress and next steps of the literacy initiative.	The school occasionally informs families and community members about the progress and next steps of the literacy initiative.	The school annually informs families and community members about the progress and next steps of the literacy initiative.	The school actively solicits ongoing input from families and community members about the progress and next steps of the literacy initiative.
	C Collaborative Support	Few families discuss their child's progress as a reader and writer with teachers.	Some families discuss their child's progress as a reader and writer with teachers.	Many families discuss their child's progress as a reader and writer with teachers.	Most families discuss their child's progress as a reader and writer with teachers.
		Few families are provided with assistance (e.g., diagnostic results, strategies) or resources (e.g., tutoring services, booklists) to help their child improve as readers and writers.	Some families are provided with assistance (e.g., diagnostic results, strategies) or resources (e.g., tutoring services, booklists) to help their child improve as readers and writers.	Many families are provided with assistance (e.g., diagnostic results, strategies) or resources (e.g., tutoring services, booklists) to help their child improve as readers and writers.	All families are provided with assistance (e.g., diagnostic results, strategies) or resources (e.g., tutoring services, booklists) to help their child improve as readers and writers.
		Few students communicate with parents and teachers about their progress as readers and writers (e.g., student-led conferences, portfolio presentations).	Some students communicate with parents and teachers about their progress as readers and writers (e.g., student-led conferences, portfolio presentations).	Many students communicate with parents and teachers about their progress as readers and writers (e.g., student-led conferences, portfolio presentations).	All students communicate with parents and teachers about their progress as readers and writers (e.g., student-led conferences, portfolio presentations).

Copyright © 2010 by Judith L. Irvin. All rights reserved. Reprinted from *Taking the Lead on Adolescent Literacy: Action Steps for Schoolwide Success,* by Judith Irvin, Julie Meltzer, Nancy Dean, and Martha Jan Mickler. Thousand Oaks, CA: Corwin, www.corwin.com. Reproduction authorized only for the local school site or nonprofit organization that has purchased this book.

PART II

Schoolwide Change in Five Stages

1

Stage 1: Get Ready

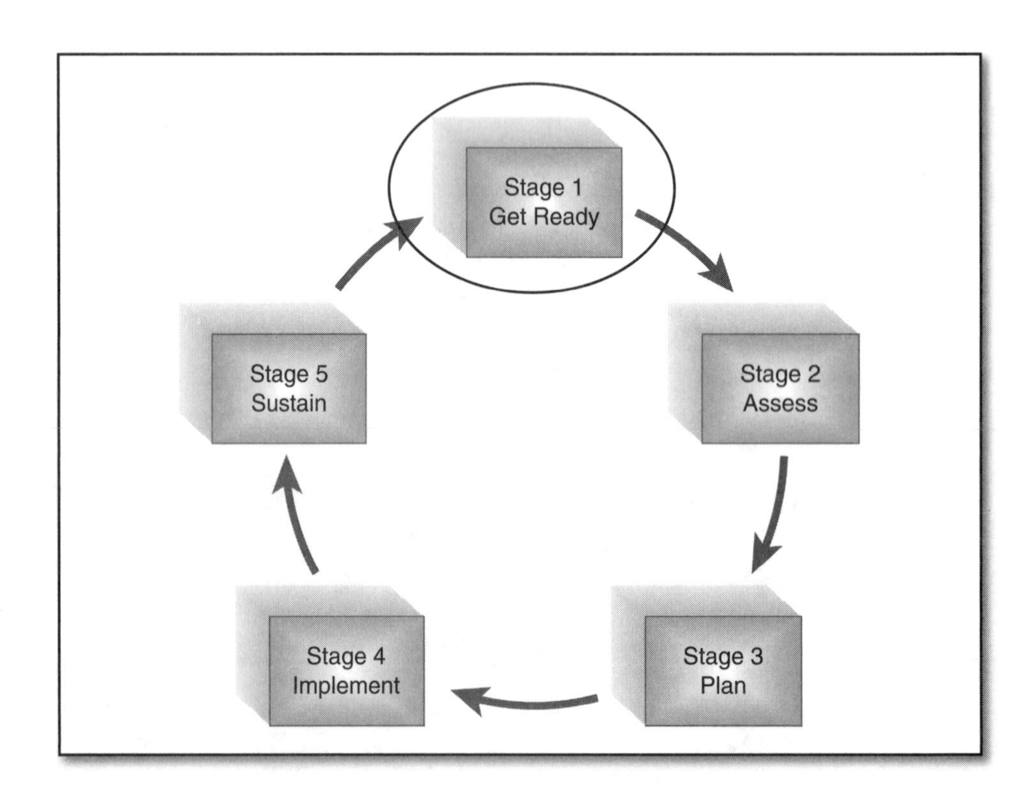

In Stage 1 of the literacy leadership process, you will complete the following:

- ✓ Build an effective literacy leadership team.
- ✓ Develop a common vision of a literacy-rich school.
- ✓ Use data to validate and communicate the need for literacy improvement.

You are now ready to get your literacy improvement effort underway. The groundwork for a successful literacy initiative begins before goals are set and action plans developed. Whether you are an administrator, a literacy coach, or a curriculum coordinator, someone has to begin the effort by assembling a team of people to work on the initiative, developing a common language and vision with the faculty, and establishing the need for a focus on improved literacy.

We recommend completing the steps of Stage 1 in sequential order: building a literacy leadership team, creating a vision, and communicating the need for the literacy improvement effort. However, you may have good reasons for completing the steps in a different order. If you have already begun a literacy initiative, you can review the content of this stage to see if there are any valuable approaches or strategies that you want to use to reenergize your initiative, increase buy-in, and/or bring new teachers, parents, and administrators on board with the initiative.

This step is important because an effective literacy leadership team is instrumental in developing, implementing, and monitoring a literacy action plan. When members of the team represent the entire school community, the team can serve as a resource for the faculty and guide the direction of the school's literacy improvement effort.

Taking the time to be certain that the right people are on the literacy leadership team is a wise investment. It is this group of people who will lead the schoolwide literacy improvement effort. Strong administrative support for the literacy leadership team's work is critical. Team members will need support to plan, vision, and discover how to build on the strengths of the school. The best efforts of team members can be derailed without strong administrative representation on the team. (Some districts have a district-level literacy team. Much of the material in Stage 1 can be carried out at the district level as well as at the school level. See Chapter 7 for concrete suggestions about how to develop and implement a literacy action plan for an entire school district.)

Select Team Members

Your literacy leadership team should include 8 to 12 members, depending on the size of your school. Team representation should be balanced by role in the school (e.g., administrator, support personnel, core content areas, and grade level). It is essential that the principal or some other designated administrator be an active member of the literacy team. Some literacy leadership teams also include student and/or parent representation.

Teachers who have significant teaching experience, knowledge of their curriculum, strong interpersonal and organizational skills, and respect from their colleagues make excellent literacy leadership team members. It is also important to include teachers who are knowledgeable about and experienced with offering literacy support to students in their own classrooms. These teachers can share their expertise with other teachers in the school. However, candidates, including new teachers, who lack some of these credentials but are enthusiastic learners and see literacy as a priority, should certainly be considered for team membership. Ideally, a team would include all of these types of teachers, as well as individuals representing library media and technology. You will want to include teacher leaders representing each of the core content areas, special education, English language learners (ELL), and at least one representative from the areas of world languages, health and wellness, physical education, and the unified and allied arts (music, business, art, technology). You may want to use the following criteria to create an initial list of likely teacher candidates to serve on the school's literacy leadership team. Teachers who

- are strong proponents of literacy,
- are considered by their peers to be school leaders,
- are comfortable inviting colleagues into their classrooms during instruction, and
- have demonstrated interest in participating in study groups or other professional development activities.

Team Meetings

Once your team members have agreed to serve, it is time to meet. Focusing on four objectives will lay the foundation for a successful team.

Objective 1: Get to know one another as team members. Building group cohesiveness is essential for the smooth functioning of the team. Be certain to discuss the following questions:

- What would members like to accomplish this school year as a literacy leadership team?
- Who has strengths in literacy, and who needs to learn more about it?
- What support do team members need to learn more about literacy?
- What expertise does each member bring to the team?
- What concerns do members have?

Objective 2: Select the team leader. Although one person can function as both team leader and meeting facilitator, shared leadership can build the capacity and strengthen the impact of the literacy team. The literacy team leader is responsible for the following:

- Scheduling and organizing meetings
- Communicating with team members about agendas and notes
- Communicating and representing the initiative to others
- Troubleshooting when the team needs outside support
- Advocating for the action plan with other leadership groups in the school and district
- Actively supporting team members and others working with the initiative

Objective 3: Select the meeting facilitator. Every meeting should have a designated meeting facilitator. This person can be the same person as the team leader, a team member with exceptional facilitation skills, or someone different at each meeting. The meeting facilitator is responsible for the following:

- Making space for all voices to be heard
- Making sure multiple viewpoints are aired and a variety of possibilities are discussed before closure on a given issue
- Bringing clarity to team decisions while avoiding simplistic answers
- Providing time and space for people to deal with difficult issues
- Turning a concern into a question
- Reminding the group that the agreed-upon ground rules are important and need to be honored

REAL SCHOOL EXAMPLE

In the organizational meeting of a high school literacy team, most team members thought that the principal, a strong leader with excellent interpersonal skills, would be the team leader. However, he declined to play that role. Instead, he insisted that the literacy team be teacher-led. The team then selected the literacy coach as its leader. The literacy coach was both knowledgeable and enthusiastic about infusing literacy skills throughout the curriculum, and she had the deep respect of the faculty. In addition, she was a hard worker and had excellent communication skills. In short, she was perfect for the job! The principal did agree, though, to be the meeting facilitator. His ability to ensure that all voices were heard and his skill at helping the team clarify difficult issues brought order and purpose to the team. In addition, his agreeing to play a key role at literacy team meetings empowered the team and validated its work.

Source: Thanks to Northeast High School in St. Petersburg, Florida, for this example. Used with permission.

Objective 4: Decide basic logistics about how the team will function. Establishing ground rules and procedures safeguards the smooth functioning of the literacy team. Your discussion should include the following:

Ground rules for team discussions. Setting ground rules for discussion prevents the voices of one to two people from controlling the conversation. The following is a sample list of ground rules for discussion:

- Everyone has a right to share an opinion.
- All ideas are thoughtfully considered.
- Everyone participates.
- The facilitator moderates but does not dominate.
- Decisions are made by consensus, not majority rule.

Team norms. It is helpful to develop agreements about how documentation, communication, logistics, and responsibilities will be handled. This discussion helps to avoid actions that default to the preferences of some team members but do not meet the needs of others. By setting norms, members have recourse beside personal recrimination when the agreements are not followed. Here are some sample norms that a literacy leadership team might set:

- Members will receive e-mail reminders of meeting dates, times, and locations.
- Members bring materials to each meeting.
- A member takes notes at each meeting and sends meeting notes to team members. This task rotates among team members.
- Members responsible for data collection should send information to the team leader at least two days prior to the next meeting.
- The team facilitator solicits roundtable responses to make sure that everyone has a say before making important decisions.
- Meetings always start and stop as scheduled.
- Refreshments are provided on a rotating basis by team members.

Meeting agendas. It is helpful to the meeting facilitator and to the team to have an agenda for each meeting. This keeps the conversation on track and assists the team to remain focused, greatly enhancing the chance that the meeting will be productive.

Communication with the faculty and the district. The team needs to decide how it will communicate with other entities in the school and the district to keep people informed about activities related to the literacy initiative, progress toward goals, ways that colleagues can be supportive or get more involved, and actions being taken by the team. This ongoing responsibility can be facilitated by answering the following questions.

- How will the team connect with other entities in the school (departments, professional learning groups, grade-level teams)?
- How will the team make the work public? (For example, who will post news about the literacy initiative on the school's Web site?)

Now that you have a literacy leadership team and have made decisions about meetings, communication, and logistics, the team is ready to begin leading a schoolwide literacy improvement initiative. The next step is to get on the same page about what a schoolwide literacy initiative involves and why a schoolwide literacy initiative is important.

This step is important because many people do not have a clear vision of what a literacy-rich school looks, sounds, and feels like. Teachers within a school may not even share a common definition of literacy. Before you can expect to agree on your school's literacy goals, it is important to come to a common understanding about literacy.

In the early stages of a literacy initiative, it is important to create a schoolwide vision and understanding about literacy and what your school would look, sound, and feel like if the literacy initiative were successful. Developing a common language about literacy, exploring examples, and providing opportunities for structured discussion will help people collaboratively develop a common vision of a literacy-rich school. This vision will then help to guide the literacy improvement effort.

Develop a Common Language About Literacy Among Literacy Team Members

In our experience, literacy leadership teams work most effectively when members share a common language to discuss literacy and learning. Teams who develop and use a common vocabulary around literacy and learning can then extend these understandings to teachers and students throughout the school. This shared vocabulary needs to include adherence to a common naming protocol for instructional strategies, student learning strategies, and collaborative routines. When all departments use the same name and procedures for a particular literacy strategy or approach to learning, two important actions are made possible. First, students can access and transfer their experience to their work in different classes across content areas. Also, when a shared language for discussing literacy and learning is in place, all members of the school community can support and assist each other in using effective literacy teaching and learning practices. Here are several approaches you can use to develop a shared vocabulary:

- Team professional development on a literacy topic (developing vocabulary, literacy support in different content areas, writing to learn), either school, district, or conference-based
- A professional study group in which teachers select a literacy topic to research and apply to their various content areas
- Use of the information in Resource C (Examples) and Resource F (Glossary) in this book as a basis for study

How will the literacy leadership team help teachers and students develop a common language about literacy and learning across the school?

Examine the Characteristics of a Literacy-Rich School

Unless literacy is front and center in the minds (and actions) of the entire school community, it tends not be emphasized in a way that benefits students.

> A schoolwide culture of literacy encourages teachers to demonstrate their own enthusiasm for reading, writing, communicating, and thinking as a stage of all aspects of classroom learning. When every member of the school community takes responsibility for literacy efforts, a culture of literacy becomes pervasive. (Irvin, Meltzer, & Dukes, 2007, p. 103)

Schools that implement successful literacy improvement initiatives actively build a culture of literacy.

The following examples are two activities that team members can use to develop a common vision of what a school successfully focused on literacy development looks like. The team can repeat these activities with other colleagues to help establish a schoolwide literacy vision.

Activity 1: Team members look through the following list of evidence that literacy development is a priority. Team members then individually rank each statement on a three point scale:

1 = we don't do this; 2 = we do this occasionally; 3 = we do this well

Following the rating, the team can discuss individual ratings, what the school already does well, and where the school can improve.

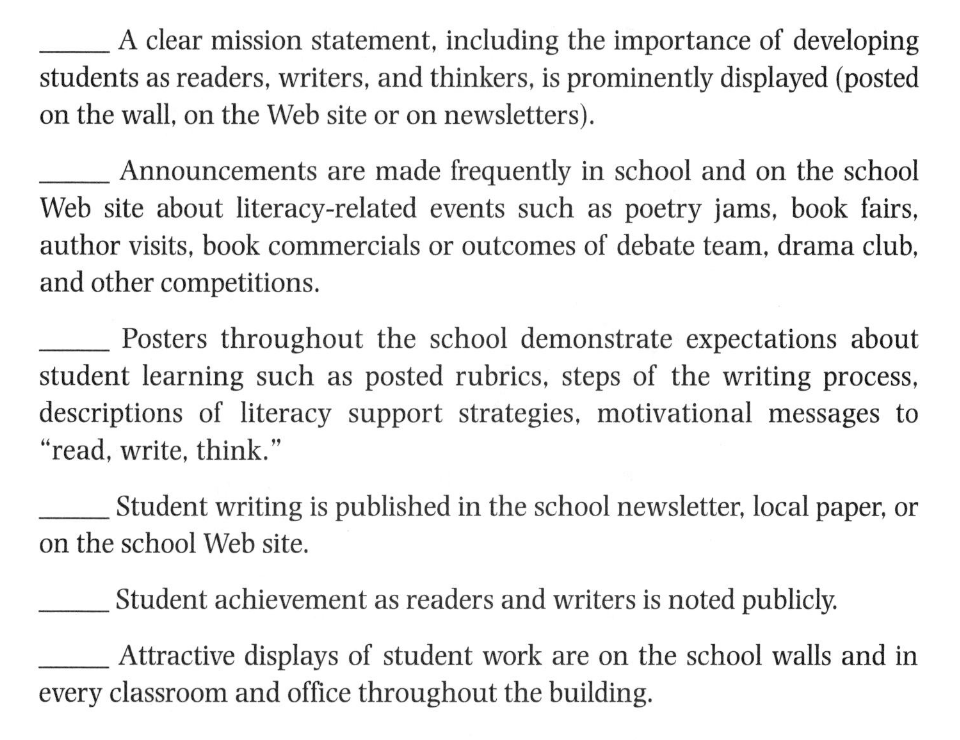

_____ A clear mission statement, including the importance of developing students as readers, writers, and thinkers, is prominently displayed (posted on the wall, on the Web site or on newsletters).

_____ Announcements are made frequently in school and on the school Web site about literacy-related events such as poetry jams, book fairs, author visits, book commercials or outcomes of debate team, drama club, and other competitions.

_____ Posters throughout the school demonstrate expectations about student learning such as posted rubrics, steps of the writing process, descriptions of literacy support strategies, motivational messages to "read, write, think."

_____ Student writing is published in the school newsletter, local paper, or on the school Web site.

_____ Student achievement as readers and writers is noted publicly.

_____ Attractive displays of student work are on the school walls and in every classroom and office throughout the building.

Activity 2: Another way to develop a common language and vision is to read descriptions of schools that have implemented literacy-rich practices. Resource A contains three descriptions of literacy rich schools—one at the upper elementary, middle, and high school levels. Read the vignette that is aligned with your school level and underline the practices that show how the school actively promotes literacy development for all students. Write each practice on a separate sticky note, group the practices, and construct a concept map like the one in Figure 1.1.

Literacy leadership team members sometimes get discouraged by how far their own school is from implementation of the activities portrayed in the vignettes. The team needs to remember that developing and sustaining a successful literacy improvement effort is a multiyear process. The school's literacy action plan will be revised and updated based on progress toward goals at the end of each school year.

Get Everyone on Board

One goal of a literacy improvement initiative is to get the entire school community involved. Everyone can play an important role in promoting literacy and learning. No one would say that improving literacy is a bad idea, but sometimes the team will meet with resistance. Some teachers may not participate because they resent the perceived implication that they should become reading teachers. Veteran teachers, as well as less experienced teachers, may feel overwhelmed or fearful that they do not know enough to effectively integrate literacy learning into their content instruction. It is important for school leaders to understand the reasons for teachers' reluctance to participate actively in a literacy improvement initiative so that these can be addressed

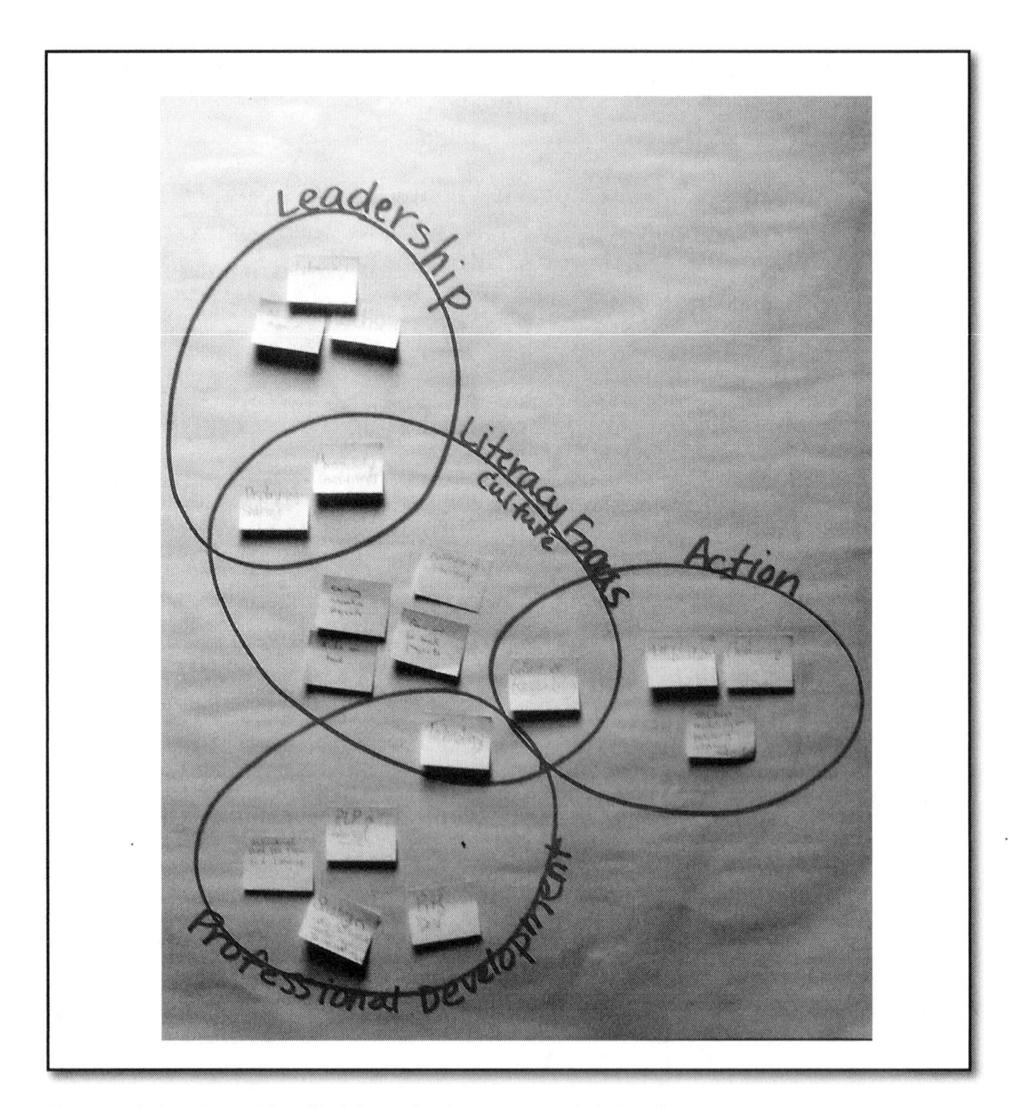

Figure 1.1 One School's Map of a Literacy-Rich School

directly by the team. When literacy leaders address teachers' concerns, this reassures teachers that they are not being asked to become reading teachers but are being asked to contribute their content expertise to the important endeavor of improving students' abilities as readers, writers, speakers, and thinkers of their content area.

The following are strategies for getting everyone on board. These strategies can be carried out in small groups at faculty meetings, with literacy team members facilitating in each group, or in department or team meetings with literacy team representation.

- Clarify teacher roles and the expectations for implementation of content area literacy support.
- Examine and discuss beliefs about literacy and learning.
- Communicate the professional development opportunities that will be in place to enhance teachers' and administrators' current knowledge about literacy and learning.

- Clarify the structures, policies, and other support that will be put into place to support the literacy initiative.

Discuss as a team how you can employ the strategies listed above and brainstorm other approaches you can use to get everyone on board with this literacy improvement effort.

This step is important because some stakeholders do not see the need to embark on a literacy improvement effort. When confronted with the data on how students in your school are performing against the demands of college, citizenship, and the world of work, this opinion often changes. Collecting baseline data will help the team track progress toward your goal to have students improve as readers and writers.

The team needs to document and communicate the need for a schoolwide literacy improvement initiative for three reasons. First, documentation and communication open the way for dialogue and allow people to consider what can be done. Second, data provides a context for goal setting and data-driven decision making. It is critical to collect baseline data so you can document progress. Third, documentation can do much to bring naysayers or reluctant colleagues on board by making a clear connection between the need for literacy improvement and what their role will be.

It is important to make the case that urgent collective action to improve student literacy is required. In some school cultures, this is the galvanizer that gets teacher buy-in. Even if this is not the case in your school, you will want to collect some baseline data so that you can gauge the impact of your literacy improvement initiative over time.

Create a Map of Reading and Writing Assessments

To establish baseline data, begin by reviewing the reading and writing assessments given in your school. What kinds of data about student performance as readers or writers are available? What does each assessment tell you about your students as readers or writers? When is each given? To whom? With the team, use Tool 1 (see Tool 1 in Resource B) to fill in the grid as shown in the following example with the aim of getting as robust a view as possible of the data available about student performance.

Tool 1: Student Performance Data Assessment Grid

Reading or Writing Assessment	Who Takes It?	When Was It Last Given?	Do You Have Multiple Years of Data?	What Does This Test Tell You About Students as Readers or Writers? (e.g., Is the score based on the reading of narrative text, expository text, or both?)
Write to Learn	9th and 10th graders	February	2 years	Skills in mechanics and organization
MAP	All students	April	3 years	Reading comprehension of expository text

The team now has a picture of the baseline data it collects at the outset of the literacy initiative and can track progress. Once the team has created or reviewed an assessment grid, the team can discuss if there are gaps between what different assessments measure and what teachers need to know to help students grow as readers and writers. Some questions include the following:

- What else would be good to know about students as readers and writers?
- Is there a way to get that information?
- Do all teachers know what tests are given to whom and how to read the reports associated with each test?
- Do teachers understand what each assessment can tell—and might not be able to tell—about students' performance as readers and writers?
- Do teachers know how to use this data to guide instruction?

Chapters 4 and 6 show a number of ways that data can be used effectively as part of a literacy improvement initiative.

Do the data collected provide enough information about students as readers and writers? What questions are not answered? How do teachers currently use these data? How could they use the data more effectively?

Create a Data Overview

You can also create a data overview, which includes a summary of student data, analysis of the data, and essential messages for the faculty. The purpose of a data overview is to display where the school strengths and challenges are relative to literacy and learning. It can be as complex or as simple as the team wants to make it. Multiyear or multigrade data can be especially useful to look for patterns and trends that give insight into the strengths and weakness of the current program as opposed to the strengths and weaknesses of a specific cohort of students.

Use the Steps for Creating a Data Overview described in the following box to make a data-driven case for focusing on literacy at your school. The outline will also enable the team to establish a before and after picture of literacy teaching and learning in your school. You can work on the data overview as a team, or you can ask a small group of literacy leaders in the school to put the data overview together. You may also wish to ask a district administrator to help you collect and analyze the data for your school. The literacy leadership team will use the data overview to help establish literacy improvement goals and to help all stakeholders embrace the need for the literacy initiative.

Steps for Creating a Data Overview

1. Summarize student performance data.
   a. Examine the data.
   b. Decide on the essential messages of the data.
   c. Determine current strengths and weaknesses for your students as readers and writers.
   d. Summarize the data using charts and text.
2. Share the Data Overview with the faculty.
3. Revisit the Data Overview in Stage 2 when you to develop your literacy action goals.

Starting with Chapter 1 and continuing through Chapter 5, we provide you with one school's literacy action planning process that we call Central School. While we also use actual examples throughout the book, we thought it would be helpful to provide a continuing example based on the work of a fictional team to showcase the stages of the literacy leadership process. You will find a Data Overview in PowerPoint for Central School in Figure 1.2.

What are the key messages of the data that you want to present to colleagues? What do you hope to achieve by presenting these data? How will the team present the Data Overview to the school? How will you invite colleagues to engage with the data you present?

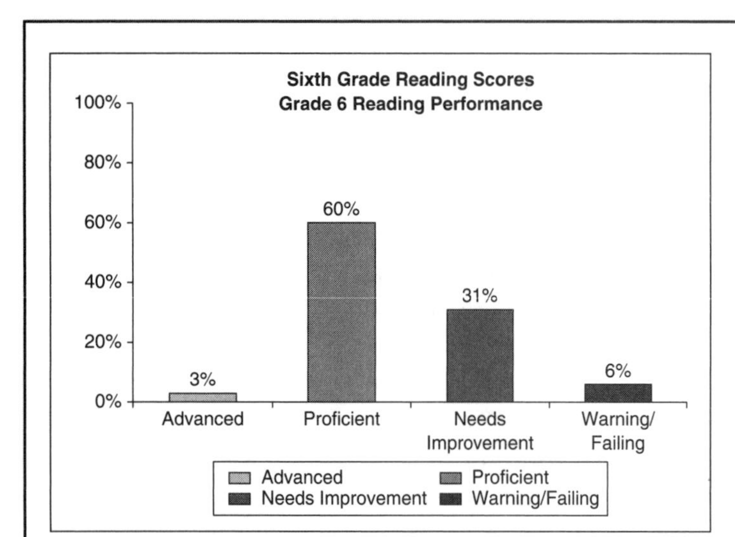

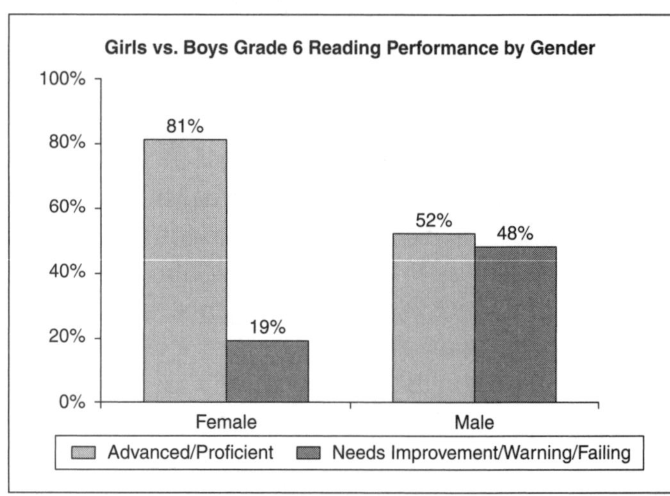

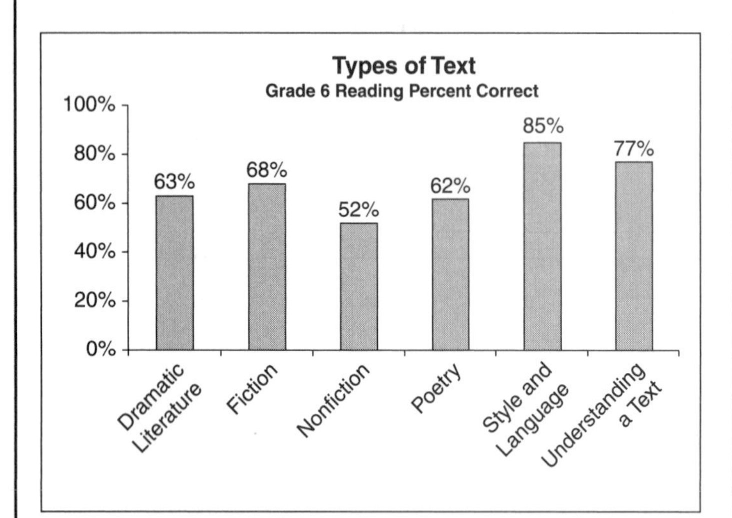

Our thoughts about the data

- Our sixth graders score above the state average, but we still need to target 37% not meeting standards.
- Our boys are not performing as well in reading as our girls.
- Nonfiction is still an area of weakness for our sixth graders.

Data-based key messages

Although . . .	We still need to work on . . .	We could do this by . . .
Reading scores are above the state average	• Providing interventions for students not meeting the standard • Raising the bar for boys • Working on improving nonfiction comprehension	• Using *Soar to Success* instead of study hall with students not meeting the standards • Improving student engagement through more choice in reading and writing assignments • Reading more nonfiction in all language arts classes • Using literacy support strategies in all science and social studies classes

We will know we are succeeding . . .

- When we put interventions into place, and we see that students in the lower two performance categories are able to meet or exceed the standard.
- When the gap between the scores for girls and boys narrows.
- When the percentage of items correct in the area of nonfiction is higher.

Figure 1.2 Sample Data Overview for Central School

NEXT STEPS

Your journey toward improved student literacy and learning in your school has begun. As you and your colleagues work together to build everyone's understanding about literacy and the need to focus upon it, you will see enthusiasm growing. Students will become more engaged with reading and writing, and teachers and administrators will be more willing to learn how to provide literacy support for students across the entire school and community.

It is now time to move to Stage 2 where you will assess your school's strengths and areas of challenge in more depth and begin the process of developing goals for your literacy action plan. The literacy leadership team will work hard during Stages 2 and 3 to develop literacy action goals that are realistic yet make a difference for students.

2

Stage 2: Assess

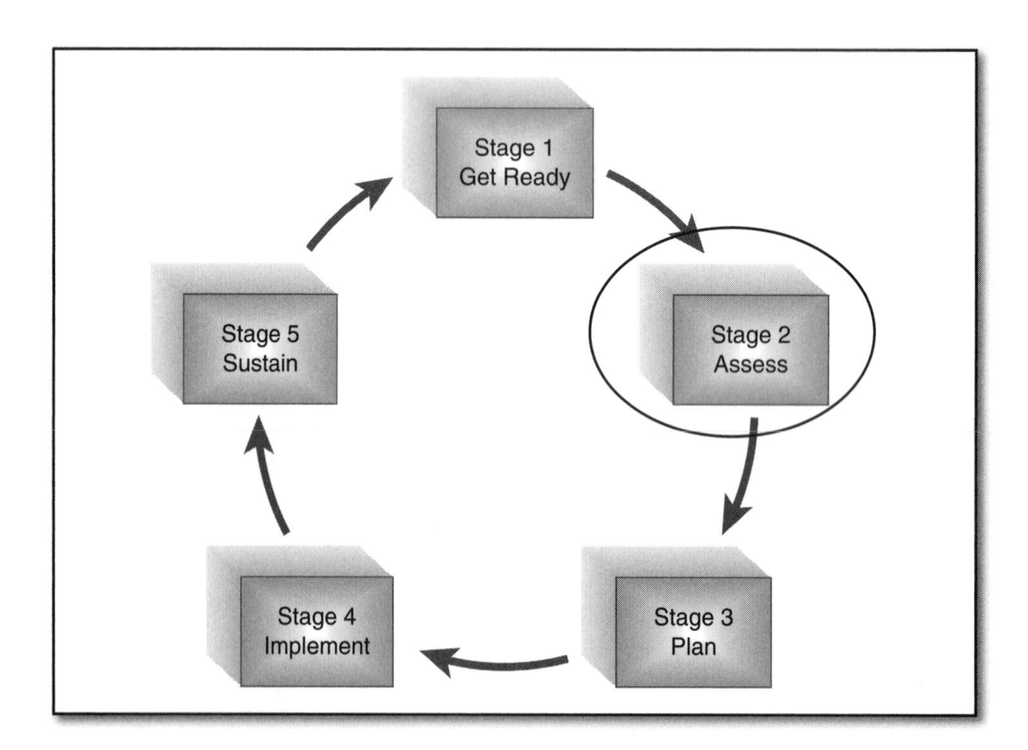

In Stage 2 of the literacy leadership process you will complete the following:

- ✓ Identify the strengths of your school.
- ✓ Summarize and analyze your data.
- ✓ Use the literacy action rubrics to assess your school's current capacity to support systemic literacy development.
- ✓ Develop relevant, feasible, and measurable literacy action goals.

Now that your literacy leadership team is up and running, you have examined your school data, and you have created some common language and vision about literacy, it is time for the team to assess the current implementation of literacy in your school and identify goals for your literacy action plan. The literacy leadership team can work through the activities described in Stage 2 to develop literacy action goals based on the strengths and needs of your school.

Developing clear, relevant, feasible, and measurable literacy action goals to guide your literacy improvement effort can be a challenge. The four steps of Stage 2 of the literacy leadership process are designed to support the literacy leadership team as you engage in a series of discussions and activities to do just that. By the end of Stage 2, the team will have developed literacy action goals that can be used to guide the literacy improvement initiative.

It is helpful if the team can schedule a retreat or longer periods of time to meet in which to complete the activities in Stages 2 and 3 of the literacy leadership process. But if this is not possible, Stages 2 and 3 have been broken into steps that can be accomplished during a series of meetings. The steps in Stage 2 are intended to be completed sequentially because they build directly upon one another. It is helpful to designate a meeting facilitator who will support the team to complete the four steps recommended for Stage 2. Or you may want to rotate facilitation among team members. Whoever is facilitating may want to read the description of each step ahead of time to have a sense of what is involved.

STEP 1: IDENTIFY SCHOOL STRENGTHS

This step is important because starting from strengths builds a sense of community and pride and identifies school capacities that can be used to support the work. Identifying school strengths helps the literacy leadership team begin by focusing on what is working instead of on what needs to be fixed.

Every school has strengths. In your school, there might be strengths such as caring faculty members, strong music or sports programs, students who are resilient and energetic, adequate resources, a supportive district, and/or a parent community that is actively supportive of the school. Since an effective literacy improvement effort builds on the current capacity of a school, it is important to begin planning for literacy improvement by first identifying and celebrating the school's strengths. Hearing what team members perceive to be strengths is enlightening and reinforces the importance of multiple perspectives.

In Step 1, team members will collaboratively develop a *School Strengths Concept Map,* such as the one in Figure 2.1, to focus the attention of literacy team members on your school's strengths. The school's name goes in the center of the map. In the outer circle, team members write down all of the strengths of the school they can identify. Think about how teachers work together, the school's environment, programs or extracurricular activities, how students are supported for success, innovations that seem to be working, and support provided by administration or the district. Team members should be specific in what they identify as strengths.

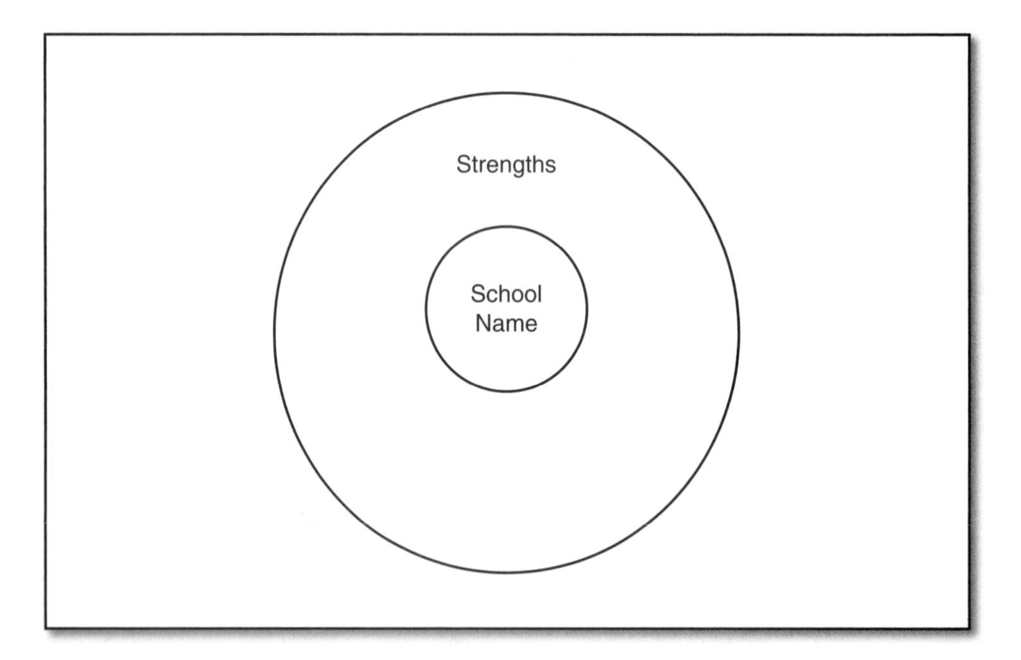

Figure 2.1 School Strengths Concept Map

Team members might want to complete individual concept maps first and then combine their maps into a team concept map like the map in Figure 2.2. Giving people time to complete individual maps allows each person to think about the school's strengths from his or her perspective. Or team members might want to brainstorm strengths together. Sometimes the activity of filling out the chart together can energize the team. The essential component is to ensure that everyone contributes ideas.

Once the team has created a School Strengths Concept Map, post the map in a prominent place to remind team members of the school's strengths as they build goals and action plans to improve literacy and learning throughout the school.

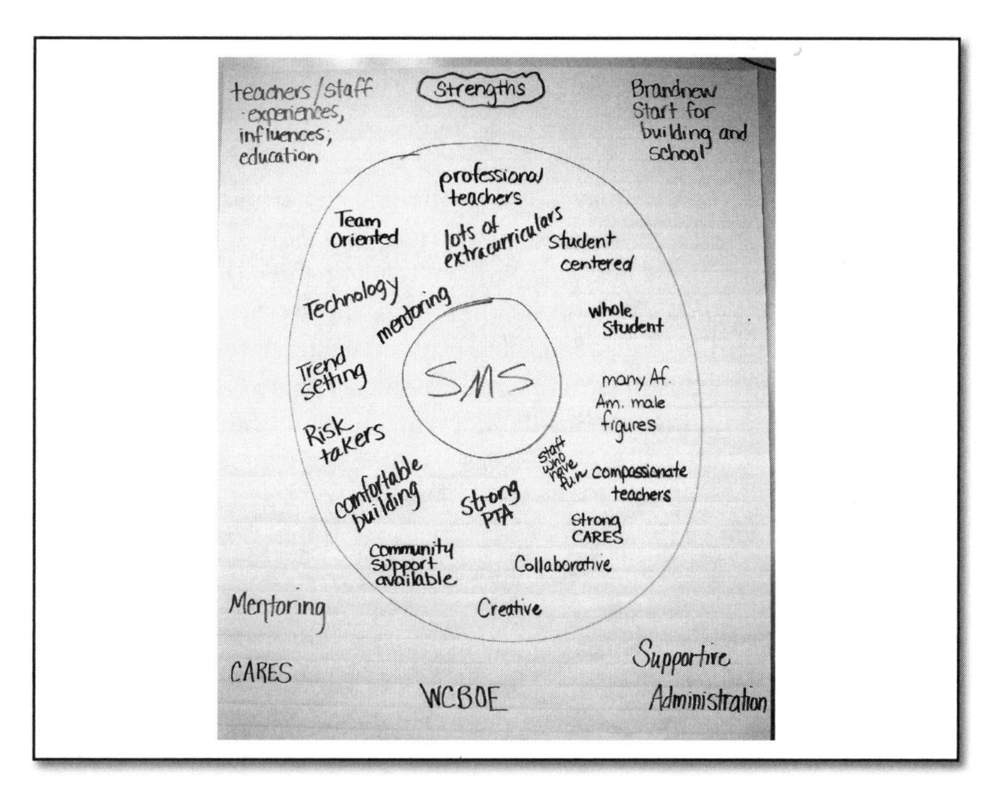

Figure 2.2 School Strengths Concept Map From One Middle School

How can a literacy improvement effort build on your school's strengths?

STEP 2: SUMMARIZE KEY MESSAGES FROM YOUR SCHOOL DATA

This step is important because discussion of the data allows the team to frame questions they have and to identify places where they need to collect additional data. In a data-driven decision-making process, such as this one, it is important to make sure that the team's goal setting and decision making is guided by data on student performance in conjunction with what the school is held accountable to do.

Developing a *Data Summary Chart* allows the team to discuss what the data indicate at the onset of the literacy initiative. It also ensures that the literacy leadership team has a chance to own the data by deciding together what the data are telling them is needed.

In Step 2, literacy team members examine student performance data and the data overview presented to the faculty in Stage 1. Prior to the meeting, a team representative may wish to consult with the school or district data analyst and the principal to ensure you have appropriate data for the team to examine. The data should include results from student reading and writing assessments and whatever else you chose to focus on in the Data Overview you created in Stage 1. If possible, disaggregate the data by discrete literacy skills and analyze it to reveal any achievement gaps that are present for your students.

To facilitate sharing of the data, create a wall chart, handout, or PowerPoint presentation. Team members examine the data individually or in pairs. Then each individual or pair writes a summary sentence using the following sentence frame: *Although* ___________(something good), *we still need to work on* _________. For example, a school may have good overall writing scores, but they find that the girls far outperform the boys on the writing assessment. One of their summary sentences might look like this: *Although our writing scores are above the state and district average, we still need to work on the average score of our boys, which is more than 20 points lower than the average score of our girls.* By limiting the response to a single sentence, team members must focus on what they determine to be the essential findings of the data. Encourage team members to focus on the most important findings of the data as they construct their sentence frames. You may want to ask different team members to examine different assessment results. Once all team members are finished writing their sentences, the meeting facilitator combines responses into a two-column data summary chart, one column labeled *Although (Strengths)* and the other column labeled *Needs.* Post the chart in a prominent place for further reference by the team during the goal setting and action planning processes. An example of one literacy team's data summary chart can be found in Figure 2.3.

Given a summary of the data presented, what are the implications for a literacy improvement effort for our school?

This step is important because the team needs to analyze where the school currently does and does not support systemic literacy development. The team uses the literacy action rubrics to assess the school's level of literacy implementation and to develop team consensus about where to focus the literacy improvement effort over the next year.

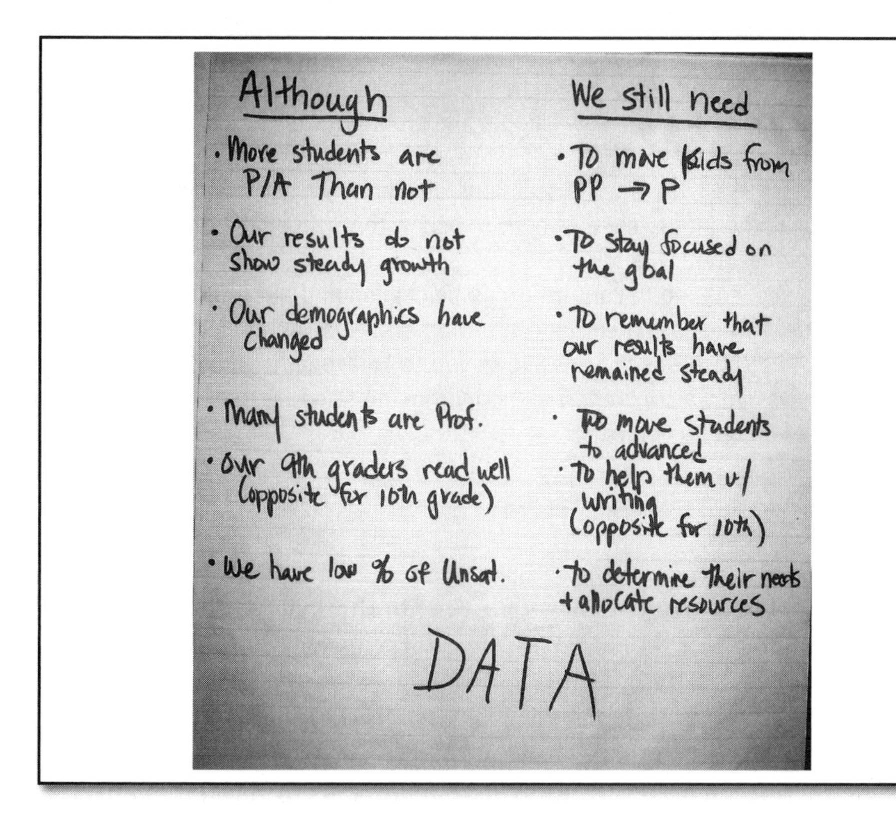

Figure 2.3 One School's Data Summary Chart

In Step 3, literacy leadership team members will use the literacy action rubrics to assess current school literacy practice relative to several critical dimensions aligned to the *Taking Action Literacy Leadership Model.* At the end of this step, the literacy leadership team will have reached consensus about their assessment of the strengths and challenges of the school in terms of literacy support and development. The act of reaching consensus takes into account multiple perspectives about the school's current status and enables the members of the literacy leadership team to get on the same page about the school's current practice in each area. However, many team members may not be familiar with consensus building and how it utilizes a different process than "majority rules." We recommend that the team explore the concept of consensus by reading and discussing the following rationale for why consensus building is powerful.

Reaching Consensus

Unlike a majority-rules voting approach that results in winners and alienated losers, consensus building develops mutually advantageous solutions that everyone can live with. No vote is taken, and the final ranking is not an average. Instead, agreed-upon decisions are made by discussion and negotiation. Consensus building requires patience and the determination to respectfully

(Continued)

(Continued)

hear and weigh all points of view. The process promotes the best thinking of the group and reflects a diversity of experience and opinion. The value of the consensus process lies in the open discussions of school literacy practices, discussions that will lead ultimately to a plan of action that will enable the school to address students' literacy needs.

The process of coming to consensus can be challenging but is ultimately very rewarding, as it builds a shared understanding of where you are and where you want to go. The consensus process allows you to knit together multiple individual perspectives into a coherent understanding, informed by the expertise and knowledge of all team members.

During Step 3, team members first take time to think about their individual perception of how the school currently addresses each component of the rubrics. The opportunity to think and reflect before the group discussion prepares each team member to actively contribute to the consensus-building process. After team members complete their individual assessment, the team will use the consensus decision-making process to develop a collective assessment of the school's current capacity to support literacy and learning.

Choose Which Rubrics to Use to Develop Literacy Action Goals

The first decision that team members need to make is which rubrics they will work with to develop their initial literacy goals and literacy action plan. Some teams prefer to work with one rubric at a time; others take on two to three rubrics. You may want to refer to the data summary chart from Step 2 to remind everyone of priority areas of need as well as productive starting points. Literacy teams often choose to begin with Rubrics 1, 2, and/or 4 since these rubrics apply to the entire school community. Other teams choose to focus on Rubric 3, *Literacy Interventions*, because of the many students performing below grade level. If this is the team's decision, we strongly encourage you to also choose at least one other rubric that stresses the broader components of a whole school initiative. Teams typically save Rubric 5 to use later in their initiative.

Team members should individually rank the set of five school-based rubrics from highest (5) to lowest (1) in priority, thereby indicating which rubrics they think address the most pressing literacy improvement issues for the school. Team members can refer back to *Introduction to the Literacy Action Rubrics* to review the components and indicators of each literacy action rubric. If team members are unsure what components would look like in action at their level of schooling, they may want to refer to Resource C (Examples) that contains descriptions of each rubric component.

Once everyone has ranked the rubrics individually, the meeting facilitator records the rankings and the totals next to each rubric. Then the team needs to reach consensus about which rubric(s) will be used as the basis for the literacy action plan.

If there is disagreement on the rankings, team members should take turns explaining their thinking. After everyone has shared his or her thinking, the meeting facilitator suggests what he or she understands to be the three top priority rubrics based on the discussion. Then the team decides how many of the priority rubrics to use in building the initial literacy action plan. The team can revisit the remaining rubrics after action steps on the initial plan are successfully underway.

The goal is to develop a literacy action plan that is clear, strong, and doable. While it is tempting to want to ensure that the plan is comprehensive, trying to address all of the rubrics in your initial literacy action plan can be overwhelming, time consuming, and self-defeating. Remember that the purpose of the literacy leadership process is to efficiently develop a literacy action plan that meets student needs, builds on school capacity, and addresses current areas of weakness that, if addressed, will have a positive impact on student literacy and learning. Developing a plan and moving to the implementation phase quickly is important because it is crucial that momentum and progress be achieved during each year of your literacy improvement initiative.

Individually Assess School Implementation Using the Rubrics

When the team has decided which rubrics to include in the assessment, individual team members should rank their perception of the school's implementation on each indicator of each component of the selected literacy action rubric(s). Team members should do this independently, without discussion, by placing a check where they think *typical school practice* falls on the rubric. The individually ranked rubrics will form the basis for the discussion, consensus building, and goal setting that follows.

As individual members rank the components of the rubrics, they should jot down the evidence they used to make their decisions. This could include student test scores, knowledge of particular programs, specific team or department practices, and classroom observation. Team members write their evidence in the spaces around the rubric component or on a separate piece of paper. Thinking carefully about evidence deepens the conversation about the school's ratings on the rubrics. As team members consider and write down the evidence for their decisions, they go beyond a first reaction to a more studied and thoughtful ranking. This provides the foundation for the consensus discussion and group recording of evidence which follows.

A team member might ask, "But how do we know what others in the school are doing?" Team members should rank the school based on what they know of the school and jot down that perspective on the top of the rubric (e.g., from the perspective of the science department or from the perspective of my own teaching). When all of the perspectives are pulled together in the next step of the activity, these more local perspectives will add depth and accuracy. Someone might also ask, "What happens if some people do this but not everyone?" That is fine. The meeting facilitator encourages team members to read the description of each level as carefully as possible and make a match as accurately as possible. The goal is not to mark down or give extra credit but to accurately reflect *based on the perspective of each individual* where the school should be ranked on each component. This opportunity to think and reflect before the group discussion helps guarantee that the group as a whole will benefit from everyone's perspectives.

Each individual creates an average score based on his or her ranking of the indicators within each component. When a component contains two or more indicators and an individual does not rank all of the indicators at the same level, the rating becomes the lower level plus ".5." Team members then address indicators separately as they develop their action steps to implement the goal. Figure 2.4 shows one team member's individual ranking of school performance on components related to literacy action Rubric 2: *Literacy Across the Content Areas.*

Discuss and Reach Consensus on Rubric Ratings

Once everyone has completed the independent ranking based on his or her perspective of each component, the team must come to consensus about the school's current level of implementation. The meeting facilitator then records and leads a discussion based on team members' independent rankings. One way to do this is to list the components of each of the selected rubrics on a large

Literacy Action Rubric 2: Literacy Across the Content Areas

Desired Outcome	Components	Level 1 *Little or No Evidence of Implementation*	Level 2 *Evidence of Emerging Implementation*	Level 3 *Evidence of Consistent Implementation*	Level 4 *Evidence of Exemplary Implementation*
Teachers consistently integrate high quality reading, writing, and vocabulary instruction to improve all students' literacy development and content learning.	A Classroom Instruction	Content area reading and writing instruction and vocabulary development are strongly emphasized in only a few classes on a given day.	Content area reading and writing instruction and vocabulary development are strongly emphasized in some classes on a given day. ✓	Content area reading and writing instruction and vocabulary development are strongly emphasized in most classes on a given day.	Content area reading and writing instruction and vocabulary development are strongly emphasized in almost all classes on a given day.
		Few teachers use classroom routines to involve students actively in reading, writing, and learning.	Some teachers use classroom routines to involve students actively in reading, writing, and learning. ✓	Most teachers consistently use classroom routines to involve students actively in reading, writing, and learning.	Almost all teachers consistently use classroom routines to involve students actively in reading, writing, and learning.
		Few teachers select, teach, model, and use instructional strategies to strengthen content learning while supporting literacy development. ✓	Some teachers select, teach, model, and use instructional strategies to strengthen content learning while supporting literacy development.	Most teachers select, teach, model, and use instructional strategies to strengthen content learning while supporting literacy development.	Almost all teachers select, teach, model, and use instructional strategies to strengthen content learning while supporting literacy development.
		Few teachers encourage students to select and use literacy support strategies that match the content area demands and the task at hand. ✓	Some teachers encourage students to select and use literacy support strategies that match the content area demands and the task at hand.	Many teachers encourage students to select and use literacy support strategies that match the content area demands and the task at hand.	Most teachers encourage students to select and use literacy support strategies that match the content area demands and the task at hand.
	B Curriculum Alignment	Few content area courses include the development of specified literacy habits and skills, types of text, and amounts of reading and writing.	Some content area courses include the development of specified literacy habits and skills, types of text, and amounts of reading and writing. ✓	Most content area courses include the development of specified literacy habits and skills, types of text, and amounts of reading and writing.	All content area courses include the development of specified literacy habits and skills, types of text, and amounts of reading and writing.
		Course content and literacy development does not build by grade level. ✓	In some departments, course content and literacy development builds by grade level.	In most departments, course content and literacy development builds by grade level.	In all departments, course content and literacy development builds by grade level.
		Only a few students have access to rigorous course content and strong literacy support.	Only some students have access to rigorous course content and strong literacy support.	Most students have access to rigorous course content and strong literacy support. ✓	All students have access to rigorous course content and strong literacy support.

Figure 2.4 One Individual's Rating of Rubric 2

wall chart (sticky chart paper works well) and use the chart to record team members' rankings. The checks indicate each team member's assessment.

When everyone's individual rating on each component has been recorded, the team discusses where the team's ratings are in sync and where they are widely divergent. The role of the meeting facilitator is to lead the discussion and decision making on a group consensus ranking. After each component is discussed, the meeting facilitator indicates consensus by placing a colored labeling dot at the level the team feels is truly reflective of the school's current level of practice (see Figure 2.5). Note that this is *not* an average of the individual ratings. The exact placement of the dot is less important than describing trends, recognizing strengths, and understanding the needs of the school. This is not a time to argue for a particular assessment rating on a specific component but rather to develop a collective understanding of what the team members believe to be the current level of practice in the school relative to systemic support of literacy development.

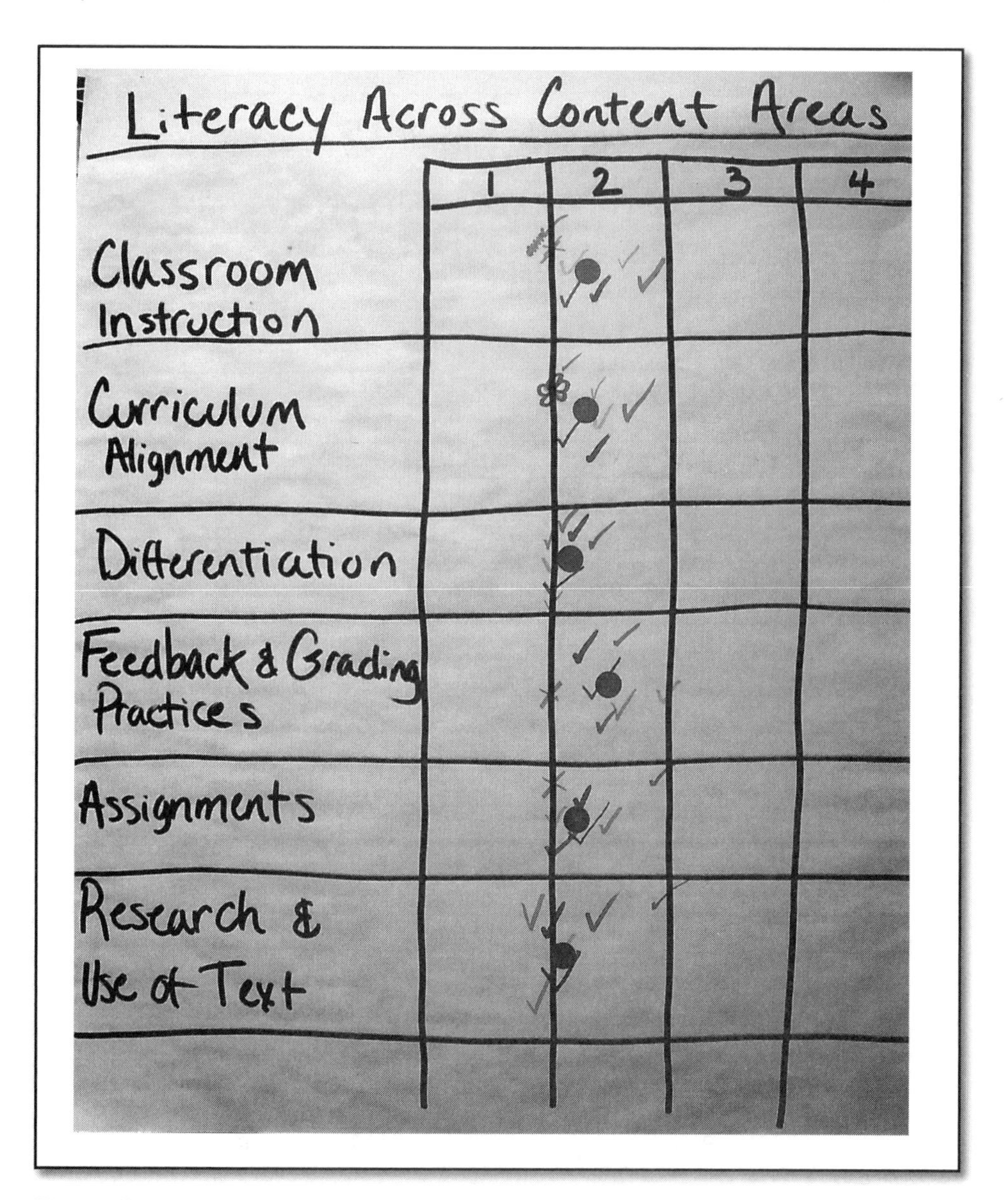

Figure 2.5 Group Consensus Chart From Rubric 2

At the end of the discussion, the team should have a completed chart such as the one in Figure 2.5, which shows the team's consensus rating for each component on each of the rubrics selected.

Provide Evidence for the Ratings

To move the conversation along and to document perceptions at the outset of the initiative, ask a team member to record the evidence that others cite for their ratings. The recorder can take notes on a computer, projecting the document for all to see, or can write on a large wall chart. The recording of evidence keeps team members focused and shifts the conversation away from which ranking is more correct to a deeper discussion of the component being ranked. An example of one team's evidence summary for Rubric 2 can be found in the chart that follows.

REAL SCHOOL EXAMPLE

Group Evidence Chart for Literacy Across the Content Area Rubric

A. Classroom Instruction

- *Literacy instruction occurs daily in reading classes; often in math and science but not every day*
- *Vocabulary development occurs in classes; strategies may not be based on enough understanding or may not be used consistently*

B. Curriculum Alignment

- *Standards implementation strong in some classrooms but not all*
- *Literacy expectations and connections to content are recognizable in core content areas but not so much in others*
- *Some teams craft more choice, more rigor for students than others. Perception of some teachers that student motivation influences instructional choices*

C. Differentiation

- *Teachers use flexible grouping but not for literacy differentiation*
- *Flexible grouping more for management than for differentiation*
- *Accelerated Reader levels on books in library—student choice for independent reading*
- *Not much use of leveled texts except for Accelerated Reader*
- *Some teachers choose Web sites accessible at students' reading levels*
- *Some teachers don't know literacy support strategies to use for scaffolding students' gaps*
- *Students may use strategies but not independently (not internalized yet)*
- *Students respond to some consistently used strategies (e.g., Venn diagram) as "boring"*

D. Feedback and Grading Practices

- *Teachers offer specific feedback; often not timely (turnaround time is long)*
- *Teachers offer clear, understandable rubrics; students expected to work toward them*
- *Schoolwide good intentions about opportunities for students to improve, revise, resubmit work; however, "organization" to manage this is hard for teachers*
- *Late work debate: Guidelines? Consistency? Statute of limitations? Demonstration of learning versus busy work? We believe that students should have opportunity to turn in late work, but we're uneasy about our practices*

E. Assignments

- *Reading and writing assignments may not mean much to students; they don't see themselves in the work, not meaningful to them*
- *Valuing reading and writing assignments across all content areas isn't consistent*
- *Expected critical thinking stops short of summarizing; nowhere near synthesis*
- *In gifted and talented classes expectation for higher order thinking is more prevalent*

F. Research and Use of Texts

- *Students are not engaged in synthesis of multiple texts, although they are meeting expectations to conduct and apply research*
- *PowerPoint, posters, and video presentations of learning in some classes*

Thanks to Northeast High School, Pinellas County, Florida, for this example. Used with permission.

STEP 4: DRAFT LITERACY ACTION GOALS

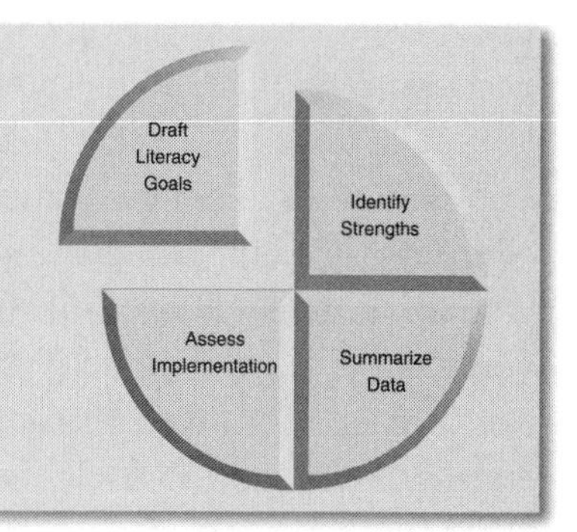

This step is important because developing clear, measurable, and feasible goals for progress is critical to an effective school improvement plan. Without clearly defined goals, it is impossible to determine if growth is being made, where additional attention is needed, and what might be the most productive action steps to take.

At this point, the literacy leadership team has the information it needs to develop effective, measurable, feasible literacy action goals. By the end of Step 4, you will have developed a set of relevant, measurable literacy action goals to guide literacy improvement at your school over the next year. These goals will drive the literacy action planning that the team will complete in Stage 3 of the literacy leadership process.

It is important to articulate the school's most urgent literacy needs and to develop measurable literacy action goals. First, team members will examine the Group Consensus Charts, the School Strengths Concept Map, and the Data Summary Chart and individually identify three to five components that they think should be the focus of the literacy action plan. Team members look at rubric components that they feel are important for the school to address but which were ranked low in terms of implementation (ranking of Level 1 or 2 on some or all indicators). Or team members may choose a component ranked at a Level 3 that represents an area of strength for the school but one they want to see elevated to Level 4 implementation. Team members should also think about the following:

- What does student data indicate about students' needs?
- Which of these priority components is feasible to address in the next year? It is critical that progress be made in the first year of a literacy improvement initiative in order to generate momentum and increase buy-in.
- Review the School Strengths Concept Map created in Step 1. Some of these strengths may be used to address challenge areas.

Constructing clear, concrete goal statements to guide your literacy action plan is not an easy task. To draft clear goal statements, revisit the needs that team members collectively identified as most important and as feasible to address. Then, articulate these as measurable goal statements. You can use the language of Level 4 from the rubrics to construct meaningful goal statements. You may wish to concentrate on a particular aspect of a component from one of the rubrics that is important for students in your school. For example, if your goal is for all teachers to make assignments that are more relevant to students, you can revisit Component A on Rubric 1: Student Motivation, Engagement, and Achievement Rubric to help the team choose language necessary to build a clear, achievable goal. Or you may construct a goal statement that pulls from more than one component on a rubric.

As you construct goal statements, be certain to follow these guidelines:

- Develop goals that you can meet with collaborative effort and resources.
- Develop goals that, if met, would make a positive difference for students.
- Develop a limited number of goals (2–4) that will direct your literacy improvement efforts over the next year.
- Develop goals that are measurable and toward which the team can track progress.
- Write the goal statements in clear, specific language that is jargon free and can be understood by everyone in the school community.

As you develop your literacy action goals, keep in mind that goals can be written in a variety of formats. You may wish to write a goal in which you state what the students will do, such as, *Students will routinely use literacy support strategies in each of their content area classes.* Or you may wish to write a goal in which you state a number or percentage to improve or change, such as, *The number of students scoring in the bottom quartile in reading on our state assessment will decrease by 10%.* Other goals will be written from the perspective of what teachers or administrators will do, such as the four listed in the Sample Goal Statements that follow.

We recommend taking some time at this point for the team to discuss the qualities that make a good goal statement. Read through the Sample Goal Statements, and use the questions to evaluate the goal statements and collectively determine the attributes of clearly written literacy action goals.

Sample Goal Statements

1. All teachers will routinely incorporate reading and writing strategies designed to enhance literacy and learning.
2. All members of the school community will embrace the idea that all students can succeed academically and will provide opportunities to help students meet high expectations.
3. Student work will be prominently displayed in classrooms, hallways, and common areas to showcase students' progress and achievement relating literacy to content area learning as a message that our students are valued and celebrated.
4. Our school will offer a continuum of research-based literacy interventions for struggling students aligned with student needs and implemented with fidelity.

Which goals would, if met, make the most difference for kids? How would you measure progress related to each of these goals? Which goals are specific enough to be put into action? Which goals are too vague? What makes a good goal?

REAL SCHOOL EXAMPLE

When the Instructional Leadership Team (ILT) of a vocational and career academy met to develop literacy action goals and a plan, it was important to them to build on the professional development they offered the previous year on differentiation. In addition, they had previously identified writing as an area they needed to target for improvement. As members of the subgroup discussed their primary literacy action goal, they wanted to make sure that it related to Writing to Learn

(Continued)

(Continued)

and Differentiation. Teachers were also enthusiastic about the concepts of "rigor" and "relevance" for students, and many had attended a seminar where William Daggett presented. The ILT's final goal was, "Students will routinely engage in reading and writing to learn strategies with an emphasis on rigor, relevance, and differentiation." The literacy action plan included ways to build on and monitor the implementation of the previous professional development and targeted areas while adding an emphasis on reading.

Thanks to Chicago Vocational and Career Academy in Chicago, Illinois, for this example. Used with permission.

The following sample goal statement is associated with with the Central School example from Chapter 1. This goal statement, based on Rubric 2, could be suitable for a literacy improvement initiative at the upper elementary, middle, or high school level. The implementation map in Stage 3 provides an example of how to build an implementation map to address this goal statement. In Stage 4, we provide an example of implementation and troubleshooting processes that the Central School team could use. In Stage 5, we show the Central School team's analysis of the overall plan's outcomes and processes for revising the plan for the next school year. Thus, by following the actions of the fictional Central School literacy team, you can better understand to your literacy leadership team will be doing throughout Stages 3, 4, and 5 of the literacy leadership process.

Central School's Literacy Action Goal Statement based on Rubric 2: All students will learn and routinely use reading and writing support strategies to enhance literacy and learning across all content areas.

NEXT STEPS

Now that the literacy leadership team has completed the four steps of Stage 2, be sure to take time to celebrate the efforts of the team before proceeding to Stage 3. The team's work in Stage 2 may be the first opportunity that team members have had to express their views about important issues related to literacy and instruction. Team members have worked hard and used collaboration, thoughtful analysis, and consensus building to develop literacy action goals using the rubrics. As a result, the team has strengthened its voice and is more prepared to assume increasing leadership responsibility as the year progresses.

In Stage 3, the team begins the work of drafting the implementation maps to reach each goal. The implementation maps will provide clear direction about how action steps will be successfully implemented. Although the team proceeded through Stage 2 in sequential steps, you may find it necessary to refer back to a rubric, review your school's strengths, or revise a goal statement as you move forward with implementation mapping in Stage 3 of the literacy leadership process. This recursive process ensures that the action plan remains a vibrant and viable document, matched to the needs and building on the strengths of the school.

3

Stage 3: Plan

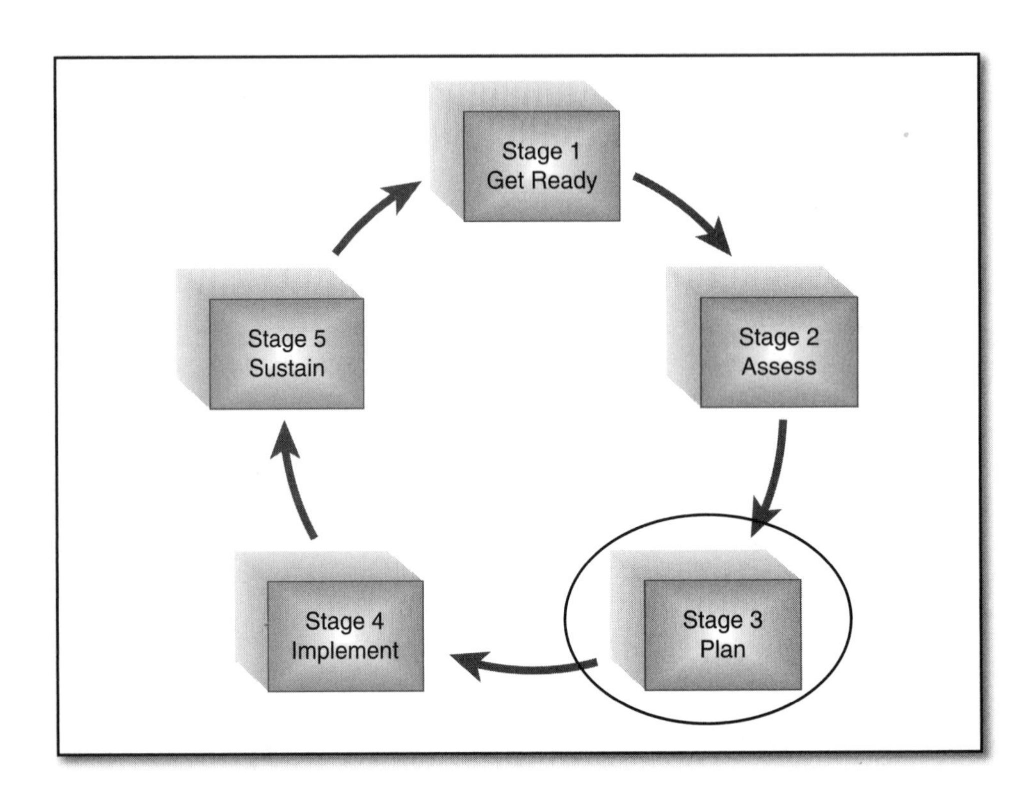

In Stage 3 of the literacy leadership process, you will complete the following:

- ✓ Develop an implementation map for each of your literacy action goals.
- ✓ Solicit support and feedback from the whole school community.
- ✓ Revise and publish a formal literacy action plan.

The focus of Stage 3 is on developing a relevant and doable literacy action plan that incorporates feedback from stakeholders and leads to action. For each literacy action goal created by the team in Stage 2, the literacy leadership team develops an implementation map. Thus, if the team has developed three literacy action goals you will have three implementation maps. Each implementation map comprises a set of action steps designed to support progress toward one of the team's goal statements. Collectively, these implementation maps will make up the school's formal literacy action plan, along with information about members of the team as well as the planning and design process that the team used to build the plan.

In Stage 3, the team will also solicit feedback from the school community about the action steps in each implementation map to create buy-in and to ensure that the work of the literacy leadership team is clear and inclusive from the outset. The team then discusses the feedback, revises the implementation maps accordingly, and publishes the formal literacy action plan. The four steps of Stage 3 are designed to be completed sequentially, as they build directly upon one another.

In Step 1, the team develops an implementation map for each literacy action goal created in Stage 2, using the template (Tool 2 found in Resource B). The six headings on the template are shown in Figure 3.1.

It is helpful to have the whole team working on the implementation map for each goal statement, allowing for input from all team members. If you have a large team, many (e.g., four) goal statements, and/or limited meeting time, we suggest you complete an implementation map for the first goal statement as a team. After that, the team can break into smaller working groups, with each subgroup completing an implementation map template for one of the remaining goal statements. The subgroups can present their completed maps to the team so the team can provide feedback and make additional suggestions.

Develop an Effective Implementation Map

The time you spend developing your implementation map will pay off as you enact your action steps. When developing the parts of the implementation

Action Step	Timeline (Target Date)	Lead Person(s)	Resources Needed	Specifics of Implementation	Measure(s) of Success

Figure 3.1 Parts of the Implementation Map

map, it is important to be very specific and listen carefully to the input of each team member as you work toward action steps that are both significant and achievable. As you develop your maps, keep the following in mind:

- Create one implementation map template for each literacy action goal statement.
- Write the literacy action goal statement at the top of the map.
- Use the data from Stage 2 to help you build specific action steps and measures of success on each map.
- Fill in the remaining parts of the implementation map for each action step. Make sure that each implementation map is clear, easy to understand, and complete before sharing it with others outside the team.

As you read the following guidelines for each part of the implementation map, look at the sample we provide in Figure 3.2. You may wish to discuss the sample with your colleagues to make sure you understand how to complete each section of the implementation map.

Action Steps. Clear, concrete action steps are critical to an effective implementation map. State your action steps carefully. For example, instead of stating, "Have higher expectations for students in classroom discussions," word your action step in such a way that it can be measured: "Teachers will use higher level thinking questions and prompts in all content classes multiple times weekly." Make sure that each action step directly links to the goal statement. Try to make the action step explicit, walking a line between being too general and too specific. While literacy action goal statements are often stated as student outcomes, action steps usually specify what teachers will do to assist students to get the stated outcome (although an action step might also address what students, parents, or administrators will do, as appropriate).

Timeline. The timeline should include dates for implementation of each action step as well as when progress will be reviewed. Dates for implementation should be reasonable but also should express some urgency, stressing the importance of taking the action steps in a timely manner to ensure that implementation begins soon. Reviewing progress on action steps should not wait until the end of the year. Rather, literacy team members should evaluate the progress both on implementation and toward goals on a regular basis, as specified in the literacy action plan.

Lead Person(s). For each action step, identify a person or a team of people responsible for making sure that the action step is completed in a timely manner. This does not mean that the people responsible must actually complete the actions themselves. Instead, lead people oversee and guide implementation of specific action steps, guaranteeing that the step is not forgotten.

Resources Needed. The resources needed to complete an action step depend on the nature of the activities. Some resources are clearly fiscal such as those required to pay stipends, consultants, materials, and fees. Some resources are in kind, such as volunteer services. Others are related to time, scheduling, or the use of specific materials or existing facilities or technology. The implementation map should clearly list the resources needed to achieve each action step. Many plans have failed because the resources were not adequately identified or allocated to support the scope of the activity.

Specifics of Implementation. An important part of the implementation map includes a description of what needs to occur for the action step to be successfully implemented. Here is where the team describes the specific tasks and events that are designed to move the plan forward. For example, professional development might be needed in order to make a specific action step successful. It is important to specify if you are referring to professional development from outside sources, support from literacy or instructional coaches, or formal and informal professional development delivered by literacy leadership team members. It is also important to specify when the professional development will occur, whom it will involve, and who is in charge of arranging it.

Measure(s) of Success. The implementation map should indicate measure(s) of success for each action step. Without defining what successful completion of an action step looks like, it is impossible to judge whether or not the school has accomplished the action steps and made progress toward the literacy action goal. The more specifically the team defines successful implementation or progress toward a goal, the more likely the team will be able to assess results and move ahead with the literacy improvement effort. Defining what success would look like is a critical element of the plan. For example, "meeting notes" could be cited as the evidence that meetings occurred as planned. However, it is more helpful to describe what is to be accomplished by the meetings and have the measure(s) of success be directly related to this: *Grade-level teams will meet twice monthly to use a protocol for looking at student work. Meeting notes will document conclusions and recommendations drawn from the work.* Measure(s) of success can also involve data collection approaches such as informal surveys of faculty practice, faculty responses to professional development, walk-through data, and the results of benchmark assessments.

You may want to review the Central School example shown as Figure 3.2 of a completed implementation map that corresponds to the sample literacy action goal statement highlighted in Stage 2. A blank copy of the Implementation Map can be found as Tool 2 in Resource B.

Literacy Action Goal Statement: All students will learn and routinely use reading and writing support strategies to enhance literacy and learning across all content areas.

Action Step	Timeline (Target Date)	Lead Person(s)	Resources Needed	Specifics of Implementation	Measure(s) of Success
The literacy team will select a common set of literacy support strategies.	August to September	Literacy team members with input from entire faculty	Time to meet and consider strategies. *Common Reading Comprehension Strategy Selection* Tool	• After reviewing student data and seeing where students need additional support, the literacy team will discuss several strategies. • The literacy team will select three to five strategies that address these needs. • Input will be solicited from teachers to see if others should be added. • The literacy team will agree on a common set that teachers will learn and then model for students. These will be posted on the intranet.	List of common literacy support strategies selected and distributed to all teachers. Posting of description and examples of strategies on school Web site for all teachers to access.
All teachers will participate in at least two professional development sessions to learn the common set of strategies.	September to October	Literacy coach will schedule Teachers Possibly outside consultant	Time and stipends for professional development Handouts, supplies for presentations	Literacy coach and literacy team members will work together to present the common strategies to the faculty and invite participation and discussion about the purpose of the strategy and how the strategy can be applied to different content areas.	Professional development evaluations show that teachers understand and feel confident in the implementation of the strategies.
Each department will discuss the literacy demands of their content areas and make a plan for how to use common strategies in their instruction.	October to November	Department chairs will lead discussions Literacy coach	Meeting time Meeting agenda prepared by the literacy team	Each department will meet two times: Meeting 1: Discuss the literacy demands of the content area and how the common strategies connect to those demands. Meeting 2: Discuss the use of selected common strategies and make plans for implementation using the gradual release model (explicit instruction, model, guided practice, independent practice)	Plan for the use of strategy implementation submitted by each department.

Action Step	Timeline (Target Date)	Lead Person(s)	Resources Needed	Specifics of Implementation	Measure(s) of Success
All teachers will have multiple opportunities to visit demonstration classrooms, engage in peer coaching, and/or work with a literacy coach to see strategies in action.	December to January	Literacy coach Peer coaches Literacy team members	Schedule for presentations Sub money to release teachers Protocol for peer coaching Observation sheets for demonstration lessons	• Literacy team members will develop a schedule for demonstration lessons. • Literacy coach will recruit and support peer coaches. • Literacy coach will set up a schedule to work with teachers in each department. • Teachers will observe lessons. • Literacy coach and teachers will debrief each lesson.	Completed demonstration lessons with evidence that others observed. Peer coaching documentation indicates peer coaching is occurring. Literacy coach log of activity indicates the literacy coach is meeting with teachers regularly and modeling in classrooms.
All teachers will model and teach students the agreed upon literacy support strategies multiple times to strengthen content literacy and learning.	January to February	Teachers Literacy team members Assistant principal to assist with walk-throughs	Walk-through form that focuses on literacy Documentation form for strategy use	• At each department or team meeting, teachers will discuss the strategies they used and how they can improve instruction. Literacy team members will record data and bring to next team meeting. • Administrators and literacy team members will conduct walk-throughs twice a month. • Literacy team will review documented use of strategies and walk-through data and discuss ways to raise, improve, or sustain literacy use in content area classrooms.	Walk-through data collected shows increasing use of the common strategies across classrooms. Documentation of strategy use indicates regular use in all departments.
All students will understand and routinely use the literacy support strategies as needed.	March to June	Literacy team Literacy coach Students	Time for focus group Focus group questions	The literacy team members will conduct focus groups with students to determine student strategy knowledge and use.	Student focus group data reveal widespread knowledge and use of literacy support strategies.

Figure 3.2 Sample Implementation Map Based on Rubric 2 for Central School

After each implementation map has been developed, review and discuss each part as a team. Is every step clear? Are the parts specific? Are the resources feasible to obtain? Do the measures of success specifically assess each action step?

STEP 2: SOLICIT FEEDBACK FROM THE SCHOOL COMMUNITY

This step is important because the team needs to get widespread buy-in and ownership of the literacy action plan for implementation to be successful. Faculty members deserve to understand the plan, what it is trying to achieve, and what they are going to be expected to do. Public review and feedback can also strengthen the plan by surfacing additional concerns, approaches, and ideas not considered by the team up to this point.

In Step 2, the literacy leadership team shares the implementation maps with the wider school community and solicits feedback. This step is designed to inform the faculty of the literacy leadership team's efforts and to gather input, ensuring that everyone's voice is heard.

Your presentation to the faculty should describe the process the team went through in Stages 1, 2, and 3, share the literacy action goals along with a rationale for why they were selected, and include a brief summary of the implementation maps. Literacy leadership team members can each take a section of the presentation, or one or two members who feel comfortable presenting to a group can take the lead. We strongly recommend that an administrator take an active role in the presentation because it is important to assure the faculty that the literacy improvement effort has administrative support.

To complete this step, the team needs to decide how to gather input from the faculty. We have found either of the following options to be successful in gathering feedback from the entire school.

- *Option 1: Group Feedback:* After a presentation to the faculty of the implementation maps developed by the literacy leadership team, teachers work in groups (departments or teams) to review the goal statements and corresponding maps. A recorder from each group fills out a group feedback form and returns the completed form to a designated member of the literacy leadership team.

- *Option 2: Individual Feedback:* After a presentation to the faculty of the implementation maps completed by the literacy leadership team, solicit feedback on the goal statements and implementation maps from individuals. Distribute an individual feedback form for teachers to complete and return to a designated member of the literacy leadership team. This feedback can also be solicited electronically using a survey tool.

Either option can support getting buy-in from teachers and staff throughout the school. At a literacy leadership team meeting, you can discuss the team's goal for getting feedback and determine what you hope this activity will accomplish. Then, select which option is better for your school and make a plan for how feedback will get back to the team. A sample feedback form is shown in Figure 3.3.

The form can be used either by individuals or by groups. If used by a group, select a recorder for the group; recorders turn in their forms to Sue Jones. If used by individuals, return the form to Mr. Grey.

Group Members: LaTasha, Merissa, David, Lynn

Individual member: ______________________________

1. Goal Statements

In your groups, read and discuss the goals your literacy leadership team selected for the school year. Place a check on the line below each goal to indicate the degree your group agrees or disagrees with the goal. Then write down any suggestions you have for modifying the goals.

Goal Statement 1: All students will learn and routinely use reading and writing support strategies to enhance literacy and learning across all content areas.

Agree---X---Disagree

How we would modify this goal:

(For example)...Be more specific about strategies.

2. Implementation Map

In your groups, read and discuss the implementation map for each goal, reaching consensus about whether you agree or disagree with the plan. At the bottom of each map, use the following scale to indicate the views of your group:

1 = strongly disagree; 2 = disagree; 3 = agree; 4 = strongly agree

Then write down the suggestions and comments of your group members, indicating specifics that will improve the implementation map.

We need to know more specifics about instructional strategies. Which ones? How many? Are they new strategies?

3. What support do you need to implement this goal?

Figure 3.3 Completed Feedback Form for Central School

What are the elements of an effective presentation to the faculty? How can you reassure the faculty that this is not just another initiative?

STEP 3: REVISE LITERACY ACTION GOAL STATEMENTS AND IMPLEMENTATION MAPS

This step is important because the feedback allows the team to review and discuss the plan one more time before finalizing it. Feedback also allows the team to review the concerns of the faculty, get additional ideas and insights, and ensure that the action steps address the goal statements and guide implementation. To other stakeholders, a literacy action plan that has been vetted by the faculty is much stronger then one developed by a small committee.

In Step 3, the task of the literacy leadership team is to review the feedback, make any necessary revisions to the implementation maps, add additional information needed to preface the plan (e.g., rationale for a focus on literacy, connection between the plan and school and district improvement goals, process engaged in by the team to develop the plan, names of team members) and then present the complete literacy action plan to faculty, parents, students, the school board, and the larger community. Reviewing the feedback from faculty and incorporating their suggestions is essential for the plan's success. Although this step can be time consuming, it is well worth the effort as it builds the foundation for buy-in from the larger school community. Then the team is ready to share the literacy action plan with all stakeholders: faculty, staff, parents, students, and the community.

The literacy leadership team can review and discuss the feedback forms, deciding how to address faculty suggestions and concerns. It is helpful to conduct a List-Group-Label activity, where team members list the main ideas of all feedback, then group comments that seem to be related. The team can then label each collection of comments by what they have in common. To accomplish this, the team can use the following procedures:

- First, make a *list* of the feedback. You may wish to sort the forms (you could do this by department or grade level). Team members can put each suggestion on a sticky note.
- Next, *group* the suggestions that relate to the same issue or topic.
- Then, *label* each group of suggestions. You may wish to put the grouped and labeled ideas together in a concept map on a wall chart so that you can see all of the information at once.

Using a List-Group-Label protocol is particularly helpful if there is a lot of feedback and much of it is specific. Otherwise, the team is at risk of trying to revise based on every comment. The team does not have to incorporate all feedback but should be alert for patterns in the responses that indicate something that should be addressed.

Once the team has sorted the suggestions, the team should discuss each category of suggestion and decide which part of the literacy action plan is affected and if a revision should be made. Again, a consensus process, as opposed to a voting process, should be used. The team has to feel the primary ownership of the plan, and voicing why a change should or should not be made is important for team unity. However, the team risks being perceived as unresponsive if no changes are made. Because of this, everyone needs to be able to articulate clearly the reasoning behind the team's decisions when the revised literacy action plan is made public to the faculty. Once you have made revisions to the literacy action goal statements and implementation maps, the team leader should schedule a meeting with school and district administrators to be sure that the appropriate resources are allocated and that there is leadership support for the entire literacy action plan.

REAL SCHOOL EXAMPLE

The superintendent welcomed teachers to the fall inservice day and praised the hard work accomplished by the literacy teams. The superintendent reinforced the need for developing strong literacy skills among all students given the 21st century literacy skills demands. A keynote by an outside consultant was given that stressed how to integrate literacy and learning. Together, this literacy kickoff for the district established the need for the initiative, set the direction, and began to create a common vision and language about literacy.

The faculties of the middle and high schools then reconvened as separate schools to talk specifically about each school's literacy goals. In each school, the two literacy leadership team leaders explained how each team developed the literacy action goals and implementation maps. They each showed pictures of the activities and the consensus grids for their schools. Then, they broke into groups—the high school meeting by departments, and the middle school meeting by interdisciplinary, grade-level teams. Each goal and implementation map was discussed, and the individual faculty members filled out an electronic feedback form provided by the literacy team leaders. Literacy team members also demonstrated a literacy support strategy. When each literacy team met the next day, they considered all of the feedback and revised each literacy action goal and implementation map. They found that revising their goals and implementation maps using the faculty feedback made them much more specific. Teachers said they appreciated having some input into the process and began discussions about how they could contribute to the literacy action goals.

Source: Thanks to Marinette School District, Marinette, Wisconsin, for this example. Used with permission.

STEP 4: PUBLISH THE FORMAL LITERACY ACTION PLAN

A formal literacy action plan can be used to promote the literacy improvement effort, communicate to all stakeholders what action steps the school community will be engaged in and what resources will be used, and to coordinate school-based plans across the district. Some of the components you may wish to include in the final plan are

- Your school's mission statement or the school or district's improvement goals and how the literacy action plan connects to it;
- A rationale for the need for a literacy improvement effort that may include information from the Data Overview you created in Stage 1 of the literacy leadership process;
- Your vision for a literacy-rich school;
- The process you engaged in to develop the goals and implementation maps;
- The role, function, and membership of the literacy leadership team; and
- The literacy action goal statements and corresponding implementation maps.

The literacy leadership team can present the finalized literacy action plan to the faculty and other stakeholders. This may be done through presentations at faculty meetings, parent meetings, district level meetings, and school board meetings. Some schools actually print out a formal copy; other schools create a word document embedded with nice-looking graphics and save it as a PDF file. The literacy action plan can also be published in the school's newsletter and posted on the school's Web site. The plan does not have to be lengthy and should be updated each year with the date of the plan clearly visible.

What is the best way to publish the school's completed literacy action plan? What do we want to include in our literacy action plan?

NEXT STEPS

The literacy leadership team should be proud of having developed and published a final literacy action plan that addresses student needs, builds on school capacity, and is grounded in the team's collaborative assessment of current school practice. You have carefully developed literacy action goals and created detailed implementation maps for each goal statement. You have actively sought feedback and support from teachers, administrators, and other stakeholders.

Now, the literacy leadership team is ready to proceed to the real work of a literacy improvement initiative: implementation. After all, if the plan stays on paper and is not enacted throughout the school, there is no reason to think there will be changes in outcomes. Stage 4 is when the team begins monitoring implementation of the literacy action plan during the upcoming school year—and when the rewarding work begins!

4

Stage 4: Implement

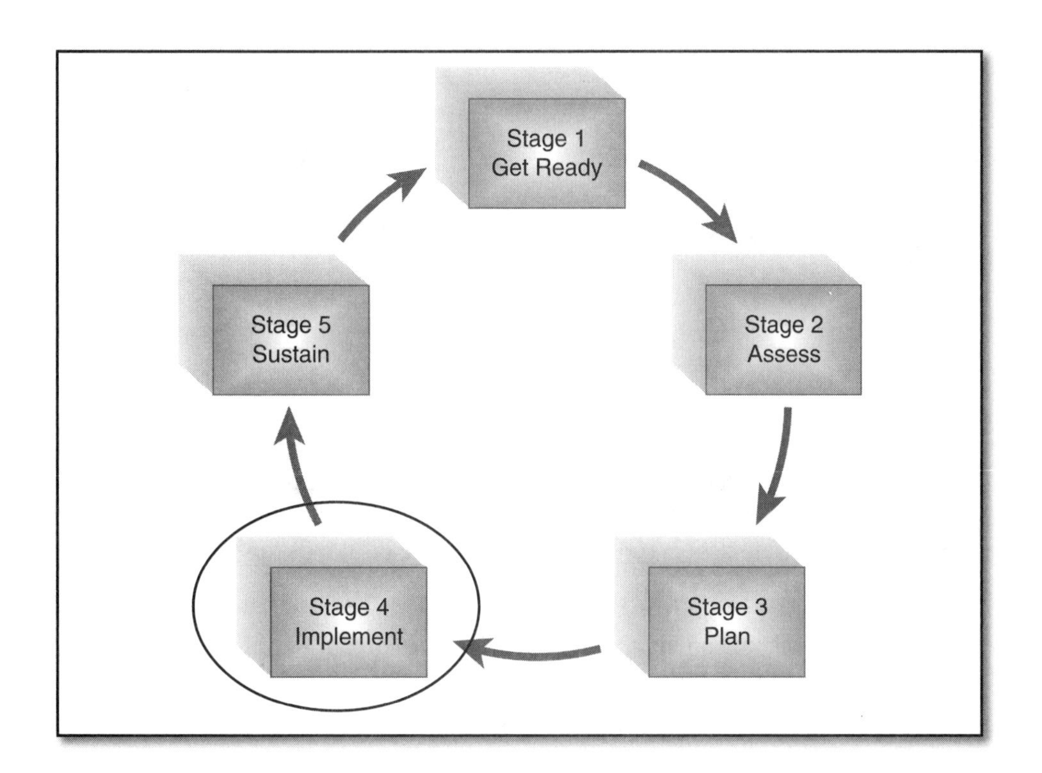

In Stage 4 of the literacy leadership process, you will complete the following:

- ✓ Organize for success.
- ✓ Monitor and troubleshoot issues with implementation.
- ✓ Use data to track progress toward your literacy goals.
- ✓ Sustain momentum and celebrate accomplishments.

In Stage 1, your team laid the groundwork for initiating and sustaining a literacy initiative in your school. In Stages 2 and 3, you assessed your school's strengths as well as the literacy needs of students, developed goals, created implementation maps, and published a literacy action plan. Now, in Stage 4, you are ready to implement the plan.

Stage 4 is, of course, critical. After all, no matter how well your literacy action plan has been designed, nothing will happen if the maps are not implemented with fidelity. Stage 4 includes four steps to ensure that the implementation maps actively produce literacy and learning schoolwide.

Unlike in Stages 2 and 3, the steps in Stage 4 are recursive rather than sequential. Organizing and holding literacy-related events that build enthusiasm and generate participation (Step 1), monitoring implementation and troubleshooting (Step 2), monitoring progress toward goals (Step 3), and sustaining momentum and recognizing and celebrating accomplishments (Step 4) need to occur throughout the year. You should therefore use the steps and activities throughout Stage 4 as needed to guide and direct the literacy improvement initiative at your school.

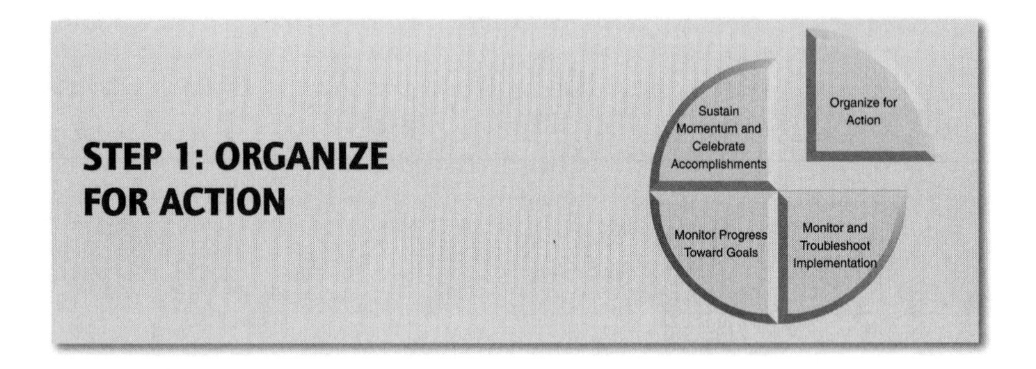

STEP 1: ORGANIZE FOR ACTION

This step is important because the team needs to galvanize schoolwide action and organize itself to oversee the initiative. Swift, concrete action ensures that everyone understands the following:

- Literacy improvement is a priority.
- The entire school community can work together to make a difference for all students.

The literacy leadership team needs to engage in some planning about how to begin the implementation of the literacy improvement effort. Step 1 includes four activities that the team plans and carries out to get the initiative off to a good start:

- Develop a brand statement.
- Implement kickoff activities.
- Plan how to involve students.
- Organize for productive team meetings.

Brand the Literacy Initiative

In our work with literacy teams, we have found that it is helpful to *brand* your initiative. A brand statement gives the initiative an identity and can serve as both a focusing tool and a constant reminder of the work being done. On the most basic level, branding your literacy initiative allows for the team and the school to organize action around an effort that has a name.

Creating the brand statement supports additional discussion among team members about what your literacy improvement effort is really about and what you are collectively trying to do. The brand can create expectations for all stakeholders and can embody the values implicit in the literacy initiative.

What do we mean by a brand statement? You are familiar with the concept of a brand statement in commercials and on billboards. Marketing executives use brands to represent what they want the consumer to associate with a particular product or idea. The team can create a brand to represent what is essential in the school's literacy improvement effort. It is a way of succinctly packaging the team's promise of better literacy and learning for all students. The brand statement should be catchy, clever, short, and memorable. Most importantly, it should represent the values and goals of the literacy improvement effort. The best brand statements appeal to both teachers and students and capture the spirit of the literacy effort.

Brand statements can be words only, words and symbols, or a picture with a caption. Examples of brand statements used by schools we have worked with include the following:

- Literacy Lights the Way to Success (with candles)
- Got Book? (with pictures of famous adults posted throughout the school)
- Read to Succeed (a student is shown running up a stack of books).

Figure 4.1 shows one school's student-written literacy brand statement presented on a banner in the front of the school and on T-shirts.

One way to develop a brand statement is to have literacy leadership team members brainstorm ideas in pairs or triads. The meeting facilitator then writes all of the ideas up on the board or on a piece of chart paper and has team members put dots on the two to three ideas that they like best. The team discusses the two to three ideas that got the most votes and comes to consensus either on a single brand statement for the faculty to approve or the top two or three for the whole school community to vote on.

Some schools have students participate in the writing of a brand statement through contests or classroom activities. This takes longer but is a great way to generate student enthusiasm and participation at the beginning of the literacy improvement effort. If you develop your brand statement through contests or class activities, it is best to have one department (e.g., social studies or language arts) assume responsibility for the contest. Students will have to understand

Figure 4.1 One School's Literacy Brand

what a brand statement is and be shown several examples before they submit their ideas to the literacy team. The literacy team can select a winner or ask students and teachers to vote for their favorite.

If the literacy team writes the brand statement, be certain to give the rest of the faculty and students a chance to respond to the statement and make suggestions for revision. You want the brand statement to reflect the values of the entire school community. You can do this by soliciting feedback at a faculty meeting or in department or team meetings. You can also bring the brand statement to the student council for consideration. When asking the school community to vote, remember to inform them of the purpose of a brand statement for the literacy initiative. Once you have selected your brand statement, prominently display it in the school and ensure that everyone knows what it is and what it means.

Some people might question why a brand statement is important. A few people may object to what they see as commercializing or sloganizing. Others have seen many empty statements come and go. In some schools or districts, there is already a motto—in these cases, some schools have branded the literacy initiative so that it connects to or extends the school or district motto. Team members may want to refer to the suggestions in the chart that follows to respond to some of these concerns.

If team members or other faculty say . . .	You may want to suggest . . .
"This is one more example of commercialism in education—save us!"	The reality is that your students have been targets of direct advertising since they were small. This is a very effective tool that emphasizes what is important while building on a schema they know applied to education. Given that we are

If team members or other faculty say . . .	You may want to suggest . . .
	all competing against a myriad of outside influences for students' attention, we need to use the tools we have. It is also important to have a name for a campaign if we expect it to be successful. A name can create excitement and have a way to connect a wide range of activities to a single initiative. Calling it just "the literacy initiative" is an option but not a very compelling or exciting one!
"Another empty slogan?!"	This brand statement needs to be backed by action, active discussion, and frequent referral. It will not work if it is another empty slogan. It will be up to the literacy leadership team to make sure the brand gets out there and that significant activities are connected in people's minds to the brand. Reports on progress toward goals, action steps, activities—all need to carry the brand of the literacy initiative.
"We already have a motto."	Is this a motto about what the school does or a message to students? Often, mottos or names of school improvement initiatives are geared toward what the adults are doing, not what students are doing or a description of the community as literate. If the motto is deeply embedded in the consciousness of the school—that is, everyone knows it—is there a way to imbed a literacy-related takeoff of the motto?

Plan and Implement Your Schoolwide Literacy Kickoff

A kickoff is designed to get the literacy improvement effort off to a good start. The kickoff is a time to build enthusiasm for the literacy improvement initiative and remind everyone of the roles and responsibilities related to the initiative, how teachers will be supported (professional development opportunities, including coaching), and how everyone will be held accountable (collaborative examination of student work, sharing of strategy use, literacy walk-throughs). Be sure to invite district-level people as well as other principals and community members or partners of the school to the kickoff. You might even consider writing up a short notice about the kickoff for the local newspaper or radio station.

You may want to schedule an interactive keynote address to the faculty about the fundamentals of literacy learning with an outside consultant or an expert at the district or school level as the speaker. Such an address establishes a basic understanding of the importance of literacy and the challenges that content literacy often present for students. Sometimes an outside expert can lend credibility and energy to the initiative. However, it is also important to establish the literacy leadership team as the leaders of the initiative to reinforce the school-based, self-sustaining nature of the initiative. To this end, we recommend that you include members of the literacy team as co-presenters with any outside presenters.

The kickoff is also a good time to present an implementation calendar to the faculty and to provide a way for the faculty to vision, voice concerns, and solve problems together. How much you want to accomplish with the kickoff depends on how much of the visioning and establishing the need for the initiative you were able to implement in Stage 1. In addition, if the literacy team met over the summer to develop the plan, then you may want your kickoff event to include getting the faculty's feedback on the literacy action goals and implementation maps that you developed in Stages 2 and 3.

Kickoff events can take multiple forms and may occur during a single day or over a number of events or meetings. A well designed kickoff takes into account a school's culture, available meeting and release times, teacher expectations, typical ways of communicating, and levels of enthusiasm and degrees of awareness of the literacy improvement initiative. You can use the Potential Activities for Faculty Kickoff chart as a checklist for the team to use in prioritizing what should be included as part of the kickoff (see Tool 3 in Resource B).

Tool 3: Potential Activities for Faculty Kickoff

Stage 1	**Include in Kickoff**	**Do Not Include in Kickoff**
Introduce the literacy leadership team and its charge and responsibilities. Explain how members were chosen.		
Make a case for importance of the initiative (e.g., present 21st-century literacy skills needed by students to make the case that all students need literacy support).		
Introduce the *Taking Action Literacy Leadership Model* to the faculty.		
Use the vignette activity to envision a literacy-rich school. (Stage 1, Step 2)		
Stage 2		
Present school strengths map or repeat activity with faculty. (Stage 1, Step 1)		
Present current data about students as readers and writers and discuss improvement goals.		
Introduce the rubrics or use one or more with departments, grade-level teams, or professional learning groups to self-assess.		
Present the literacy action goals that the team developed and get feedback.		

Stage 3	Include in Kickoff	Do Not Include in Kickoff
Present the formal literacy action plan and get feedback from the faculty.		
Communicate the types of professional development opportunities planned for teachers and administrators.		
Ask faculty what professional development they need and how they would like the professional development delivered (whole faculty, by departments or teams, during faculty meetings, on workshop days or during common planning time).		
Ensure that everyone understands his or her role and the expectations for implementation of content area literacy support.		
Clarify the structures, policies, and schedule that will be put into place to support the work.		
Provide time for teachers to examine and discuss beliefs about literacy and learning.		
Present the implementation calendar and solicit feedback.		
Stage 4		
Introduce the brand statement or describe how this will be developed. Get feedback or suggestions from entire school community.		
Describe how the implementation maps will be rolled out and how the team will monitor implementation and progress toward goals during the school year.		
Introduce a common set of specific instructional strategies (selected by the literacy leadership team) that enhance content area literacy and learning.		

Include Students in the Literacy Initiative

Although improved student performance is the focus of a schoolwide literacy improvement initiative, literacy leadership teams sometimes forget to include students in the planning and implementation of the initiative and in the kickoff events. We have found that when students are brought into the initiative as partners and contributors, the initiative has a much better chance of success at all levels. Many schools include student members on the literacy leadership team. Other schools regularly schedule ways to get student input and feedback through surveys and focus groups. Some schools establish a student literacy leadership team that supports the work of the school's literacy leadership team. The student team provides insight into how the literacy initiative is being seen by students and how the initiative might be improved or strengthened. The following chart shows some suggestions for actively involving students in the literacy improvement effort (see Tool 4 in Resource B).

Tool 4: Involving Students in the Literacy Initiative		
	Needed	Not Needed
Sponsor a student contest to develop a poster and/or logo to publicize the brand statement.		
Form a student literacy team.		
Have students discuss what assists them to be better readers, writers, and thinkers and report back to the literacy leadership team.		
Ask one or more student groups to complete one of the rubrics to assess their school and build a student-centered goal to share with the literacy leadership team.		
Have student focus groups give feedback about the literacy initiative and how it can be more relevant to students.		
Have the student literacy team organize literacy-related activities such as poetry slams, readings, and book clubs.		
Have the student literacy team publicize the literacy initiative through announcements, the school newspaper, and community media.		
Survey students on their perceptions of specific aspects of school environment, culture, and policy.		
Nominate students to serve as student representatives to the literacy leadership team.		
Other:		
Other:		

Organize for Productive Team Meetings

It is helpful to have an agenda for each meeting in the implementation phase. An agenda keeps the conversation on track and assists the team to remain focused, greatly enhancing the chance that the meeting will be productive. Meeting topics might include the same action items each time the team met, changing only the specifics to help move the literacy initiative forward. For example,

- Share success from classroom, departments, and teams.
- Share questions and concerns that have emerged since the previous meeting.
- Discuss the data around any implementation challenges so far. What do we notice? What do we wonder? What actions do we need to take?
- Discuss the specifics of implementation. What questions are we exploring related to implementation during the next meeting? Establish procedures, deadlines, and responsible parties for needed data collection for next meeting.

- Debrief on what went well during this meeting and any suggestions that team members have for making meetings more productive.
- Remind everyone of the decisions made at the meeting and the date, time, and place of the next meeting.

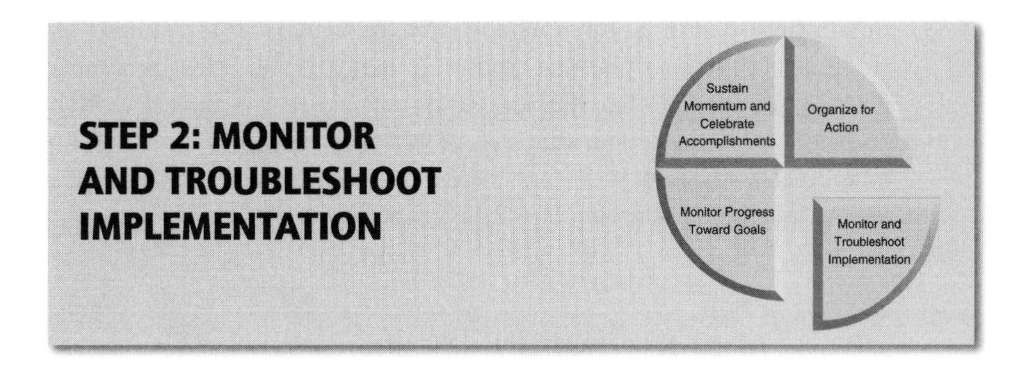

STEP 2: MONITOR AND TROUBLESHOOT IMPLEMENTATION

This step is important because many literacy action plans look good on paper, but implementation occurs only in pieces or not at all. To be certain that the plan results in improved literacy teaching and learning, it is crucial that team members monitor how well the plan's action steps are being implemented.

In Step 2, the team asks, "To what extent are we following the implementation maps as designed?" A specific map might not get implemented as intended for many reasons, including time demands, conflicting initiatives, or change of administration. A major responsibility of the literacy leadership team is to make sure that quality implementation is occurring as planned. To complete an evidence-based review of implementation, the team can use the following protocol at each team meeting:

1. Select one literacy action goal statement and the associated implementation map to review. We recommend rotating this review so all implementation maps are examined at least twice throughout the year. Of course, the team might review more than one map at the same meeting.
2. Review each action step of the implementation maps, including the specifics of implementation and the measures of success. Compare these with actions taken to date, paying particular attention to evidence that indicates progress toward implementation.

Action Step	Timeline (Target Date)	Lead Person(s)	Resources Needed	Specifics of Implementation	Measure(s) of Success

Figure 4.2 Parts of the Implementation Maps

3. The team can use the Implementation Monitoring Template to determine whether or not, and to what degree, implementation of an action step has occurred as planned. You may want to have a team member actually fill out the chart during the discussion so you have a written record of your discussion that can be put into the notes from a given meeting. Or you may just want to use the categories of the chart as a way to focus the discussion (see Tool 5 in Resource B).

Tool 5: Implementation Monitoring Template			
Literacy Action Goal Statement:			
Date of Meeting:			
Attendees:			
Action Step	**Where Are We Now?**	**Are We on Track? (Yes/No/Somewhat)**	**Actions the Team Needs to Take (Based on the Action Points of the Model)**

If the team uses the Implementation Monitoring Template and finds that implementation is on track and an action step has been successfully completed, the team may need to develop next steps to deepen and sustain momentum of the initiative. The completed sample that follows shows how the Central School team might have completed this review using the Implementation Monitoring Chart.

Implementation Monitoring Chart Central School Example			
Literacy Action Goal Statement: *All students will learn and routinely use reading and writing support strategies to enhance literacy and learning across all content areas.*			
Date of Meeting: October 15			
Attendees: All team members plus assistant principal for curriculum			
Action Step	**Where Are We Now?**	**Are We on Track? (Yes/No/ Somewhat)**	**Actions Needed to Deepen or Sustain the Work**
The literacy team will select a common set of literacy support strategies and decide which departments or teams will be responsible for teaching the strategies.	The literacy team selected four strategies: Think Alouds, Question-Answer Relationship, Graphic Organizers, and Quick Writes. Departments have the option of choosing two additional reading to learn strategies.	Yes	Need to encourage other departments to focus on a few strategies—invite department members to attend core department meetings—and ask departments to review when students have been introduced to strategies in each class and how often students are using the strategy; strategy descriptions need to be posted on the teacher resource site.
All teachers will participate in at least two professional development sessions to learn a common set of strategies.	Literacy coach and selected teachers presented the common strategies to the faculty at the Literacy Kickoff and invited participation and discussion about the purpose of each strategy and how the strategy can be applied to different content areas.	Yes	A second session on literacy strategies will be offered to teachers at the November systemwide inservice. This one will match specific content literacy demands to selected strategies.
Each department or team will discuss the literacy demands of their content areas and use the common strategies in their instruction.	Core departments (math, science, social studies, English) are routinely using the four strategies. Other departments need additional content-specific professional development.	Somewhat	Team will refer to the Support Teachers Checklist to develop ideas for professional development. Team leader will talk with principal about locating resources for professional development.
All teachers will have multiple opportunities to visit demonstration classrooms, engage in peer coaching, and/or work with a literacy coach to see strategies in action.	This step will be addressed in January and February.	Has not yet occurred	The team leader will work with the school literacy coach in developing a calendar of demonstrations and classroom visits.

In the following section, we present a series of troubleshooting checklists related to four of the five action points (Support Teachers, Use Data, Build Leadership Capacity, and Allocate Resources) in the *Taking Action Literacy Leadership Model.* Depending on the results of the review of implementation, you can use the appropriate checklist to troubleshoot issues and jumpstart implementation in a specific area. The checklists describe a range of problems that can derail a literacy initiative, so the team may want to review these checklists periodically to make sure all is moving forward appropriately.

For example, if the team determines that professional development is not translating to the types of changes in practice outlined in the action steps of the implementation map, the team can refer to the Support Teachers Checklist to troubleshoot potential pitfalls and generate solutions. Or if the team feels that too few teachers are participating in the literacy initiative, the team may use the Build Leadership Capacity Checklist for ideas to inspire more participation among teachers and staff.

Use Troubleshooting Checklists

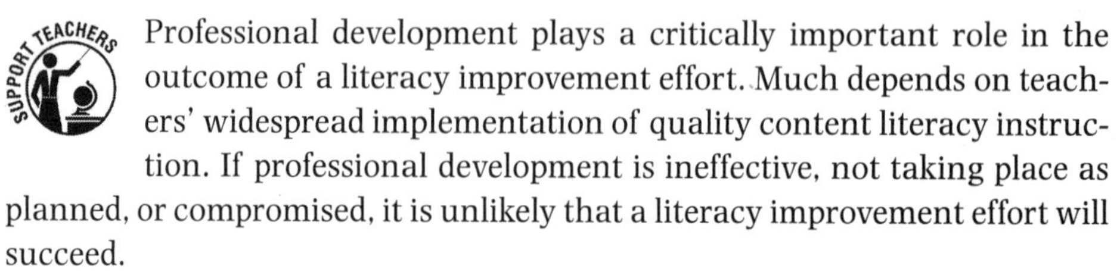

Professional development plays a critically important role in the outcome of a literacy improvement effort. Much depends on teachers' widespread implementation of quality content literacy instruction. If professional development is ineffective, not taking place as planned, or compromised, it is unlikely that a literacy improvement effort will succeed.

Professional development can be implemented using multiple formats, including a workshop series, coursework, coaching, demonstration lessons, structured conversations among colleagues, and online modules. Monitoring the implementation as well as the effects of planned professional development is critical because professional development that does not result in changed classroom practices is a waste of resources and time.

We recommend that the team read through the checklist below and determine which areas, if any, need attention. You may want to ask each team member to make an individual assessment first before discussing responses with the group. As you identify trouble spots, you can use the Support Teachers Checklist to help you determine next steps to take as a team (see Tool 6 in Resource B).

Tool 6: Support Teachers Checklist

	Yes	No	If no, team members can do the following:
Teachers are receiving professional development that includes teaching and modeling of literacy strategies aligned to goals and action steps.			Meet with the professional development committee and discuss the professional development required to implement the literacy action plan successfully. Decide together how to make this support available to teachers.
Faculty members are satisfied with the quality of the teacher professional development that has taken place.			Determine what participants perceive as impediments to high quality professional development. Use that perception data to adjust future professional development activities.

Tool 6: Support Teachers Checklist			
	Yes	**No**	**If no, team members can do the following:**
Professional development is being tied to the authentic issues that teachers face in their classrooms.			Survey teachers to determine what they consider to be the most pressing issues for students as readers, writers, and thinkers. Find time for teachers across various content areas to share concerns and insights and tie professional development to these areas of challenge.
School administrators are attending and reinforcing essential messages from the professional development.			Meet with the principal and revisit the plan, clarifying the roles and responsibilities of the principal associated with each goal and set of action steps. Develop a process for moving forward with more active engagement by the principal.
School administrators and/or the literacy coach follow up professional development with classroom observations and coaching to make sure teachers are implementing suggested activities.			Ask the team leader to meet with the administrators and/or literacy coach to set up a schedule of follow-up classroom visits.
Participation in planned teacher professional development is high.			Meet with teachers who are not attending professional development. Work toward finding solutions based on feedback from those teachers.
Professional development is provided live or through video models when introducing new instructional strategies.			Meet with the library media specialist to determine if video and DVD resources are available through interlibrary loans. Create a hot linked list of examples available on the Internet for teachers to have as a reference point.
Coaching and mentoring are available to team members and participating teachers.			Meet with the administrator responsible for curriculum and instruction to discuss opportunities for co-planning with a coach or peer. Seek insights from department chairs about literacy-savvy content teachers who would be willing to mentor team members and participating teachers.
Evidence suggests that professional development is positively impacting classroom practice.			Ask literacy leaders to do classroom observations and discuss which teachers would benefit from targeted support to improve classroom practice.
Teachers and support personnel are being provided opportunities for collaborating, brainstorming, and sharing strategies.			Examine the master schedule to determine where time can be allocated during the school day for opportunities to collaborate. Establish an electronic collaboration tool so that teachers and staff can conduct collective action research and communicate with experts.
Professional development is taking advantage of teachers' professional expertise.			Meet with department chairs and team leaders to assess which teachers have literacy expertise and recruit them to be peer presenters.
Literacy team members open their doors, demonstrating effective literacy practices in their own content areas.			Bring in an outside consultant to demonstrate instructional strategies related to your literacy action plan (e.g., a specific strategy, differentiated instruction). Coordinate opportunities for classroom exchanges and co-teaching, to shift the culture from one of isolation to one of shared responsibility for student learning.

To monitor and troubleshoot implementation, the team needs to collect, review, and analyze the kinds of data you outlined in each implementation map as measures of success. Use this data to determine if implementation is going as planned. This is called collecting data on *fidelity of implementation.* After all, if you are not implementing the initiative as designed, there would be little reason to expect positive effects on teacher practice or student learning.

Some common issues that literacy teams face as they endeavor to collect and use data to monitor implementation are provided in the following example. We recommend that the team read through the issues and determine if any areas need attention. You may want to ask each team member to make an individual assessment first before discussing responses with the group. As you identify trouble spots, refer to the Use Data Checklist to help you determine next steps for the team to take (see Tool 7 in Resource B).

Tool 7: Use Data Checklist

Indicator	Yes	No	If no, team members can do the following:
We are collecting the data we said we would collect.			Revisit who is responsible for collecting the data and determine what support is needed.
We are analyzing and drawing conclusions from the data we have collected.			Determine what is preventing the data from being analyzed. Is it a matter of time for the team to meet? Is it a lack of a process for data analysis?
We have the data we need to answer our questions about implementation.			Determine what additional data are needed and how these can be collected.
The data suggest that we are on track with implementation.			Identify goals or action steps where more data are needed to determine if implementation is on track.

A schoolwide literacy improvement initiative requires a collaborative effort to launch and sustain it. Building the literacy leadership capacity of administrators, literacy coaches, reading and media specialists, team leaders, department chairs, curriculum coordinators, and teachers is, therefore, a priority.

If you have evidence that teacher leaders or school administrators may not be involved or supportive of the initiative, this may be negatively impacting implementation. While specific leadership roles and responsibilities may not be explicitly spelled out in the implementation map, you may want to review and discuss the Build Capacity Checklist to troubleshoot where implementation may be breaking down and what the team can do about it.

The following chart illustrates some common issues that many literacy leadership teams face as they work to build capacity. We recommend that the team read through the issues and determine if any areas need attention. You may want to ask each team member to make an individual assessment first before discussing responses with the group. Then the team can use the suggestions in the Build Capacity Checklist to discuss what next steps make sense to take (see Tool 8 in Resource B).

Tool 8: Build Capacity Checklist			
Indicator	**Yes**	**No**	**If no, team members can do the following:**
The Faculty as a Whole			
The faculty as a whole is becoming more knowledgeable about literacy.			Dedicate part of every faculty meeting to discussing the progress and accomplishments of the literacy initiative. Invite team members to make presentations at faculty and parent meetings. Publicize the work of the team on the school's Web site and publications.
Members of the faculty are serving as resources to others through providing demonstration classes and sharing resources.			Publicly acknowledge faculty who are serving as resources and mentors. Ask teacher leaders to recommend colleagues with whom they could collaborate and support as future presenters and mentors. Provide planning time for teacher pairs to develop classroom demonstrations.
Content area teachers are buying into the goals and action steps of the implementation maps.			Determine which teachers are on board and which are not. Continue to work with the teachers who are enthusiastic and willing to integrate literacy support with content learning. Continue to offer support and professional development to all teachers.
The literacy action plan is understood by most teachers outside of the literacy leadership team.			Periodically, ask to have some time at a faculty meeting or at department or team meetings to reintroduce the plan and report on progress thus far. Invite faculty members to suggest additional ways to help make the literacy initiative successful.
Administrators and Literacy Coaches			
Administrators and literacy coaches are meeting regularly with designated team members to support progress toward goals.			Ask the principal to free up administrators to meet with the literacy team. Be sure that administrators and literacy coaches are notified in plenty of time to put team meetings on their calendars. Send out minutes of the meeting to keep the work of the team on their minds.
Media and Technology Specialists			
The media and technology specialists provide time and support for the action steps of the implementation maps.			Include the media and technology specialists in the events and activities led by the literacy leadership team. Send reports and minutes of the meetings if specialists are not attending team meetings. Ask the specialists to identify teachers who are experienced in multiple literacies and ask them for suggestions for integrating media and technology with literacy instruction.
Department Chairs and/or Team Leaders			
Department chairs and team leaders are providing adequate support for the literacy action plan.			Discuss the plan with department chairs and team leaders. Solicit ideas for how department and/or team leaders can support and advocate for quality implementation of the map. Allow time during department meetings to air additional questions and concerns.
Parents and Community Members			
Parents and community members are aware and supportive of many events and activities of the literacy action plan.			Publish the activities of the literacy leadership team and participating teachers in the newsletter and/or on the Web site. Invite parents and community members to activities sponsored by the team. Include a parent and/or community representative on the literacy team.

The literacy leadership team needs to be aware of the challenges that may face team members and other literacy leaders, including the challenges of time, increased workload, and the potential stress of fulfilling dual roles of teachers, administrators, and literacy leaders. Troubleshooting issues can prevent minor problems from growing into barriers that can derail the work. For suggestions of how to troubleshoot issues specifically related to how the team is functioning, see Chapter 5.

Resources are essential to the implementation of an effective literacy improvement effort. Schools led by administrators who strategically allocate resources such as time, space, personnel, professional development, funding, technology, and materials are more likely to meet the goals set out in the literacy action plan. However, finding adequate resources may involve a reallocation of resources or using resources in different ways than in the past.

If resources are more limited than anticipated, the literacy leadership team should brainstorm potential solutions. Sometimes, creative thinking can unlock a solution that might otherwise be overlooked. For example, team members might advocate for revisions to the master schedule to allow more time for teacher meetings. Another tactic might be for the team to help stakeholders understand the importance and benefits of sharing resources.

We recommend that the team read through the issues listed on the Allocate Resources Checklist and determine if any areas need attention. You may want to ask each team member to make an individual assessment first before discussing responses with the group. Then, the team can use the Allocate Resources Checklist (see Tool 9 in Resource B) and discuss what next steps make sense to take.

Tool 9: Allocate Resources Checklist

Indicator	Yes	No	If no, team members can do the following:
Resources described in the implementation maps are available as anticipated.			Schedule time with the principal to confirm that these resources were reasonable to expect and to discuss current availability. Schedule meetings with those who control specific resources (e.g., technology, time, space) and discuss why the resource is needed and how it connects to the plan's goals. Report the results of each meeting to the principal and discuss options.
Resources are being used effectively to support the action steps outlined in the implementation maps.			Revisit the resources identified for each action step. Determine if the resource is critical to successful implementation. If so, meet with the principal or team administrative leader to determine alternatives for supporting the action step.
District leaders are providing adequate support for implementation.			Ask to meet with key district leaders to communicate the plan, what has been accomplished, why this work is important, and what types of support would be helpful. Discuss how the literacy action goals are aligned with the district's goals and ask district leaders about other resources they have to support the work.

Indicator	Yes	No	If no, team members can do the following:
The literacy action plan is aligned with and connected to the School Improvement Plan so that resources can be shared.			Meet with school administrators and discuss how the literacy action plan connects to other instructional improvement initiatives at the school. Then, discuss how the literacy improvement initiative can be used to connect to other initiatives. The results of this discussion can be shared with the entire faculty so everyone can understand the connections. Ask the administrator to publicly state ongoing support for the plan and expectations that everyone will work collaboratively to fully implement the plan.

STEP 3: MONITOR PROGRESS TOWARD GOALS

This step is important because by collecting and analyzing data connected to the goals of the implementation maps, the team can examine how well the initiative is achieving the intended outcomes. If you are not making progress toward the literacy action goals you established, it is critical for the team to recognize this lack of progress and take action.

Now that action is being taken toward completion of the implementation maps, the literacy leadership team needs to examine evidence that shows the initiative is making a difference for classroom teaching and learning. Certainly, you will use student performance data on the state assessment or on district mandated tests as one outcome to examine. But other sources of data can be used strategically to determine if progress is being made. Four valuable types of data to collect and analyze include the following:

- Samples of teacher assignments and student work
- Teacher survey data
- Student feedback data
- Literacy walk-through data

Through examination and analysis of these data, the team is then able to assess progress toward goals as well as report findings to other stakeholders (e.g., students, parents, school board members, district leaders, members of the business community). Remember, the team does not bear the total responsibility for collecting all appropriate progress monitoring data. The team should be assisted by administrators, data coordinators, and district office personnel. While data are the team's best ally, too much data can be overwhelming and a single-minded focus on data collection and analysis can overshadow implementation and other important roles of the literacy team, bringing momentum on literacy improvement to a halt.

Collect Evidence From Teacher Assignments and Student Work

Many protocols can be used to look at teacher assignments and student work. There are also protocols to analyze student performance data on benchmark or summative tests. The benefit of collecting and analyzing this type of data is twofold: (1) it is based on artifacts that can be collected fairly easily, requiring no additional assessment time; and (2) the exercise can be repeated at different points in the school year to determine if progress is being made.

Teacher Assignment Data. The type of data you collect and protocols you use depends on the goals specified in your implementation maps. For example, you may want to see if increasing numbers of teacher-made tests include higher order critical thinking questions. To answer this question, it may be helpful to collect copies of tests that were given during a specified time period and to analyze the questions asked and tasks assigned using Bloom's taxonomy. The results will provide one measure of how much critical thinking is being typically required of students. Then the process can be repeated to measure progress over time.

Collecting and Analyzing Student Work. Collaborative examination of student work builds teacher buy-in and promotes literacy development as a collective responsibility. Many protocols are available for the collaborative examination of student work. This can be a productive way for the team to involve teachers in looking at the type and quality of work students are doing.

To use student work as a way to gauge progress toward goals, the team again needs to determine what it wants to know. For example, the literacy action goal may be to increase the amount of writing students engage in while responding to reading. To answer if progress is being made toward that goal, samples of student work can be collected and analyzed by the team at various times during the initiative. If raising the quality of student writing is one of the goals of the initiative, then samples of student work can be scored against rubrics, or work that has been scored by teachers can be collected and analyzed.

We encourage the team to examine the literacy action goals and determine if collecting and analyzing student work would be helpful in determining progress toward that goal over time. If the answer for a given goal is *yes*, then the team should plan how to get baseline data near the beginning of the initiative against which progress can be documented and measured.

Collect Evidence Using Teacher Surveys. Since many of the action steps of the implementation maps depend directly on the actions of teachers, student performance data may not tell the whole story, at least not early in the initiative. The literacy team may want to collect evidence of the impact of teacher professional development or professional learning communities using teacher surveys over time. Or the team may want to know if teachers are implementing specific instructional strategies and instructional practices. Depending on the goal, the team may also want to examine changes in teacher perceptions over time of their students' abilities and strategies as readers and writers.

Although this is self-report data, and, therefore, subject to some variability in response rates and reliability, the team can use survey data to plan further professional development that responds to needs, to track trends over time, and to establish whether efficacy and participation is growing. To strengthen the chances of collecting usable data, when creating survey questions, make sure that you are only asking one question per item and that the response choices are set up so that the data show progress over time. For example, you may want your response scale to show frequency of strategy use or use of a specific classroom practice. Consider using a free or inexpensive computer-based survey tool like SurveyMonkey or Zoomerang so that the data can be easily compiled and analyzed.

You might also survey teachers to determine what they know about various aspects of literacy support, a precursor to their being able to provide this support in the classroom. If the goal is to provide excellent content literacy support, teacher knowledge is critical to ascertain and measure. These data are also important for determining professional development needs and showing progress in teacher efficacy over time.

Collect Student Feedback. Student perceptions offer compelling evidence about student engagement in classroom instruction and activities. Two strategies that the team can use to gather student feedback are focus groups and surveys. Student focus groups are a good way to talk directly to groups of students and get their understanding of the initiative and how they experience teaching and learning. Members of the literacy leadership team can meet with students from across grade levels or by grade level and can discuss students' experiences across content areas. Team members might want to develop a focus group protocol to answer specific questions. For example, the team might ask students how teachers model strategies for students, what strategies students find helpful when reading and writing, or how students perceive specific project-based assignments. An example of one focus group protocol targeting how students perceive the assignments is in the box on the next page.

Example of Student Focus Group Protocol

Questions the team wants to answer. Do students perceive that their assignments help them learn content and become better readers and writers? Do assignments help students produce quality work?

Directions to the focus group: Think of an assignment that you recently completed that you worked on for more than one class period.

- What was the purpose of the assignment?
- If you were confused, what was the cause of your confusion?
- If you needed extra help, what could you do?
- How do you know you have completed quality work?
- Did the assignment help you become a better reader or writer? Why or why not?
- What grade do you expect to get on the assignment? Why?
- What suggestions do you have to make the assignment more interesting?
- What literacy support strategies have you learned in this class?

If the team wants to know students' perceptions of the literacy initiative's areas of focus, another potential student focus group activity is to have students rate their perception of how well one of the literacy action rubric's components is implemented in the school. The team might also want to conduct a more general student focus group activity and repeat the exercise over time with either the same or different students to get a view of how students perceive the impact of the initiative over time. Questions might include the following:

- Your school is part of a districtwide literacy project. Did you know that? If so, what do you know about the literacy project?
- What is your school's literacy project brand statement or motto? How did you find out about it?
- Do your teachers use any literacy support strategies in your classes? If so, what are they?
- If your teachers use literacy support strategies in your classes, how did you learn to use them, and when do you use them now?
- Think about the reading assignments you have had this year. What made the assignments easy or hard? What made them meaningful? What helped you complete those assignments successfully?
- Think about the writing assignments you have had this year. What made the assignments easy or hard? What helped you complete those assignments?
- In what ways does the school encourage you to read for pleasure?
- In what ways do your teachers help you read and write more effectively?

Another approach to collecting student feedback is through the use of student surveys. As with teacher surveys, ask questions that are targeted to get information about progress toward goals, make sure you are asking only one question per item, and consider using electronic survey tools to collect and analyze the data. The benefit is that students can be periodically surveyed over the course of the initiative. Be aware, though, that student survey data can be unreliable, depending on student understanding of the questions and the level of student engagement with the material.

Collect Evidence From Literacy Walk-Throughs. One systematic way to collect data focused on progress toward goals is to conduct regular *literacy walk-throughs.* Literacy walk-throughs consist of a series of brief (5–8 minutes) classroom visits using targeted data collection tools. Data are not analyzed until several classroom visits have occurred. Literacy walk-throughs provide a glimpse into the everyday instructional practices in the school and over time can provide systematic data about progress toward goals. Literacy walk-throughs can be spontaneous to see the typical behavior of teachers and students, or they can be planned and very specifically targeted to identify aspects of literacy instruction that support progress toward literacy action goals. The focus is on the interactions between teacher and students; the level of student engagement; the amounts and types of reading, writing, presenting, and critical thinking; and on the quality of student work. A literacy walk-through can be conducted by a single person or a team, which might include school administrator(s), curriculum support person(s), district-level administrators, members of the literacy leadership team, and team leaders and/or department chairs.

The focus of the walk-throughs can be collaboratively determined ahead of time based on student performance data, elements of the implementation map and/or school improvement plan, or specific evidence of classroom practice related to recent professional development sessions. Literacy walk-throughs can also focus on a variety of classroom artifacts and interactions, including the following:

- Word walls with content area vocabulary
- Literacy strategy instruction
- Student work exhibiting thinking about texts
- Student writing about content area learning
- Evidence of the schools literacy vision
- Students reading a variety of text at multiple levels
- Evidence of differentiated literacy instruction

The literacy team can summarize the results to discuss with faculty, to guide professional development planning, and to provide a clear picture of progress toward goals. We recommend that literacy walk-throughs be conducted during two week intervals and then not conducted for three to four weeks. This allows the team to examine trends with respect to the goals of the literacy action plan. The emphasis is always on collective data, not individual feedback to teachers.

To develop literacy walk-through forms that support monitoring the progress toward goals, the literacy team should brainstorm ways that they can collect evidence of progress toward a goal based on observations in classrooms. That is, what would be regularly observed if the goal were reached? This evidence becomes the indicators on the form. Then the team needs to establish a rating scale that makes sense and can show progress if it is observed. Lastly, the team needs to try out the form, observing in pairs and calibrating their ratings, then discussing as a group which indicators are unclear and need revision. Literacy walk-through forms created by the team should be shared with the faculty so that the whole process is transparent and everyone knows the focus of the literacy walk-throughs.

Literacy walk-throughs are not intended to "catch" teachers. Instead, the intent is to provide an effective tool that helps everyone understand literacy goals through clarification of what it looks like in the classroom. They also allow for systematic data collection to inform everyone on ongoing progress. For more information about literacy walk-throughs, see Chapter 6.

Report on Progress Toward Goals

When people get ongoing feedback about performance, they tend to try harder, stay more focused, and reach more goals. In the event that the data do not show progress toward goals, the team can troubleshoot and bring the data back to the faculty for collective discussion and problem solving. Either way, understanding what is and is not working is critical to the team's responsibility to monitor implementation and progress toward goals.

The team only wants to use the data collection tools that make sense given the school's specific literacy action goals. No one has the time or energy to collect data for its own sake. Note that some of these ideas were suggested in Stage 1 as a way to collect some baseline data for the initiative. They are discussed again here because they can be productively repeated to show progress over time. As the team improves its data collection and analysis skills, it will become clearer what types of data provide the most relevant information.

The literacy leadership team can inform school colleagues about the progress being made toward goals in multiple ways. At the end of each team meeting, one member can complete a simple form that describes what the team learned and accomplished at the meeting and invite comments and suggestions from colleagues. Whenever the team analyzes data that relates to one of the goals in the literacy action plan, they can summarize the outcomes and make the information available to others; bigger news can be posted on the school's Web site or e-mailed to members of the school and district community. Make sure good news is shared with parents and the local media. Time to share progress and update the faculty on the work of the team can also be a regular feature of each faculty meeting.

REAL SCHOOL EXAMPLE

One rural district of six K–8 schools looked at their student performance data and set a literacy improvement goal related to improving students' abilities to read nonfiction texts. A literacy leadership team made up of teacher leaders from across the six schools was convened by the district curriculum coordinator. The district hired an outside literacy consultant to occasionally work with teacher leaders, lead teacher workshops, and meet with district administrators. The teacher leaders participated in professional development related to literacy support strategies designed to improve student comprehension when reading nonfiction text. The teacher leaders tried out the strategies in their own classrooms and then provided teacher professional development for their colleagues during release days. The consultant also facilitated teacher workshops. District administrators developed literacy walk-through forms with the consultant and conducted regular walk-throughs to develop a picture of implementation. The curriculum coordinator surveyed teachers to ask about current level of knowledge and use of the common strategies introduced over the course of the year. At the end of each year, the literacy team analyzed the reading performance data with the curriculum coordinator and reported the results back to teachers. After the first year, the team decided that more teachers needed to be involved with looking at data, have practice matching strategies to student needs, and have time to share with their colleagues. The consultant introduced the teacher leaders to a protocol for examining student work. Administrators provided time for the teachers in each school to use the protocol, look at student work, and have discussions about the use and effectiveness of specific strategies. Administrators asked teachers to identify which literacy support strategies could be used to strengthen students' abilities to understand nonfiction. Student performance data showed a steady increase over the three years of the initiative with greater increases occurring in schools where teachers reported more use of the strategies and the walk-through data showed higher levels of implementation.

Source: Thanks to Union 92 in Hancock County, Maine, for this example. Used with permission.

STEP 4: SUSTAIN MOMENTUM AND CELEBRATE ACCOMPLISHMENTS

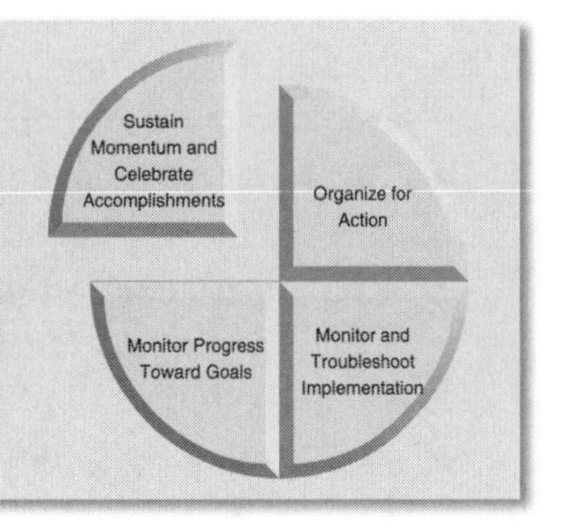

This step is important because celebration and recognition encourages teacher and student involvement and commitment to the literacy improvement initiative. When people feel acknowledged for their time and effort, they are more likely to support and promote implementation of the literacy action plan.

We recommend that the literacy leadership team find ways to recognize and celebrate accomplishments of team members, faculty members who have implemented effective literacy practices, and students who have contributed to the literacy improvement effort. The following are a few suggestions for providing recognition.

Recognize Faculty Members Who Have Implemented Effective Literacy Practices

- Set aside time in faculty meetings for faculty members to describe their efforts and share successful literacy practices
- Provide opportunities for teachers to describe and demonstrate their accomplishments to others in the district
- Remunerate teachers for time spent on the literacy initiative outside of their contract hours
- Provide coupons and gifts from local businesses for exemplary literacy initiative implementation
- Periodically cover classes to provide time to share ideas and experiences in departments or teams
- Create and display posters of faculty members reading books

Recognize Students Who Have Contributed to the Literacy Improvement Effort

- Create meaningful leadership roles in the literacy improvement initiative—this can include membership and leadership in a student literacy team or membership on the school's literacy leadership team
- Display students' exemplary literacy work throughout the school
- Provide opportunities to participate (in student panels or individually) in dialogue with the faculty about literacy-related issues
- Highlight students' literacy efforts on the school's closed circuit television and on the school's Web site
- Award for participation in literacy-related activities such as speech and debate, journalism, and contributions to the school's literary magazine
- Recognize participation in book clubs
- Provide coupons and gifts from local businesses for exemplary literacy accomplishments
- Create and display posters of students reading

Another way of recognizing accomplishments is to make meetings celebratory and festive. Providing food goes a long way toward making people feel appreciated. If budgets are tight, think about asking the Parent Teacher Organization or a local business to sponsor refreshments at student and faculty events and professional development sessions.

NEXT STEPS

Stage 4 is focused on implementation, the heart of a literacy improvement effort. After all, if the implementation maps are not implemented with high fidelity, there is no progress to monitor and no success to celebrate. The implementation phase will probably last the entire school year or, at minimum, for the remainder of the school year once the plan is in place. But what happens at the end of the year when classes are over, grades are turned in, and the student achievement results have been published? Is the team's work complete?

Far from it. At this juncture, the team is ready to move to Stage 5, where you will review what was accomplished during the past year and engage in a process to sustain and/or update the plan. It is unlikely that you met all of your goals in one year. If you did not meet some of your goals, it is time to refine your plan to make sure the job gets done. If you did meet all of your goals, congratulations! In either case, it is time to return to the literacy action rubrics and see what else you need to put into place to continue your quest to significantly improve student literacy and learning and prepare all students for college, careers, and citizenship in the 21st century.

5

Stage 5: Sustain

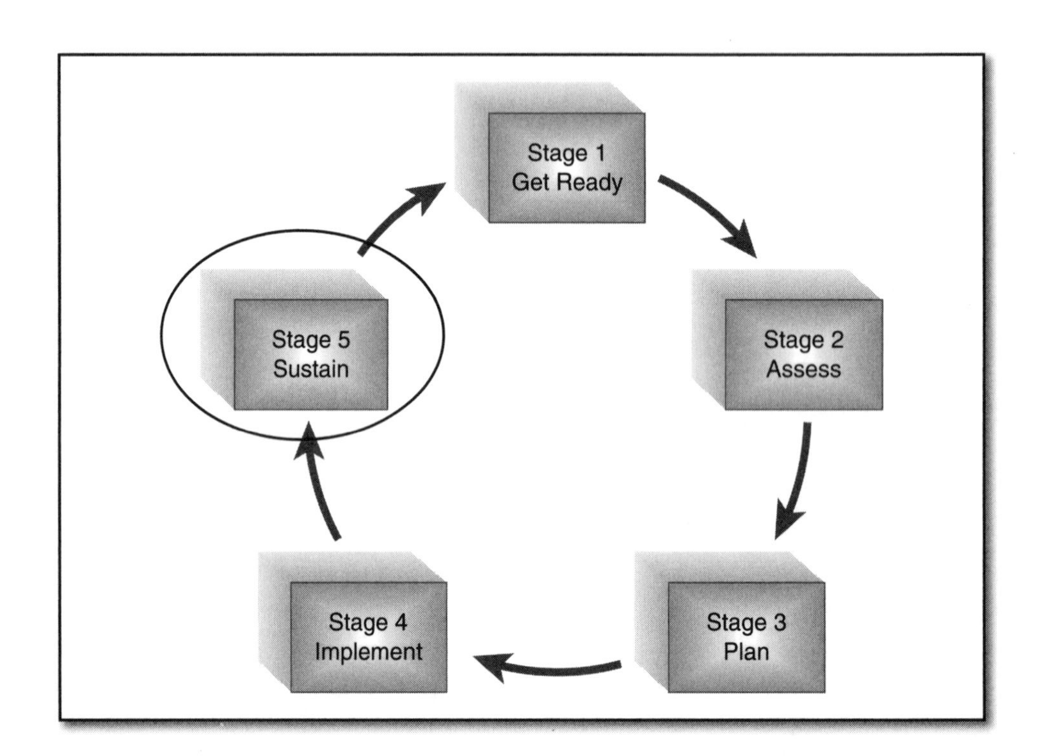

In Stage 5, you will do the following:

- ✓ Summarize progress toward your goals.
- ✓ Revise implementation maps and update the literacy action plan.
- ✓ Analyze your success as a literacy leadership team.
- ✓ Plan how to sustain momentum.

The literacy initiative is now well underway. During Stage 4, the literacy leadership team monitored implementation and kept track of what was happening throughout the year, noted successes, and made adjustments as needed. Now, the school year is over, and it is time to step back and reflect on what has been accomplished. In Stage 5, the team takes stock of the past year of the initiative, determines if goals were met, and summarizes the work that was accomplished by faculty, students, and team members. Based on this information, the team decides how the literacy action plan needs to be revised and updated and how the team will sustain momentum into the following year.

Since Stage 5 involves review and revision, approaches and tools used in earlier stages of the literacy leadership process are revisited. In Step 1 of Stage 5, you assess and summarize the progress made toward your literacy action goals. To complete this step, the team revisits the literacy action rubrics, repeats selected steps from Stages 1, 2, and 3, and collects other data for the assessment. In Step 2, you update and revise the next year's implementation maps and literacy action plan. In Step 3, you analyze and reflect on your accomplishments as a literacy team and determine what you need to maintain the team's effectiveness and efficiency. In Step 4, team members think about the activities and policies you need and plan how to sustain momentum for the literacy initiative.

As you work through the steps of Stage 5, it is important to remember the value of making each team member feel appreciated and included in decision making. Therefore, this is a good time to revisit procedures for reaching consensus discussed in Stage 1 and to review your ground rules for successful team meetings and collaborative decision making.

STEP 1: SUMMARIZE PROGRESS TOWARD GOALS

This step is important because taking time to assess and summarize progress toward each goal allows the team to make data-driven decisions when updating the literacy action plan.

In Step 1, the team revisits the literacy action goals and implementation maps to form a summative assessment of progress. This assessment begins with a return to the literacy action rubrics. As in Stage 2, team members complete an assessment based on the same literacy action rubrics used the previous year. Individual team members rate their perception of the school's current implementation on each indicator of each component of the literacy action rubric(s). As before, team members reflect independently, without discussion, by placing a check where they think typical school practice falls on the rubric. The individual ratings form the basis for the discussion, consensus building, and reflection that follows.

When using the rubrics for a second time, it is even more important that individual members write down the evidence they used to make their decisions, including student test scores, knowledge of particular programs, team or department focus, and classroom observations. Thinking carefully about evidence deepens the conversation about the school's progress on the rubrics. Reviewing evidence also provides a foundation for the consensus discussion that follows.

Once everyone has completed the independent rating process, the team must once again come to consensus about the school's current literacy practice. Use the same format (e.g., a sticky wall chart, checks, dots) you used in Stage 2 so that you can easily compile the results and make decisions. Remember, this is a time of open discussion. The exact placement of the dot is not as important as seeing trends and recognizing current strengths.

To provide the team with additional summative data, a recorder should take notes about the evidence that team members cite for their ratings. As before, the recorder can take notes on a computer, projecting the document for all to see, or on a large wall chart. The recording of evidence keeps team members focused and shifts the conversation away from ratings to deeper discussion about the component.

Once you have reached and recorded consensus the team can compare the new charts with the previous year's charts and examine changes in ratings. This will provide valuable data for assessing progress toward goals. An example of one team's comparison charts for Rubric 2 can be found in Figure 5.1.

In this example, improvement is evident in two components—classroom instruction and curriculum alignment—when the data from Year 1 and Year 2 are compared. In these areas, teachers made considerable progress in focusing on literacy support strategies and modeling so that students are consistently involved in literacy activities. Teachers also reported gains in how courses are aligned across grade levels and the extent to which students had access to rigorous course content and strong literacy support. Modest gains were also realized in the area of teacher assignments. Three components (differentiation, feedback and/or grading, and research) remained flat between the two years, suggesting that more attention needs to be given in those areas in the coming year.

Other data that the team can use to assess progress include student performance data, student and faculty focus group replies, survey results, and walk-through data. These data, along with the rubric data, will help you evaluate whether or not you have met your goals and successfully implemented your action plan.

The team can use the Progress Toward Goals Summary Chart (see Tool 10 in Resource B) to record the kinds of data you used to assess progress toward a particular goal. You can then discuss the implications of these data with respect to the specific goal, drawing conclusions about what the data reveal, and the degree to which the school has made progress in a given area.

Year 1

Year 2

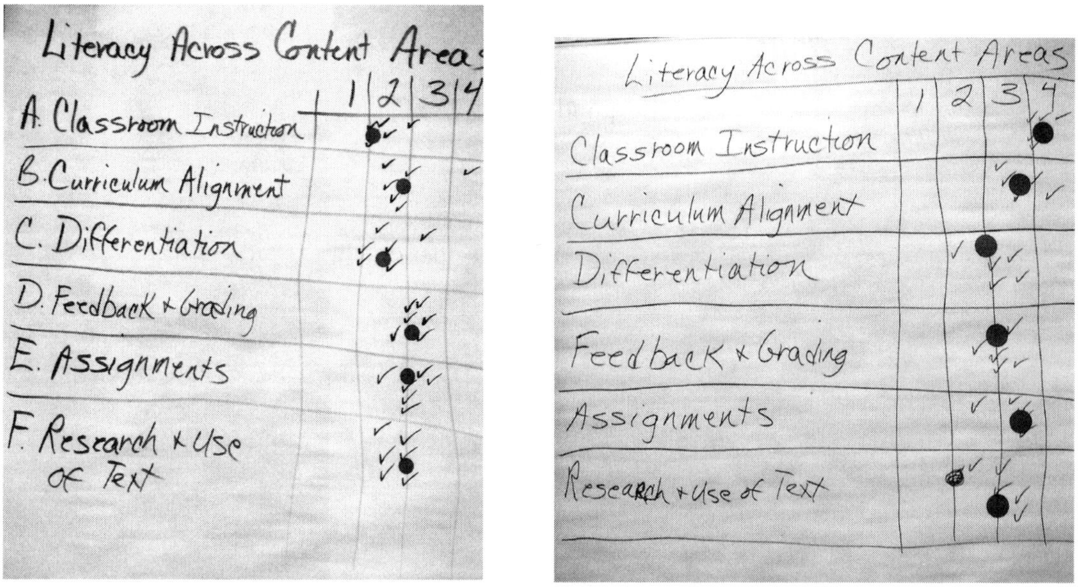

Figure 5.1 One Team's Comparison of Rating on Rubric 2 From Year 1 to Year 2

Tool 10: Progress Toward Goals Summary Chart

Literacy Action Goal:

What data do we have that will tell us if we have met this goal? (check all that apply)

- _____ Analysis of teacher-designed assignments
- _____ Literacy action rubrics
- _____ Teacher feedback (focus groups or survey data)
- _____ Student feedback (focus groups or survey data)
- _____ Literacy walk-through data
- _____ Student performance data
- _____ Other (be specific) ________________________

Summarize what the data and evidence reveal relative to meeting the goal.

Did we meet the goal? Yes/No

What did we do that directly supported success?

Did we fall short of the goal? Yes/No

Do we need to revise the goal for next year? Yes/No

What revisions would make a strong goal for next year?

For a more detailed assessment of individual implementation maps, the team can also complete the Implementation Review Chart (see Tool 11 in Resource B) to summarize how well the action steps associated with each goal were accomplished during the past year of implementation and what needs to happen next in this area to deepen or expand the work.

Tool 11: Implementation Review Chart		
Literacy Action Goal: **Was the goal met? Yes/ No / Partially** **Evidence that we met the goal:**		
Action Step	**Was the Action Step Accomplished?**	
	Progress	*Continued Needs*
	Progress	*Continued Needs*
	Progress	*Continued Needs*

List the Action Steps from the Implementation Map in the first column. The team then uses the next column to indicate progress in accomplishing the action step as well as continued needs related to that action step. The following is a sample Implementation Review Chart that might have been completed by the Central School literacy team. When you finish your review process, develop a summary statement of what was accomplished and what remains to be addressed. The statement can be shared with others and included in the updated literacy action plan.

Implementation Review Chart (Central School Example)

Literacy Action Goal Statement: All students will learn and routinely use reading and writing support strategies to enhance literacy and learning across all content areas.

Was the goal met? Yes/No/(Partially)

Evidence that we met the goal: Focus groups with students indicated that some students recognized the strategies and could describe how they used them. Teacher surveys indicated self-report of knowledge, and use of reading and writing support strategies increased from the beginning to the end of the year.

Revision to goal for next year's literacy action plan? No change.

Measurable Action Step	Was the Action Step accomplished?	
The literacy team will select a common set of literacy support strategies and decide which departments or teams will be responsible for teaching the strategies.	*Progress* The team selected and the faculty approved four literacy strategies to be used schoolwide: Think Alouds, Question-Answer-Relationship (QAR), Graphic Organizers, and Quick Writes.	*Continued Needs* The team needs to expand the number of content-embedded literacy strategies regularly used in each content area for next year.
All teachers will participate in at least two professional development sessions to learn a common set of strategies.	*Progress* Eighty percent of teachers participated in at least two literacy professional development sessions.	*Continued Needs* Twenty percent of teachers were unable to complete both sessions. Those teachers, as well as new teachers, will need professional development in the application of literacy-based content strategies for next year. Professional development will be offered again to all teachers in order to deepen their understanding and use of literacy in their content areas.
Departments or teams will discuss the literacy demands of their content areas and use the common strategies in their instruction.	*Progress* All departments met with the school literacy coach to discuss the literacy demands of their content areas.	*Continued Needs* Some departments embraced the literacy focus enthusiastically (English, social studies, and, and to some extent, science). Other departments (math, physical education and wellness, foreign language, and fine arts) are still exploring the best ways to integrate literacy within their content. These department members need professional development provided by individuals with specific experience in literacy in these subject areas.
All teachers will have multiple opportunities to visit demonstration classrooms, engage in peer coaching, and/or work with a literacy coach to see strategies in action.	*Progress* Sixty percent of the faculty participated in demonstration teaching and/or peer coaching. The most enthusiastic departments were English and social studies. Several math and science teachers conducted demonstrations for a few of their colleagues.	*Continued Needs* Forty percent of the faculty did not participate in this action step. At the end of the year, however, the math and science departments agreed to participate in demonstration classrooms taught by a teacher or consultant who is experienced in literacy-embedded content instruction. The cadre of demonstration teachers needs to be expanded.

STEP 2: REVISE IMPLEMENTATION MAPS

This step is important because decisions should be based on the data collected and analyzed during implementation when updating the literacy action plan. This way the team builds directly on what has occurred, addresses targeted student and teacher needs, and includes action steps that will be worthy of teacher and administrative support.

In Step 1, the team analyzed and discussed progress toward meeting goals. The team is now ready to make decisions about which goals to keep and revise, which to discard, and which to add. Using the Progress Toward Goals Summary Chart and the Implementation Review Chart as a guide, complete the following:

- Examine each literacy action goal statement.
- Decide whether or not to keep the goal.
- Decide if you need to revise the goal and, if so, how.
- Write a revised or new goal statement as needed.

The team can use the Implementation Map Template found in Resource B (Tool 2) to discuss and develop new action steps with associated timelines, lead person(s), resources needed, specifics of implementation, and measure(s) of success. You may want to revisit Chapter 3 for tips on how to develop an effective implementation map.

Return to the Literacy Action Rubrics

If you have met last year's literacy improvement goals or feel that goals need to be discarded, revised, or combined, the team can return to the literacy action rubrics for help in revising established or developing new goals and implementation maps. The team may want to select a rubric in a goal area where the team did not focus this past year and repeat the process of using the rubric to develop a goal statement and associated implementation map, as outlined in Stages 2 and 3. For example, the team may not have tackled Literacy Action Rubric 3:

Literacy Interventions, during the first year of the literacy initiative, but student performance data may indicate that students performing in the lowest quartile need some intensive support. Or the data may indicate that related areas need attention. For example, although teachers may have done a good job of integrating reading, writing, and vocabulary into content area instruction, walk-through data may indicate that students have limited opportunities to participate in literacy activities outside of their scheduled classes. In this case, the team may choose to return to Literacy Action Rubric 4: Literacy-Rich School Environment, Culture, and Policies. The wording in the literacy action rubrics can guide you as you revise goals and action steps.

REAL SCHOOL EXAMPLE

One middle school literacy team was very satisfied with the teacher professional development it had led throughout the past two years. There was clear evidence that teacher practice was changing and that students knew and were using strategies regularly when reading and writing. But when revisiting the components of Rubric 1: Student Motivation, Engagement, and Achievement to see if there were indicators that were not being addressed, they realized that the district's technology initiative was not at all connected with the literacy initiative. So, the team members focused on Component D and drafted a new goal statement and action plan around this area. The team also decided that it was time to address the issue of Literacy Interventions so they used Rubric 3: Literacy Interventions *to develop a goal to address assessment and use of data to guide instruction. Finally, team members revisited their initial goal for the use of a common set of literacy support strategies and revised it to include a deliberate focus on critical thinking. For the action steps associated with this goal, they included successful strategies used in the past to get teacher buy-in, and change teacher practice such as workshops, study groups, presentations at faculty meetings, and invitations to observe in team members' classrooms.*

Source: Thanks to Plymouth Community Intermediate School in Plymouth, Massachusetts, for this example. Used with permission.

You may have a good reason to start the process all over. Perhaps all of the literacy improvement goals in last year's plan were met. Perhaps the team feels that last year's goals were not specific enough to guide improvement or that schoolwide improvement goals have shifted requiring an alignment with those priorities. Perhaps last year's goals were too easy to attain or too difficult. If you choose to make a new start, the team will need to repeat Stages 2 and 3 of the literacy leadership process and complete the assessment, goal setting, and implementation maps as described in Stages 2 and 3.

When the team completes new implementation maps, we recommend that representatives from the literacy leadership team meet with the school leadership team (if different) or school or district administrators to discuss the maps and troubleshoot potential challenges related to planned activities, timelines, and needed resources. We suggest that at minimum you send a copy of the implementation maps to district subject area, media, and technology supervisors for their information, input, support, and possible allocation of resources. As recommended in Stage 3, we suggest that you provide the faculty with a description of the revised goals and implementation maps as well as a description of the work that went into its design and once again solicit feedback from colleagues using the same strategies recommended in Chapter 3. The team will then need to set aside time to examine the feedback and make any necessary revisions to the maps. Once the implementation maps have been finalized, you can update the formal literacy action plan to include a summary of progress toward last year's goals as well as the process used to review and revise the implementation maps, the current membership of the literacy leadership team, and a closing narrative that summarizes the major literacy-based activities planned for the next school year.

As described in Stage 3, you can publicize the final literacy action plan through presentations at faculty meetings, parent meetings, district-level meetings, and school board meetings. The updated literacy action plan can also be published in the school's newsletter and posted on the school's Web site.

STEP 3: ANALYZE SUCCESS AS A LITERACY LEADERSHIP TEAM

This step is important because literacy leadership team members need to review how well they functioned as a team, how they will bring new members onto the team if needed, and what norms for team functioning need to be revisited, reemphasized, or established. This reflection will allow the team to support continuous improvement and make the team even more effective in the following year.

You have reviewed your data and progress over the past year. If you have evidence of improved student motivation and engagement, chances are that the team's effort contributed to this progress. Likewise, new support structures for students or successful teacher professional development may have resulted in positive changes in classroom practice. Perhaps, you have evidence of improved student outcomes or positive changes in climate or culture. When you have clear evidence of results, you can attribute these results to the hard work of team members and their colleagues!

You have taken time to review the team's efforts to improve literacy and learning and have designed a literacy action plan for the next school year. Now, it is time to reflect on how you did as a team and what attention needs to be paid to team functioning to assure that the team's efforts continue to be productive. Review the items in the chart that follows. This chart is also reproduced as Tool 12 in Resource B. If you find that any of the statements are not true, you may need to focus some attention on the issue in order to function more effectively. It may be helpful to have team members rate these items individually before the team discusses the responses as a group. The team can then make a plan to address issues that you identify, using one of the suggestions provided in the chart.

Tool 12: Literacy Leadership Team Assessment			
The team is working well to make good decisions.	Yes	No	If not, discuss the extent to which the team is (or is not) doing the following: • Supporting and including a variety of viewpoints and perspectives • Soliciting contributions from all team members • Establishing an environment of inclusion and safety • Working to reconcile disagreements and reduce tension by using consensus building • Exploring and validating differences and suggesting areas of consensus
Team members are working to expand or deepen their knowledge about literacy.	Yes	No	If not, analyze what is preventing members from increasing their professional knowledge. Consider the following: • Need for professional development • Need for adequate time to network, read, and reflect • How to reduce excessive demands on members' time • How to address lack of perceived support and recognition for efforts from colleagues and administrators • How to seek out resources to target and address these problems
The team is taking a leadership role in planning and supporting teacher professional development.	Yes	No	If not, determine which members have expertise and are comfortable with making faculty presentations or conducting classroom demonstrations. Pair up experienced team members with novice teachers, and provide time to develop leadership knowledge and skills.
The team is being effective in getting others on board with the initiative.	Yes	No	If not, ask each team member to share the team's activities with their colleagues—either individually or in a department or team-level meeting.
The team is being effective in supporting others' efforts to contribute to improved student literacy and learning.	Yes	No	If not, discuss which faculty members are attempting to implement some of the steps in the literacy action plan. Publicly acknowledge the efforts of all faculty and staff to support the initiative.
The team leader or facilitator ensures that all members have an equal voice in discussion and decision making.	Yes	No	If not, have one team member collect informal data on the amount of time that all members contribute to the discussion.

Literacy leadership teams face specific challenges in maintaining momentum when members leave the team, new members join, or when the team is merged with another leadership team at the school. In each of these situations, it is helpful to plan for the transition. If members leave the team, you should certainly provide opportunities for the team to recognize the contributions of those members who are leaving and say good-bye.

When new members join the team, it is important to make them feel welcome and to bring them up to speed on the activities of the literacy leadership team. You can summarize actions and accomplishments from the past year's work, introduce them to team norms, and explicitly support them as they cycle through the literacy leadership process. If the literacy leadership team is merging with another team, it is important to clarify the original charge and accomplishments of each team and the strengths that each can bring to the combined team. Then, you will need to work collaboratively to establish new roles and ground rules. We recommend using the following strategies to maintain team integrity and to support the team's work during transitions from one year to the next:

- Publish a summary of what the team has accomplished so that others can recognize and understand the purpose of the team's work.
- Celebrate accomplishments so that team members can be justifiably proud of what they have contributed and new team members can understand what is expected.
- Provide public recognition of the team's achievements so that school and district administrators can appreciate the contributions of team members. The principal and/or curriculum coordinator (or other school or district administrator in charge of literacy improvement) should be the one to make the recognition public, adding importance and stature to the recognition. This is also important if there is a need for recruitment of individuals to join the team.
- Develop a means for literacy leadership team members from multiple schools to contribute strategies and stories related to their literacy improvement efforts, thereby sharing ideas and expertise across the district.

STEP 4: PLAN HOW TO SUSTAIN MOMENTUM

This step is important because it is critical for the team to take the lead in sustaining enthusiasm for the work and the momentum of the literacy improvement effort. Without strong leadership from the team, the impact of a literacy improvement initiative may fade in subsequent years of implementation.

We know that transformational change can take at least three to five years, but since many initiatives come and go, educators do not typically experience ongoing consistent focus for improvement over multiple years. What can the literacy leadership team do to help colleagues maintain enthusiasm for improving literacy and learning over time? How can the team encourage reluctant teachers to participate more fully in the literacy initiative? In addition, how can the initiative grow and build on the accomplishments of previous implementation of literacy action goals?

Establish a System of Communication

One important element is to establish a system of communication that includes school colleagues as well as parents and individuals in the district office, other schools, and community. When others know that literacy improvement is a priority for the school, interest in the initiative grows. It is helpful to target communication to the specific audiences of students, teachers, school and district administrators, parents, and the community. When communicating with members of each group, highlight how they can help and provide resources you would find useful. The literacy brand statement should be visible on all communication. In this way, you build enthusiasm around the literacy improvement initiative. We recommend the following:

- Enlist help from media and technology specialists.
  - Set up a system of electronic communication for parents and community members.
  - Set up a Web site to share literacy strategies, examples of student work, and other literacy-related information.
- Urge departments and teams to invite district personnel and other stakeholders to meetings when the focus is on literacy instruction.
- Recruit a team of students and teachers to organize efforts for community, business, and family literacy outreach programs.
- Include community representatives and students on the literacy leadership team.

The team can easily provide a summary of the progress made toward goals during the past school year, post upcoming activities, offer resources, and share student successes.

Reinvigorate the Literacy Initiative

Sometimes the literacy leadership team needs strategies to revitalize the initiative if interest is waning. If this happens, the team might ask teachers to revisit the strengths shown in the school's original circle map (see Stage 2) and add new strengths developed during the past year. The team might also discuss the literacy initiative brand statement and determine if changes need to be made or if the brand statement needs to be more visible. Or the team might report key messages from updated student data, showing progress made and what still remains to be accomplished. The team may also want to revisit the kickoff activities listed in Step 1 of Stage 4 to see if there are any that need to be repeated or reemphasized.

One helpful activity is to use the Then, Now, Next Chart. The team can complete the chart as a team, or team members can facilitate this conversation with departments or grade-level teams, professional learning groups, or the faculty as a whole. By discussing the columns together and recording the group's observations on the following chart, the team creates a powerful, shared vision of sustained momentum and collaboratively rededicates the initiative to a culture of continuous improvement. Results can be summarized and published using whatever communication system the team has established (see Tool 13 in Resource B).

Tool 13: Then, Now, Next Chart			
	Then . . .	**Now . . .**	**Next . . .**
What students were, are, or will be doing			
What teachers were, are, or will be doing			
What the school environment was, is, or will be like			

The following is an example Then, Now, Next literacy chart that could have been completed by the Central School literacy leadership team.

Then, Now, Next Chart (Central School Example)			
	Then . . .	**Now . . .**	**Next . . .**
What students were, are, or will be doing	Students faked reading during silent sustained reading (SSR) and did little reading and writing in school.	Students talk about the books they are reading and read and write in school every day.	Students will analyze what they read, not just respond to it.
What teachers were, are, or will be doing	Teachers did not provide modeling or exemplars and were frustrated by students not trying.	Many teachers use a gradual release model and explicitly teach reading strategies.	Teachers will use exemplars, rubrics, and Think Alouds.
What the school environment was, is, or will be like	Walls were bare in classrooms and in the hallway; classrooms did not have books to support SSR.	Much more student work is posted on the walls in classrooms and in the hallway; all classrooms have book collections to support SSR.	There will be more talk about reading and writing and more celebration of student successes; the literacy team will have established and supported more literacy-related activities for students (poetry jams, debate club, literary magazine).

As always, celebrating successes and recognizing people's contributions are important strategies for sustaining momentum. The team should make sure it does this on a regular basis as it moves into the implementation stage of the updated literacy action plan.

Sustain Momentum Through Transitions When Key People Leave

Many schools experience turnover or transitions in teaching, instructional support, or administrative staff. This can derail literacy improvement efforts if it is not addressed. The team can review applicable items on the chart that follows to determine proactive steps that can be taken to sustain a focus on improving literacy and learning through times of transition. (see Tool 14 in Resource B).

Tool 14: Proactive Steps for Sustaining Literacy Leadership and Improvement			
1 = No evidence of planning 2 = Some evidence of planning 3 = Fully planned for			
When the Principal Leaves . . .			
Set up a strong literacy leadership team that works with the principal to implement and monitor progress on the literacy initiative.	1	2	3
Set up a strong vision and action plan that is communicated to others.	1	2	3
Put in place policies and procedures for using reading assessment data.	1	2	3
Decide when and how much content area reading and writing instruction will take place.	1	2	3
Use student performance results and other data to publicly tell the story of the literacy improvement effort so that results are clearly attached to the literacy work.	1	2	3
When the Literacy Coach Leaves . . .			
There is a clear job description for the position of literacy coach.	1	2	3
The literacy coach is expected to be an essential member of a strong literacy leadership team.	1	2	3
The literacy coach is expected to meet regularly with the principal so the principal is informed and can act and be seen as co-leader of the literacy improvement effort.	1	2	3
Literacy leaders take responsibility for many specific processes such as content area classroom support, library and media center promotion, and student book talks.	1	2	3
When Key Teacher Leaders Leave . . .			
Expectations of teachers in leadership positions are clearly defined in terms of their roles as literacy leaders.	1	2	3
Leadership selection is based on establishing a commitment to literacy improvement as a selection criterion.	1	2	3
The principal, coach, and other leaders provide explicit support for mentoring new leaders in their roles.	1	2	3
When District Leadership Changes . . .			
School leaders communicate to district leadership how new mandates are being addressed and implemented in their school.	1	2	3

(Continued)

(Continued)

School leaders provide evidence that the school's literacy improvement effort is aligned with district priorities.	1	2	3
School leaders communicate a clear vision and action plan that is actively supported by the community.	1	2	3
When There Is High Teacher Turnover . . .			
Teacher induction includes a literacy mentor and coaching support.	1	2	3
New teachers have access to content area literacy materials and professional resources.	1	2	3
Teachers have clear understanding about the amount and types of students' reading and writing, as well as reading and writing instruction expected in each of the courses to which a teacher is assigned.	1	2	3
Teachers have access to quality and ongoing professional development.	1	2	3
Teachers are involved and participate from the beginning in the use of reading and writing assessment data to drive instruction.	1	2	3
Attention and feedback from administration is focused on the quality of content area literacy development.	1	2	3

Source: Adapted from Irvin, J. L., Meltzer, J., Mickler, M. J., Phillips, M. P., & Dean, N. (2009). *Meeting the Challenge of Adolescent Literacy: Practical Ideas for Literacy Leaders.* Newark, DE: International Reading Association, pp. 218–219.

Which of the issues in the chart does the team anticipate facing as it moves into the next year of the initiative? What steps can the team take to counteract the potentially negative effects of these transitions? Are these steps that need to be included in the updated literacy action plan?

NEXT STEPS

Congratulations! You have completed all five stages of the literacy leadership process—Round 1. You have revisited steps in Stages 1 through 4 in order to update your plan and determine how to actively support a culture of continuous improvement. At this point, you will move back into Stage 4, implementation of your updated literacy action plan. By the end of another year of implementation, you will again be ready to engage in Stage 5.

Keep in mind that change is not static but dynamic. If the team is effective at accomplishing its goals, the next areas to address and the strategies that are needed to sustain momentum will become clear. Improving literacy and learning is a journey, not a destination.

Chapters 6 and 7 of this book are specifically directed to administrators at the school and district levels to help them understand how they can best support the work of the literacy leadership team. It may make sense for literacy leadership team members to review these chapters so that you can actively suggest how administrators can be most helpful in a given situation and so that you can better understand how the work might be viewed from a school or district perspective.

PART III

School and District Administrators as Literacy Leaders

6

The Principal's Role

In this chapter, you will learn about how you can complete the following:

- ✓ Build leadership capacity through establishing and working with a high performing literacy leadership team.
- ✓ Establish a culture of data use to guide instruction and determine appropriate student placement in interventions.
- ✓ Support teachers through quality teacher professional development.
- ✓ Find and strategically allocate resources to support the activities and goals of the literacy action plan.
- ✓ Use classroom literacy walk-throughs to monitor the success of the literacy action plan.

As the school's principal, you are responsible for improving student achievement and building a faculty and student culture that supports literacy and learning. Because of the central role of literacy for success throughout life, ensuring that all students leave school with strong literacy skills has to be a central mission of K–12 schools. In our experience, a focus on literacy improvement can be a powerful lever for school improvement. As the school's instructional leader, your involvement in and explicit support of a school-based literacy improvement initiative is critical. This chapter is about how you and your administrative team can use the *Taking Action Literacy Leadership Model* and the literacy leadership process outlined in this book to increase student motivation, engagement, and achievement schoolwide.

You have the responsibility to make certain that improving student literacy and learning is seen as a priority by everyone in the school as well as family and community stakeholders. Strong ongoing administrative support is critical for the success of all instructional improvement initiatives.

When you are just getting your literacy initiative underway, you need to fulfill two primary objectives: (1) assess the expertise and assets you have to put into the literacy improvement effort, and (2) raise general awareness of the importance of this issue. In the following box is a list of suggested activities that you can use to accomplish these two objectives. You do not have to be an expert in the area of literacy, but you do need to model that you are an enthusiastic learner and that you expect the entire faculty to continually improve their abilities to develop students' proficiency as readers, writers, and thinkers.

Build a Foundation for the Literacy Initiative

Assess Expertise and Understanding About Literacy Within Your School

- Have informal conversations with department heads and teachers in leadership positions about contributions that each content area can make toward students' literacy improvement.
- Explore what literacy looks like in the various content areas and how content teachers can coordinate their efforts in both curricular and instructional design.
- Seek out the expertise of administrative colleagues in other schools as well as those in your district office.
- Attend state and national conferences or administrative meetings that focus on literacy, data use, and action planning.
- Conduct a teacher professional development needs assessment (see Tool 16 in Resource B).

Generate Interest in the Initiative

- Offer professional development on a literacy-related topic for special education, content teachers, English language learners (ELL), and others involved in the literacy initiative.
- Establish a professional study group in which teachers and administrators select a literacy topic to research.
- Coordinate classroom visits to promote collaboration, team teaching, or demonstration teaching.
- Use the literary action rubrics discussed throughout this book to build the knowledge and understanding of the administrative team.
- Create a data overview and make the case for the need for a literacy improvement initiative (see Chapter 1 for tips on creating a data overview).
- Contact schools with successful literacy initiatives to determine best practices for your school.
- Send teachers and support staff to state and national conferences that focus on literacy, data use, and action planning.

SUPPORT LITERACY LEADERS

As principal, you cannot take on improving literacy and learning by yourself. A successful literacy improvement effort requires the active participation of teachers, administrators, students, parents, staff, and the larger community. If you view literacy improvement as a campaign, you are the campaign manager, making sure that everyone involved understands the goals and his or her roles and responsibilities. As the school's instructional leader, your sustained visible support for the initiative and for the people working to improve literacy and learning will greatly improve the likelihood that the school will meet the goals of the literacy improvement effort.

The *literacy leadership team* needs your active, ongoing support. Early in the initiative, it is wise to establish a literacy leadership team and make clear to the faculty that the team has your full support. If you do not have a literacy leadership team, we recommend establishing one. Or you can charge an existing leadership team with the responsibilities of developing a literacy action plan, overseeing the implementation of the plan, and monitoring progress toward goals. Team members will look to school administrators to communicate that literacy improvement is a priority and to reinforce the activities and expectations that the literacy team puts into place. It is helpful if you are able to play an active role on the literacy team because when decisions related to resource allocation or policy need to be made, you can make decisions or work with other decision makers to address the issue.

Teachers need your active support; they want to know what is expected of them, what support will be in place, how they will be held accountable for meeting expectations, and how the expectations will be monitored. In addition, your acknowledgement of teacher practice that demonstrates strong integration of literacy development with content learning is critical.

Your *literacy coach* also needs your active support. Often, school administrators turn over the literacy initiative to the coach, feeling that he or she will take care of it. Even experienced and highly capable literacy coaches depend on the principal to set expectations for how often teachers will meet with the coach, what the coach's job does and does not include, what kinds of changes are expected as a result of coaching, how and with whom classroom visits occur, and the priorities for the coach's work. Less experienced coaches need even more support and clarification from you. A literacy coach is a valuable partner with you as you lead the school to improving literacy and learning, but he or she cannot spearhead the initiative without your support.

Parents and members of the community should be able to identify that literacy improvement is a school priority, to know what you are doing to address this issue, and to understand how they can be supportive. As the school's spokesperson, it is important to

- work closely with the literacy leadership team to make the brand statement for the literacy initiative visible for those within and outside the school walls;
- update parents, the school board, and the community at large on the goals and action steps of the literacy action plan;
- display and interpret data that led to the formation of the plan; and
- communicate how you are monitoring implementation and the progress being made toward meeting stated goals.

The *district* also should understand what the school is trying to accomplish, how this aligns with district goals and priorities, and what support the school needs from the district. We discuss the district's role in supporting school-based literacy initiatives in Chapter 7.

Finally, and most important, *students* need to understand how important it is to improve their habits and skills as readers, writers, and thinkers and that supporting their literacy development is a priority of the school. Your efforts to create a strong culture of literacy and a literacy-rich environment supported by specific policies and structures are critical to the success of the literacy improvement initiative.

USE THE FIVE ACTION POINTS OF THE *TAKING ACTION LITERACY LEADERSHIP MODEL*

The action points of the *Taking Action Literacy Leadership Model* succinctly summarize the actions that school leaders take to improve student literacy and learning: build leadership capacity, use data to make decisions, support teachers to improve instruction, allocate resources, and implement a literacy action plan. Savvy principals use these as their touchstones to think about what needs their attention and to understand the combined leadership and support roles they need to play in a literacy improvement initiative. The action points are recursive and synergistic, not sequential or hierarchical. Each is a potential entry point for beginning an initiative, but together they are powerful vehicles for deepening and supporting the success of the work. Therefore, as your literacy initiative moves forward, you will most likely work with all five action points in an iterative manner.

Many principals ask us where they should begin. In our interviews and experience with school administrators who have led successful improvement efforts to improve literacy, we found that the beginning point depended on personal style and the administrator's assessment of what was needed to get things underway. Some administrators wanted to study relevant data before allocating any resources. Other administrators felt that it was important to support teachers through study groups, professional development, and peer coaching before establishing a literacy leadership team. It became obvious to us that these five actions are integrally related, and should be enacted concurrently, and occur recursively as a part of a successful schoolwide literacy initiative. In the rest of this chapter, we highlight specific aspects of each of these actions that the principal needs to focus upon relative to starting and sustaining a school-based literacy improvement effort.

Build Leadership Capacity

By establishing an effective literacy leadership team, principals can get critical assistance to build widespread support for literacy improvement, develop teacher leaders, and develop and implement a literacy action plan using the literacy leadership process described in Chapters 1 through 5.

You may already have a team in place in your school that can function in a leadership role for the literacy improvement initiative (for example, a school improvement team). If this is the case, you may not want to establish yet another committee. On the other hand, if by launching a new team you can involve a different set of people, perhaps with some overlap with other key teams, this strategic move may engage more of the faculty with the initiative (see Chapter 1 for ideas about building your literacy leadership team).

The purpose of a literacy leadership team is to develop and lead implementation of the school's literacy action plan and monitor progress toward goals. For a literacy leadership team to perform these functions effectively, it needs personal, structural, and organizational support from building administrators. Team members need to feel confident and competent in their role as literacy leaders. In our experience with literacy leadership teams from schools across the country, we often see avoidable pitfalls that can derail the successful functioning of the team. Savvy principals can meet these challenges by being vigilant and involved. Pitfalls often occur because communication has broken down; roles, responsibilities and expectations are not sufficiently clear; basic logistics are not being handled well; team members are feeling overwhelmed, underappreciated, or insecure about their literacy expertise; or teams are inexperienced in collaborative decision making. We have listed a number of these issues, along with some suggestions about how to address them, in the following chart. These issues could apply to any of the leadership teams with which you work, but if they go unchecked, they can easily undermine the success of the literacy initiative.

Issues Affecting Literacy Team Effectiveness and Possible Action Steps

Issue	What You Can Do
Sporadic teacher participation in team meetings	• Provide release time for team members to meet during the school day. • Reduce the number of faculty meetings to allow team members and other teachers to meet before or after school. • Provide help with copying and distributing team reports and locating materials. • Limit the number of committees on which team members serve. • Establish a schedule for occasional classroom coverage for team members to collaborate and plan. • Make certain that meeting agendas are clear and that meeting time is being used well to move the initiative forward. • Ask team members what the problem is, and brainstorm solutions together.
Limited experience with making and implementing collaborative decisions	• Provide professional development on the process of consensus building. • Model a process for building consensus during team meetings. o Remind team members of team norms. o Promote dialogue and conversations. o Raise a variety of possibilities while avoiding simplistic answers. o Provide time for people to deal with difficult issues. o Turn a concern into a question.

Issues Affecting Literacy Team Effectiveness and Possible Action Steps	
Issue	**What You Can Do**
Team perception of undue administrative influence	• Model a process for building consensus when addressing issues with faculty and departments. • Ask teacher leaders to assume responsibility for communicating and supporting a shared vision for literacy improvement. • Spread responsibility for meeting facilitation and follow-through on agenda items and action steps; set up pairs to be responsible if individual follow-through is an issue.
Confusion of focus	• Publish an agreed-upon list of expectations for on-topic and off-topic conversations for team meetings. • Have the team select a meeting facilitator for each meeting who will guide the team back to the topic at hand when needed. • Review the meeting minutes to determine how well the team maintained focus during the meeting.
Lack of adequate professional development for teacher leaders	• Conduct a professional development needs assessment with team members (see Tool 16 in Resource B) • Provide team members with professional development that focuses on the following: o Fundamentals of literacy instruction o Content-embedded literacy strategies o Procedures for analyzing teacher assignments and student work o Assessment-based literacy instruction o Group processing skills • Locate and share articles and professional resources on teaming and schoolwide literacy improvement. • Provide opportunities for team members to attend literacy-based conferences as a group. • Identify in-house and district experts and find ways for these professionals to share their experience and perspectives with the team.
Lack of incentives	• Provide uninterrupted time for team members to talk with each other. • Offer compensatory time for before or afterschool meetings. • Use team meetings to meet continuing education or professional development requirements. • Publicly recognize team members for their efforts. • Provide team members with opportunities to describe what they are accomplishing. • Locate funds to pay teachers for the time spent on team business beyond teacher contracts. • Provide refreshments during meetings.

No matter how supportive you are of your literacy leadership team, it is helpful to know that teams in charge of transformational change often go through a set of phases before becoming a well integrated working group. Knowledge of these stages allows you to distinguish issues specific to your literacy team from a normal trajectory of how teams evolve. Tuckman (1965) described these stages as *forming, storming, norming, performing,* and *adjourning.* To understand better what these stages look like in the context of a literacy leadership team, you may want to read the case study in Resource D. The case study is based on the work over time of a literacy leadership team at a large urban high school.

Read the Riverton High School Case Study in Resource D with your literacy leadership team. Discuss points of similarity and differences with your own literacy leadership team. What stage do you think your literacy leadership team is in? What insights do the Tuckman stages provide into the functioning of your literacy leadership team?

Use Data to Make Decisions

Data about student performance should be used on a regular basis to inform instruction, student placement, and program effectiveness. Explore with your literacy team and/or your administrative team what data you have concerning your students as readers and writers. Obviously, just testing students does not result in better performance. To leverage the power of data to improve student outcomes requires establishing a culture of data use throughout the school.

It is productive to establish some basic definitions when talking about data at your school since terms are often confused. Just as it is important to develop a common language about literacy and learning, it is helpful to have a data and assessment vocabulary. In the next section, we highlight some important concepts and ways to think about data that you can use to move your literacy initiative forward.

Formative Versus Summative Data

Instruments (surveys, tests, quizzes, inventories) that collect data about students as readers and writers can be formative or summative. If the data are collected prior to starting instruction or during instruction, this is formative data. Teachers can use these data to answer the question, "What does student performance indicate about what the student currently understands and is able to do, and what instruction is needed to further the student's learning?" Summative data are collected after instruction for the purpose of assessing what the student has learned or how well an educational objective has been met at a given time. Summative data over time also provide valuable information about the effectiveness of the instructional program and can be further disaggregated to determine for whom instructional support is working best. Decisions about resources that will be needed (e.g., teacher assignments, course offerings, additional assessments) should also be informed by these data.

Student data can also be collected using curriculum benchmarking, a process using quarterly or short-cycle assessments for all grade levels based on the mapping and alignment of subject area courses. These periodic assessments allow teachers to monitor student progress and better understand student needs throughout the school year. Based on these data, teachers can differentiate instruction, plan their use of materials, and implement grouping practices to provide timely intervention and targeted instruction when indicated.

Types of Data Available to Use

Seven types of data are typically available in schools to provide information about student proficiency in reading and writing. Each of these types of data can focus educators' attention on how to support students to improve as readers, writers, and thinkers. In addition, these data may be used to inform classroom teaching and learning, determine appropriate placement options, and provide evidence of where instructional programming needs to be improved. The purpose of each type of data is described in the following chart, and a space is provided so that you can discuss with your literacy leadership team how you currently use each type of data in your school (see Tool 15 in Resource B).

Tool 15: Types and Uses of Data

Type of Data	Possible Uses	How Do You Currently Use This Data at Your School?
Standardized assessments	To conduct item analyses; to screen students for placement; to evaluate program efficacy	
Leveled reading assessments	To determine where additional support and challenge might be needed; to determine if additional diagnostic tests are needed; to order parallel reading materials	
Diagnostic reading tests	To determine what types of interventions would be most helpful for specific students	
School or district writing prompts	To determine individual performance for instructional purposes; to evaluate program efficacy	
Course and/or grade-level assessments that require reading and writing	To look across assignments and discuss if students are demonstrating necessary proficiency and where additional explicit instruction, modeling, and guided practice might be needed; to calibrate expectations across classes; to monitor student progress; to differentiate instruction	
Student survey data	To understand reading and writing experiences and instruction from the students' points of view	
Collaborative examination of student work	To calibrate expectations across classes, to brainstorm how to provide additional support	

Source: Adapted from Irvin, J. L., Meltzer, J., & Dukes, M. S. (2007). *Taking Action on Adolescent Literacy: An Implementation Guide for School Leaders.* Alexandria, VA: Association for Supervision and Curriculum Development, pp. 167–169.

Use Data to Make Placement Decisions

In many schools, student placement decisions are based on test score data. Many schools and districts have established a tiered system of interventions that, largely based on test scores, tries to provide students with the level of assistance they need to improve as readers and writers. For example, in one school we worked with, the schoolwide literacy initiative is supporting all teachers to provide students with good content literacy instruction. Based on test scores, students who need additional assistance get placed in an intervention class or get matched with a tutor. Students who require even more intensive support work more closely with a reading specialist.

If you are just starting to put into place a tiered system of interventions in your school, you may want to reference the following sample set of placement protocols. Review these guidelines with your team and compare them with your school's current practice. Remember that the strongest placement decisions are based on multiple points of data or test scores coupled with teacher judgment.

Guidelines for Using Standardized Test Data to Make Placement Decisions	
66th percentile and above	Basic: General monitoring (content area classrooms with good literacy instruction)
41st–65th percentile	Substantial: Close monitoring (content area classrooms with good literacy instruction)
25th–40th percentile	Intensive: Further assessment (intervention class and content area classrooms with attention to literacy needs)
0–24th percentile	Critical: Diagnostic assessment and close monitoring (strategic literacy interventions and content area classrooms with attention to literacy needs)

Source: Adapted from Irvin, J. L., Meltzer, J., & Dukes, M. S. (2007). *Taking Action on Adolescent Literacy: An Implementation Guide for School Leaders.* Alexandria, VA: Association for Supervision and Curriculum Development, p. 173.

As principal, while you may not be an expert on all of the assessments given at your school, you do need to be aware that correct placement requires the review of thoughtful professionals. No "one size fits all" approach works here. Therefore, use of placement protocols should be backed up by a process that allows for reconsideration of a placement when appropriate.

One of the dangers of basing student placement into an intervention class or program on a single score or type of data is that the data may not accurately represent student's ability as a reader or writer. Students may score low on a reading assessment for many reasons, and grades and scores may warrant a closer look before a final placement decision is made. Since it is likely that you have limited resources to provide extra assistance to students who need it, it is important to establish an efficient review process that results in students getting the type of help they need.

Consider the four examples that follow. Each may indicate potential errors in placement. How would placement for these students be handled in your school to ensure that they get the support they need to develop greater proficiency as readers?

Student Data	Placement Decision	Other Considerations
Student A: low grades but upper quartile standardized reading assessment scores	Student A has automatic placement in a reading intervention class because of low grades.	Other barriers to Student A's completion of work may exist, such as lack of engagement with class assignments and materials or attendance.
Student B: low score on reading assessment but medium to high grades	Automatic placement in an intervention class because test performance is in the lowest quartile. Classroom performance indicates that Student B reads grade-level material proficiently. Student B admits to not putting much effort into completing the test.	Placement into an intervention class may be a misuse of resources. More attention to the importance of the test, what the test can tell students about reading proficiency, and a review of the format of the test may ensure more valid data.
Student C: low score on reading assessment but medium to high grades	Student C is not placed in intervention class because of medium to high grades.	Because Student C is a hard worker, the reading score can serve as a valuable alert to the fact that Student C is a very slow reader. Student C may benefit from placement in an intervention class that further diagnoses and uses a technology-based program to address Student C's specific needs as a reader.
Student D: Adequate score on district fluency benchmark; low score on state reading and/or English/language (ELA) assessment	The fluency benchmark screening does not identify Student D's problems with comprehension, so Student D is not placed in an intervention class. A check with teachers shows that Student D is struggling in classes.	Consider providing Student D some targeted reading assistance through a strategy-based program that develops reading comprehension using nonfiction texts.

Create a Culture of Data Use

As principal, you can be a powerful model for how data can be used as a tool for continuous improvement. You can present the data that you use to make decisions, and you can expect others to use data to make decisions as well. You can also share data to communicate the need to take action as well as progress made. The payoff of establishing a culture of data use can be high. Teachers who systematically collect, analyze, and use student data are more likely to provide responsive instruction. Students who understand what their reading or writing scores mean and how to sustain current levels of growth or improve performance become more actively involved in their own learning. Parents and community members who hear what the data say about the strength of the instructional program at the school are more likely to support the school's efforts.

How can you support assessment to become an integral and continuous part of teaching and learning at your school? In addition to working with the district to make sure that reading assessments are available and that student performance data get disseminated to teachers in a timely manner, you may need to set up structural support. For example, as the expectation for using data to make instructional decisions becomes an integral part of the school culture, teachers may need professional development on how to understand and analyze the data they have. Teachers also need time to analyze and discuss data about student performance as readers and writers. Think about how you can provide time for teachers to meet by team or department to discuss what information they obtain from reading assessment data and what information they need to help students to develop proficiency as readers, writers, and thinkers.

Support Teachers to Improve Instruction

One of the keys to improving student literacy and learning is to support all content area teachers to become increasingly competent and confident facilitators of content literacy instruction. To accomplish this goal, school administrators have a responsibility to help teachers engage in ongoing, job-embedded teacher professional development, such as (1) active participation in professional learning communities, (2) sharing successful instructional practice, and (3) frequent opportunities to visit one another's classrooms to observe and coach each other. In this section of the chapter, we discuss how you can support teachers to improve literacy and learning through providing quality content literacy teacher professional development.

Professional Development Formats

Because teachers are themselves a diverse group of learners, professional development should be offered using variety of formats so that teachers can deepen their learning, using options that work well for them. The expectation should be for everyone to improve his or her instructional capacity and delivery, but there should be choices in how that can occur.

Consider the following professional development formats. How many do you currently offer? What can you offer during the next school year?

Professional Development Formats

- Weekly or biweekly afterschool or evening classes for four or eight months
- A professional development period or opportunity for professional learning communities to meet during the school day
- Summer institutes with in-person or online follow-up through the year
- Friday and Saturday classes once per month for four months

- A series of day-long workshops, addressing before, during, after reading strategies, vocabulary development strategies, and writing to learn strategies held on Saturdays or during workshop days
- Peer-led workshops conducted on site during early release days
- Demonstration classrooms
- In-class modeling and coaching
- Online classes
- Targeted conference attendance followed by peer-led workshops on selected topics
- Strategy demonstrations at faculty meetings
- Monthly literacy strategy sharing events
- Literacy and learning study groups

Source: Irvin, J. L., Meltzer, J., & Dukes, M. S. (2007). *Taking Action on Adolescent Literacy: An Implementation Guide for School Leaders.* Alexandria, VA: Association for Supervision and Curriculum Development, p. 151.

Professional Development Topics

If you or someone on the administrative team has extensive knowledge about literacy, then you will probably have a sense of the professional development topics that will need to be addressed to increase the capacity of your faculty in this area. If, on the other hand, members of the administrative team do not have a strong literacy background, you may want to review the components and associated indicators on three of the literacy action rubrics (see Introduction to the Rubrics). The components and indicators associated with Literacy Action Rubrics 1, 2, and 3 provide a comprehensive list of the areas where teachers may need assistance. You may also want to conduct a professional development needs assessment of the faculty. You can use the professional development assessment in the following chart to determine what aspects of content literacy challenge teachers most and where teachers say they can use additional support (see Tool 16 in Resource B).

Tool 16: Professional Development Needs Assessment

We would like your input for our literacy professional development this year. Please rank the following literacy professional development needs, with *1* being *least important* to you and *9* being *most important* to you.

Area of Literacy Professional Development	Rank Order
How to teach and use literacy strategies to improve content reading	
How to teach students to summarize and analyze text	
How to teach content area vocabulary	
How to increase student motivation to read and write	
How to implement interventions for struggling students	

(Continued)

(Continued)

Area of Literacy Professional Development	Rank Order
How to use data to inform instruction	
How to create a literacy-rich environment in the classroom	
How to differentiate literacy instruction	
How to teach writing in my content area	
Other areas that you would like to learn more about include the following: **Elements that best support my implementation of instructional strategies into my classroom** Use the following ranking system: *** (not helpful)** **** (sometimes helpful)** ***** (very helpful)** Specific content area examples Time to talk with colleagues about possible applications Time to plan with colleagues Access to written descriptions and templates Observation of other classrooms Strategies modeled by the consultant One-to-one coaching support to implement Time to share and discuss with colleagues' attempts at implementation Feedback from others	

Source: Adapted from Irvin, J. L., Meltzer, J., Mickler, M. J., Phillips, M. P., & Dean, N. (2009). *Meeting the Challenge of Adolescent Literacy: Practical Ideas for Literacy Leaders.* Newark, DE: International Reading Association, p. 201.

Professional Development Approaches

In addition to how the professional development is delivered (format) and what the professional development focuses on (topic), you will want to think carefully about the approach that the professional development takes. Professional development is best understood as a process, not an event. Generic professional development that is not attuned to the experience, context, or need of the participants is much less likely to be effective. As you plan professional development, be certain to consider the answers to these questions:

- Does the professional development include time for teachers to talk and share expertise?
- Does the professional development provide resources and support on an ongoing basis?
- Is the professional development being offered grounded in issues that teachers have identified as challenges that they face in the classroom?

The ultimate goal of professional development is to have the instructional innovations being introduced become part of the regular practice of teaching and learning at your school. In the following chart, we describe some of the approaches associated with effective professional development, that is, professional development that has a better chance of impacting students in the classroom. Each is accompanied by actions that school administrators can take to ensure that these aspects of professional development are supported. When successfully enacted, these approaches transform professional development from isolated workshop events to part of the ongoing culture at your school. You may want to include some of these as design principles when asking staff to present to one another or when contracting for outside assistance from a consultant.

Framework for Professional Development Planning

Professional development that includes . . .	What should occur so this is successful . . .
Careful analysis of student achievement	Be certain that teachers understand how to read assessment reports and that they have the data necessary to make data-driven decisions about instruction to improve the achievement of specific groups of students.
Strategies that improve teacher performance and raise student achievement	Allocate resources toward areas that directly impact teacher and student performance (e.g., time, materials, technology, teacher professional development, coaching).
Activities that relate to the real work of teachers and to authentic issues they are grappling with in their day-to-day classrooms	Survey teachers to determine issues and needs of high priority that meet their needs and needs of their students; examine and report on student data.
Ongoing follow-up for teachers as they try out new skills and strategies	Avoid one-time professional development; provide the time and expectation for strategy sharing and coaching.
Use of professional expertise at building or district level	Create a database of teachers who demonstrate special skills and knowledge and provide them with opportunities to work with colleagues.
Time for teachers to conduct action research and classroom visitation at their own and other schools	Create a master schedule that provides teachers with time to exchange ideas, try out new strategies together, and conduct action research to find promising approaches to instructional challenges.
Ongoing assistance and support available upon request	Ensure that a school or district literacy specialist or coach sets aside time to comply with teacher requests for support.
Meaningful intellectual, social, and emotional engagement with ideas, materials, and colleagues	Use electronic tools to support learning: e-mail, moodle, bulletin boards, Internet, blogging, podcasts, and so on, as well as providing in-person opportunities to meet and discuss practice.
Support for informed dissent	Acknowledge the existence of conflict, and use it to raise important issues and focus on continuous improvement.
Acknowledgement and appreciation of the contexts of teaching and experience of teachers	Promote a model of professional learning that values teacher talk in the halls, in classrooms, in teams, and departments.

When school leaders provide the impetus, enthusiasm, expertise, and support for successful professional development, teachers are more likely to take professional learning seriously and participate more enthusiastically.

Allocate Resources

As you and your literacy leadership team develop the school's literacy action goals and implementation maps, resources will be necessary to support each action step. These should be specifically identified in terms of funding, materials, personnel, and time. Since resources are rarely as plentiful as one would wish, it is important to be strategic in finding and allocating resources. As the school principal, you can make certain that the initiative has what it needs to succeed. The chart that follows shows some key resources as they relate to a schoolwide literacy improvement effort.

Type of Resource	Reason Needed
Teacher professional development	To improve instruction to develop students as readers, writers, and thinkers
Time for teachers to meet	To review assessment data, share strategy use, examine student work, and engage in professional learning
Materials and technology	To support learning across the content areas, literacy interventions, and assessment
Dissemination resources	To promote the literacy initiative, report progress toward goals, and recognize student and teacher effort

As you continue to monitor the plan with the literacy leadership team, the data collected will show where additional resources or reallocation of resources will be helpful. For example, if reading assessment scores indicate that many students coming into seventh grade from multiple feeder schools have difficulty with comprehending nonfiction, the principal can work with the literacy leadership team to allocate the following resources to meet this need:

- Professional development (e.g., time, consultant fees, professional books) for teachers to learn additional approaches to vocabulary development and comprehension (perhaps instead of a focus on another professional development topic)
- Additional library and classroom resources (e.g., magazine subscriptions, text sets, online databases) to provide texts about curriculum topics at varying reading levels
- Time for the literacy coach to specifically model nonfiction comprehension strategies in social studies and science classrooms

REAL SCHOOL EXAMPLE

One middle school principal says that he never makes a resource decision without thinking about how it will affect the momentum and effectiveness of the literacy initiative underway at the school. This prompts him to be even more strategic in his resource use. He uses substitute teachers to release teachers to mentor and coach one another. He uses technology-based literacy interventions and assessments to maximize the investment the district has made in technology. He works closely with the assistant superintendent to stretch funds as far as possible. He makes sure that new teachers are mentored by those with strong content literacy instructional skills. Previously, resources were not as focused, but since effectiveness of the work has been shown in test scores, the principal is unwilling to sabotage success and now sees literacy improvement as central to school improvement.

Source: Thanks to Messalonskee Middle School in Oakland, Maine, for this example. Used with permission.

Funding

All schools and districts are allocated levels of funding for programs and personnel. The question to be thinking about is how those funds might be reallocated to support a focus on literacy improvement in a school. You might think about the following funding options:

- If enrollment supports a decrease in a full-time teaching position, could you combine a part-time coaching position with a part-time teaching position?
- Could you schedule and recombine into a larger group of students who might benefit from a co-teaching arrangement—deliberate pairing of an English Language Learner or special education teacher with a content area teacher?
- Could existing funding provide materials (such as leveled or parallel texts about curriculum content) that can support the literacy initiative and content learning?

At some point, though, additional funding may be necessary beyond what is normally allocated. One way to tap into additional funding is to research the instructional and professional development priorities of local and regional funding sources and determine the degree of alignment with the action steps of your implementation maps. You may find that many of these sources have goals similar to yours and may be looking to partner with a local school. You might also consider talking with administrators in the various departments or areas of your district to determine their budget and line-item priorities. For example, the district human resources department is often responsible for new teacher development and may have resources for professional development for new hires and paraprofessionals. If your district has a department of professional development, you can work with the department head to create literacy-focused opportunities for your teachers and staff.

Another option is to collaborate with district subject-area supervisors who have resources for professional development and materials that can support specific action steps in your literacy action plan. For example, if both summer school and teacher professional development are called for, you can combine these into a model in which students attend classes in the morning for credit, and teachers attend targeted professional development in the afternoon. This summer school model provides students with important course options and provides teachers with a laboratory to try out embedded literacy strategies.

When action steps in your literacy action plan relate to one or more of the areas in the following chart, you can often make a compelling case for using the funding from other sources. As you search out resources for the literacy initiative, you might take a look at funding sources both within and outside of the school district.

Potential Sources Within the District	Potential Sources in the Community
• Title 1 and/or No Child Left Behind Act (NCLB) funds • Title IID • GEAR-UP funding • Career and technical education • Individuals with Disabilities Education Act (IDEA) • Workforce development or 21st-century funds • Technology budget • Library/media services budget • School improvement funds	• Community foundations • Business mini-grants • College and/or university partnerships • Business sponsorships • Partnerships with nonprofit organizations • Grant-writing support • Parent organizations

Materials and Resources

For literacy and learning to be supported in classrooms, access to technology, books, consumable reading publications, and other materials and resources are necessary. In addition to the types of materials discussed earlier, the following options may generate supplemental resources:

- Conduct an inventory of unused materials that can be used as resources.
- Request free materials and support from publishers of literacy-rich instructional materials.
- Ask the library media specialist to provide a list of curriculum-related text and media resources available to teachers.
- Solicit parent and community volunteers to search for literacy resources from social service agencies, museums, service clubs, youth clubs, libraries, and nonprofit agencies.
- Contact business partners and grant-making organizations for resources to purchase print and other multimedia resources.

Time

Time as a specific resource needs to be used strategically in multiple ways to support literacy improvement. How can you find time to free teachers for peer coaching, team meetings, and professional development? Some ideas to capture time can be found in the following chart.

Purchase time	Hire teachers during their off-contract hours to write and create materials.
Borrow time	Add time during the beginning and end of the school day from Monday through Thursday, thus gaining an hour on Friday for professional development. Over the school year, you will gain about 40 hours.
Create new time through teacher incentives	Teachers who are engaging in certification courses or advanced degrees have time (and incentives) to pursue self-directed professional development activities.
Tier the time	Tier activities with functions that are already in place. For example, schedule an early-bird breakfast during required time before school, and use the time for teachers to share literacy strategies and activities that they have used successfully.
Use common time	Schedule blocks of time during the master schedule for teachers to work on common literacy-oriented tasks.
Capitalize on found time	Teachers sometimes find time in unexpected ways. For example, when teachers have interns who are doing independent practice during the end of their internship, they have time out of their classroom to observe or plan literacy instruction with other teachers.
Free up time	Volunteers and visiting presenters can create time for teams of teachers to work together on literacy instruction while their students are being supervised by other teams of teachers.
Reschedule time	Some schools are moving toward a year-round calendar that allows leaders to plan the master calendar to include more professional development opportunities.
Use time differently	Save department and faculty meetings for literacy-oriented activities, such as looking at student work and sharing literacy strategies implemented from professional development.
Use district professional days	Use the standard, district-allocated professional days to provide professional development that is focused on literacy in content areas. For example, if a schoolwide focus is reciprocal teaching, provide teachers with short-term activities about reciprocal teaching with the expectation that the strategy will be systemically implemented during the school year.
Use administrators and other staff	Enlist time from administrators and staff, such as library and technology specialists, who do not have classroom responsibilities to cover classes for teachers as they collaborate, coach, and mentor.

Source: Adapted from Fogarty, R., & Pete, B. (2007). *From Staff Room to Classroom.* Thousand Oaks, CA: Corwin.

Implement a Literacy Action Plan

As the principal, you are responsible for improving student literacy and learning. As we have discussed throughout this book, using literacy as a lever for school improvement makes sense and can strengthen your school's instructional program, culture, and student outcomes. By implementing the literacy leadership process described in Chapters 1-5, you will develop and implement a strong literacy action plan to inspire collective action, improve teaching and learning, and develop a culture of data-driven decision making.

One important role that the administrative team can play is to monitor the literacy action plan through literacy walk-throughs. These literacy walk-throughs provide snapshots of content literacy teaching and learning over time. In some schools, members of the literacy leadership team conduct literacy walk-throughs; in other schools, only administrators do so. In a few schools we know about, any teacher who wants to attend an initial workshop on literacy walk-throughs can be on a walk-through team. Who conducts literacy walk-throughs at your school will depend on your school's culture and district policy.

As principal, you can promote literacy walk-throughs as an integral part of your efforts to build a culture of data use. Literacy walk-throughs support all of the five action points in the *Taking Action Literacy Leadership Model.* They *build the capacity of school leaders* to understand and reinforce quality content literacy instruction. They provide *critical data* for the literacy leadership team and the faculty around *implementation of the literacy action plan.* They *support teachers* because they honor the work that teachers do in the classroom. They point out where additional coaching *resources* and instructional materials are needed. Therefore, literacy walk-throughs are an effective strategy for you to carry out in support of your school's efforts to improve literacy and learning. The next section provides an overview of this important strategy for progress monitoring.

What Are Literacy Walk-Throughs?

Literacy walk-throughs are brief, repeated, focused classroom visits during which data are collected relative to the goals of the literacy action plan. School leaders collect real-time data about literacy instructional practices used throughout the school building. When conducted regularly over time, literacy walk-throughs provide snapshots of the evolving picture of literacy support and development throughout the school. A principal in south Florida says, "What gets inspected, gets respected." Rather than viewing instructional practices and consequences as integral to the personality and competence of individual teachers, the literacy walk-through protocol focuses on practices and habits across classrooms and the school as artifacts of student behavior and engagement. This distinction is important. Teachers and administrators need to understand the difference between literacy walk-throughs and standard classroom observations or teacher evaluations.

Literacy walk-throughs allow school leaders to get a glimpse into the everyday instructional practices in the school. While brief classroom visits can be spontaneous to see the typical behavior of teachers and students, they can also be planned and very specifically targeted to identify aspects of literacy instruction that support progress toward literacy action goals. The focus of data collection is on the interactions between teacher and students; the level of student engagement; the amounts and types of reading, writing, presenting, and critical thinking; and the quality of student work. A literacy walk-through can be conducted by a single person or a team, which might include school administrator(s), curriculum support person(s), district-level administrators, members of the literacy leadership team, and/or school department chairs.

The focus of a particular walk-through can be collaboratively determined ahead of time based on priority needs from the data, or alignment with the literacy action plan and/or school improvement plan. Or planned data collection can focus on gathering evidence of practices introduced during recent professional development sessions. Literacy walk-throughs can also focus data collection on a variety of classroom artifacts and interactions, including the following:

- Word walls with content area vocabulary
- Literacy strategy instruction
- Student work exhibiting thinking about texts
- Student writing about content area learning
- Evidence of the school literacy vision
- Students reading a variety of text at multiple levels
- Evidence of differentiated literacy instruction

Developing a data collection form that supports all participants in a given literacy walk-through helps you to collect consistent data. Your form should be simple to use but also allow the team to collect data that shows progress over time and indicates where additional teaching coaching may be needed. You can use different forms for each walkthrough or repeat the use of the same forms at different points in the year. Of course, your form can address more than one area of focus. Here are some examples of how you can construct simple data collection forms for literacy walkthroughs:

Possible area of focus: *Student engagement*

1. Define what team members want to know. For example: What is the level of student engagement? What activities are correlated with high engagement? With low engagement?
2. Define engagement levels: High (80–100% engaged); Medium (40–79% engaged); Low (0–39% engaged).
3. Create a data collection form that has space to describe the learning activity observed in each classroom and the level of engagement observed.

Possible area of focus: Student reading and writing

1. Define what team members want to know. For example: Are students reading or writing? If so, what are they reading or writing? How are they reading or writing (in pairs, silently, one at a time, in small groups)?
2. Create a data collection form that has space to check off if students are observed reading and/or writing and options to check off that reflect how this is occurring and what is being read/written.

Possible area of focus: Classroom support for literacy

1. Define what team members want to know. For example: What do classroom walls show? What aids do students have to use when reading and writing? Are these aids referred to by teachers or students during classroom visits?

2. Create a data collection form that has space to describe the types of supports found (e.g., samples of exemplary work. specific scoring criteria (rubrics), helpful process information (writing process, problem solving) and boxes to check if these are referred to during the classroom visit.

Through this structured walk-through process, school leaders maintain and deepen their understanding of the literacy teaching and learning practices taking place in the school as well as the literacy needs of students and teachers. Literacy walk-through results can be summarized for discussion with staff and the literacy leadership team and used to guide professional development planning. Again, the emphasis is on collective data, not individual feedback to teachers. For example, if what was observed was typical practice for period three or for science classes or for ninth-grade students, is this what we want to have happen? Why or why not? What do we need to do to support real improvement? The following checklist can help determine answers to these questions.

Before the literacy walk-through	❑ Decide who will conduct the walk-through. If the literacy walk-through is a team effort, pair up team members. ❑ Decide how many and which classrooms (e.g., certain period of the day; department; grade level; random) will be visited. Note: We recommend that a literacy walk-through include a minimum of 5–8 classrooms and include a minimum of 30–40 classroom visits before sharing data with teachers. Plan a schedule that allows 3–5 minutes per classroom visit. ❑ Discuss the literacy action goal to be featured in the literacy walk-through. ❑ Inform teachers about the literacy walk-through process (that it is not evaluative; that it is about what the students are doing; that the report will not include individual feedback). Share the window of time for the walkthrough and the types of data that will be collected. ❑ Create a data collection form to use for the literacy walk-through.
After the literacy walk-through (20-30 minutes)	❑ Debrief with others who participated in the literacy walk-through. ❑ Compile and analyze the data. Discuss key messages that need to be shared based on the data. ❑ Decide how those who did the literacy walk-through will share the data with the literacy leadership team and/or report the data back to the faculty. ❑ Establish date and focus for next literacy walk-through.

Reporting results to teachers is an important aspect of walk-throughs. The purpose of reporting literacy walk-through data is to generate ongoing discussion about classroom practice. You may not wish to report all of the data you collected but instead just focus on some powerful points to stimulate collective reflection. As principal, you may also need to establish who will provide feedback to the teachers and in what format.

For example, the literacy leadership team might send an adaptation of the following e-mail:

> *The literacy leadership team visited 40 classrooms over a period of three days. We focused on ninth-grade classroom use of literacy support strategies.*
>
> - *We saw evidence of the active use of a literacy support strategy by teachers or students in 50% of the classrooms we visited. This is an increase from the last literacy walk-through six months ago.*
> - *We wish we saw more students working together to discuss key points of the text and generating lists of questions raised by the reading.*
> - *We wish we saw fewer students individually reading the text and answering questions in writing.*
> - *We wonder if the reading level of the text is too advanced for many of the students and how teachers could model strategies for students to use when reading difficult text.*
>
> *Discuss the following at your ninth grade team meeting:*
>
> - *What, if anything, surprises you? Why?*
> - *What affirms what you thought was true?*
> - *What are the implications of the data for teaching and learning in your classroom?*

Keeping track of data over time and revisiting the same classrooms later in the year to monitor progress on specific criteria is one way of gaining an understanding of progress toward goals. Literacy walk-throughs can be a strategy for monitoring progress over time, acknowledging the work of teachers in the classroom, fostering collective responsibility for student literacy and learning, and communicating the message that you expect that professional development will result in changes in classroom practice. It is critical that as an instructional leader you recognize quality content literacy instruction when you see it. For more information on literacy walk-throughs, see Chapter 4.

The role of the school principal and other building-level administrators in supporting a literacy improvement initiative is essential. Without effective leadership and active involvement from the principal and the administrative team, there is a high risk that the initiative will fail. However, when effective leaders are able to generate and sustain enthusiasm for improving literacy and learning from teachers, administrators, parents, and students, the sky is truly the limit.

As you can see from the content of the chapter, the five action points of the *Taking Action Literacy Leadership Model* are all critical. The order in which you implement these action points is less important than making sure your administrative team eventually addresses all of them. In Chapter 7, we focus how district administrators can use the literacy leadership process to improve literacy and learning throughout the district.

7

District Support

In this chapter, you will complete the following:

- ✓ **Identify the essential elements of the district's role in supporting school-based literacy improvement efforts.**
- ✓ **Learn a process for developing an effective district literacy action plan.**

In this chapter, we describe how district administrators can develop a strong district literacy action plan using the literacy leadership process. The district is in a powerful position to broker resources from the state and outside funding sources and to leverage resources across schools. A coordinated district effort can positively affect school-based initiatives and can galvanize action throughout the district and the larger community to improve student literacy and learning.

Literacy Action Rubric 6 is the last in the set of rubrics aligned to the *Taking Action Literacy Leadership Model.* This rubric focuses on the essential components of a robust and collaborative district effort to support school-based literacy initiatives. In this way, it is different from the other rubrics because it specifies the role of the district as opposed to the role of the school.

Sometimes a district literacy plan is developed to support school initiatives already underway. More commonly, a district plan is used to initiate school-based literacy improvement efforts. In either case, district leaders can use Rubric 6 to assess the district's current capacity, identify gaps, and define priorities. Rubric 6 consists of a set of five essential components with related indicators:

1. Communicate that improving literacy is a priority.
2. Provide teacher professional development.

3. Provide specific types of fiscal support.
4. Establish uniform policies and procedures across the district.
5. Use data to improve instruction and monitor program effectiveness.

In the next section of this chapter, we describe each of these components and the indicators that districts can use to assess current capacity. Examples of each of the components in action can be found in Resource C. A copy of Rubric 6 in its entirety can be found at the end of this chapter.

COMMUNICATE THAT IMPROVING LITERACY IS A PRIORITY

Summary of Indicators Related to Improving Literacy as a Priority

- The district promotes the importance of student literacy improvement in Grades 4 through 12, including targeted support for struggling readers and writers.
- A district literacy plan is published, implemented, regularly reviewed, and updated annually as part of the district strategic plan.
- A district literacy team that includes district and school-based educators, parents, community members, and students meets quarterly to review and monitor progress toward literacy improvement goals.
- A district-level administrator is responsible for implementation of the district literacy action plan and coordinates literacy support for students in Grades 4 through 12 with other district content specialists.
- Hiring preference is given to administrators and content area teachers with a strong literacy background.

The district is in the position to promote literacy and learning throughout the community while providing specific support for school-based efforts. Establishing literacy as a priority sends the clear message to all of those employed by the district that literacy improvement is non-negotiable and will be carried out in all schools. When the district establishes a literacy team to develop a literacy action plan, the purpose should be to support and coordinate school-based efforts, not take away school ownership and school-level decision making related to literacy improvement. These indicators, when in place, demonstrate a district commitment to literacy improvement: school and district plan alignment, hiring practices that reflect a value placed on literacy expertise, resource allocation for appropriate materials, ongoing professional development, and staffing, and literacy interventions in place to address student needs.

The district can use multiple approaches to rally the community to support literacy improvement in local schools. For example, the district can work with local cable stations to air school-based literacy events, such as poetry jams, debate team events, and "Battle of the Books" finals. The district can also work with local radio and print media organizations to produce short announcements about the importance of literacy and the school's efforts to improve literacy among students. To strengthen the message that literacy affects everyone, the district can work with local businesses to sponsor community reads and with nonprofit organizations to provide literacy resources to after-school programs, health centers, and school-to-work programs.

How does the district currently communicate literacy improvement goals to administrators, teachers, parents, students, staff, and the community at large? What evidence is there that the communication is effective? How can the district strengthen communication efforts to establish literacy improvement as a clear priority of the district?

PROVIDE PROFESSIONAL DEVELOPMENT

Summary of Indicators Related to Teacher Professional Development

- The district provides ongoing literacy leadership professional development for school administrators, literacy coaches, and teacher leaders.
- The district provides ongoing literacy professional development and expects that all content area teachers will participate.
- The district provides ongoing literacy training and professional development for intervention and special education teachers, and teachers of English language learners.
- The district provides new teachers with sufficient support and mentoring to integrate literacy development with content teaching and learning.

The district has a vital role to play as a provider of quality teacher professional development. Many educators do not know how to support literacy development for students in Grades 4 through 12. Even if teachers took a college course about content area reading, it takes practice and ongoing support to integrate the concepts of literacy development with content area learning successfully. Although there are pockets of deep literacy expertise in all schools, literacy expertise must be spread throughout the district if a literacy improvement effort is to work. Quality professional development is essential.

Content area teachers need quality professional development that focuses on strategies that improve students' abilities as readers, writers, and thinkers in all content areas. Developing the ability to integrate literacy and learning across the content areas requires discussion about the use of instructional strategies, a school culture that promotes risk-taking, a schedule conducive to teachers' trying out instructional innovations introduced through professional development, and getting meaningful feedback from peers. Quality content literacy professional development can include professional learning communities, demonstration lessons, peer coaching, discussions, and intentional collaboration. When the district sponsors professional development, the same messages and approaches can be introduced across schools; teachers who teach the same content area in different schools can come together and share ideas; and central office curriculum supervisors can work with teachers of the same content area in multiple schools, supporting them to try out effective instructional strategies. It is especially important that new teachers receive this support from assigned mentors and instructional coaches. This will ensure that new teachers understand and can meet the expectations of the school and district. (For more about professional development formats, topics, and approaches, see Chapter 6.)

Administrators, literacy coaches, and teacher leaders also need professional development that addresses their roles in supporting teachers. Professional development for these literacy leaders should include topics such as how to support effective peer coaching, what quality content literacy instruction looks like in each content area, how to conduct literacy walk-throughs, how to use data to make programmatic and instructional decisions, and how to allocate resources to support literacy and learning. District support of this type of professional development means that similar messages and approaches can be spread efficiently throughout the district. Feedback from school administrators and other instructional leaders can provide the district with good information about what other types of professional development are needed.

Literacy intervention, special education, and teachers of English language learners need professional development, particularly for fidelity of implementation when new programs are put into place. This often takes special training with technology or program materials to make the program work as intended. Special education teachers and teachers of English language learners need content literacy professional development as well because they are charged with supporting student learning across content areas. They need time to discuss and discover the best ways to meet the needs of these special populations of students. When teachers are supported and encouraged to discuss promising practices across schools, professionals in these areas can strengthen their practice, something that can be challenging when part of a small department within a school. As schools move to inclusion of special education and ELL students within mainstreamed classes, teachers need to learn how to collaborate with one another. Professional development that provides the time for teachers to discuss and work together to address the needs of specific populations benefits students because teachers develop professional relationships, share expertise, and take on collective responsibility for student success. When the district sponsors this type of professional development, teachers from multiple schools can participate in activities and training that would be cost prohibitive for an individual school to support.

Who decides what types of professional development are offered in the district? Upon review of what is planned for the upcoming year, how well does the planned professional development meet the needs of the various groups described above? What needs to happen to ensure that district sponsored professional development directly supports the district goal of improving literacy?

PROVIDE SPECIFIC TYPES OF FISCAL SUPPORT

Summary of Indicators Related to Fiscal Support

- The district allocates sufficient funds for personnel related to literacy (e.g., district administrator(s) charged with literacy improvement, literacy coaches, reading specialists).
- The district allocates sufficient funds for resources (e.g., books and materials, site licenses, technology, reading and writing assessments, interventions) to support literacy improvement in Grades 4 through 12.
- The district regularly seeks and obtains additional grant and foundation monies and community-based funding to support literacy improvement in Grades 4 through 12.

Difficult decisions about the allocation of resources are made every day in school district offices. A successful literacy initiative, however, requires that specific types of resources be allocated to support implementation. These include personnel, materials and technology, and fiscal resources to support the work. Too often, we are told that literacy is a priority in a district, but there are no real resources to support it. While we acknowledge that resources are rarely plentiful, a successful literacy initiative requires dedicated resources to succeed.

One of the essential resources of a successful literacy initiative is skilled personnel to coordinate programs and practices; provide professional development; administer, analyze, and use data to improve instruction; and generally support the literacy improvement efforts of each school.

REAL SCHOOL EXAMPLE

One large school district wanted to improve students' literacy scores at all of their schools. While the scores were not critically low, district administrators knew that the students throughout the district needed to improve in reading and writing to be successful in life, college, and the workplace. The district wanted to implement a coordinated, consistent effort for literacy improvement throughout the district, so they hired the National Literacy Project to introduce the literacy leadership process, help school-based teams develop literacy action plans, and assist with capacity building and implementation. Three middle schools and one high school were selected as pilot sites. The four district language arts curriculum specialists learned the literacy leadership process as they worked side by side with the National Literacy Project School Partners. In the second year, limited support was continued at the year one schools, and the process was repeated with four additional schools.

Source: Thanks to Jefferson County School District in Colorado for this example. Used with permission.

Does the district employ personnel that carry out some of these responsibilities? If there are school-based literacy coaches or curriculum specialists, how can the district assist with their professional development and definitions of their roles? If the district is just putting these positions in place, what are the expected outcomes associated with these positions? How can the time of literacy coaches and curriculum specialists be used most effectively? If there are school-based literacy teams, how can the district actively support their work and leverage the use of promising practices across schools?

Who at the district office is in charge of literacy improvement (e.g., district literacy coordinator, assistant superintendent, English/language arts coordinator, curriculum coordinator, secondary education director)? If literacy improvement is to be a district priority, someone at the district level needs to take ownership of this work with the public affirmation of the superintendent. In large school districts, the strategic use of district literacy coaches who have multiple school assignments can provide coordination and support for school-based efforts. Sometimes, the district can spread personnel across schools if limited resources preclude full-time coaching or reading specialist positions within each school. In the case of school-based personnel, the district can assist schools with establishing roles and responsibilities relative to the district goal of literacy improvement and can help establish criteria for performance relative to that goal.

Consider how the following positions might be actively supported by the district within or across schools to sustain a districtwide focus on literacy improvement. Clarify for each what their primary role and responsibilities should be relative to literacy improvement (see Tool 17 in Resource B).

Tool 17: Roles of Support Personnel		
Role	**Role in Literacy Support**	**District Support of This Role**
School-based literacy coaches		
District-based reading specialists		
Content area teacher leaders		
English language learner or special education teachers with a background in reading		
Library media specialists		
Technology specialists		

Materials, site licenses, and other resources are also necessary to a successful literacy improvement effort. If these are vetted and purchased by the district, it is often possible to save costs over school-by-school expenditures. The district might decide to provide matching funds to schools that choose one of the approved literacy intervention programs. Costs for the teacher professional development on how to use these programs can then be shared by schools and the district. Technology infrastructure and the purchase or development of assessments are two additional examples of resources that can be effectively leveraged by the district.

District personnel can also seek and apply for grant-funded opportunities to support the literacy initiative. Grant funding can be used for the following:

- Professional development
- Community programs aimed at involving parents and community members in the literacy initiative (working with business and community partners to obtain in-kind donations or resources for specific projects such as books for a community read, posters and banners to promote literacy, refreshments for teacher workshops, or training of tutors)
- Materials and/or technology to support the integration of literacy support in content area classrooms, assessment, or intervention programs

ESTABLISH UNIFORM POLICIES AND PROCEDURES ACROSS THE DISTRICT

Summary of Indicators Related to Policies and Procedures

- The district curriculum includes a scope and sequence for literacy development for Grades 4 through 12.
- The district requires schools to develop school-based scheduling to safeguard that all students have access to rigorous course content and strong literacy support.
- The district expects all school administrators to function as strong literacy leaders.
- Teacher evaluation processes include the expectation that all teachers consistently integrate literacy support into content area instruction.
- The district works with parents and community members as close partners in the literacy improvement effort.

For a literacy improvement initiative to be sustainable, policies and practices must be in place to set the clear expectation that the primary role of all administrators is that of instructional leader. For example, the district can require that school principals work closely with a school-based literacy leadership team to establish school-based literacy goals, develop a school-based literacy action plan, and the monitor both the implementation of the plan and progress toward goals (see Chapters 1–5 for a review of these tasks). The district can reinforce this message by providing ongoing support for school-based administrators to develop their knowledge and understanding of their roles and responsibilities as literacy leaders.

In addition, the district should clarify the expectations and the latitude that schools have to select common literacy support strategies, put intervention programs in place, hire literacy coaches, and rearrange their schedules to promote optimal literacy learning. When the district sets policies that allow for flexibility but hold school-based leaders accountable for improving literacy and learning, it is much more likely that students will get ongoing support to improve as readers, writers, and thinkers.

Other important components of district policy should include a commitment, a plan, and resources to involve parents and community members in the literacy improvement effort. Districts can sponsor parent and community meetings to introduce and explain the literacy initiative, to teach parents and guardians the common literacy strategies being used at a particular school, and to help parents and guardians provide literacy enrichment for their students. In addition, the district can set the expectation that schools will include parents and community members in the literacy initiative through meetings, newsletters, Web sites, representation on the school-based literacy leadership team, and an active parent and community volunteer program.

USE DATA TO IMPROVE INSTRUCTION AND MONITOR PROGRAM EFFECTIVENESS

Summary of Indicators Related to Data Use

- The district requires that schools administer reading and writing assessments in addition to state testing for all students in Grades 4 through 10.
- The district provides quality data in interactive and electronic formats to schools in a timely manner.
- The district expects data use to drive decision making about placement and classroom instruction on an ongoing basis.
- The district analyzes and uses data to make decisions about program effectiveness and resource allocation to support student growth as readers and writers in Grades 4 through 10.

District leaders cannot make informed decisions about instructional programming in their schools without quality data. Although many districts and schools are data rich, they may be information poor. That is, data are collected but are not organized and reported in ways that serve educators to best support students. If you identify places where the district can strengthen its collection, communication, and use of assessment data, these become action steps that the district can take to improve the use of data and can be included in the district literacy action plan.

Think about the data that your district collects relative to student performance as readers and writers. Using the following chart, discuss with others how well you currently communicate answers to the questions that students, teachers, parents and others want to answer (see Tool 18 in Resource B).

Tool 18: Data Questions and Decisions

Stakeholder	Questions and/or Decisions	Reading and/or Writing Assessments We Give	How We Communicate Results	How We Use the Data Internally
Students	How am I doing? What should I do next?			
Teachers	Have my students met my learning goals? How effective was my instruction? Should Student A take *X* class? Would Student B benefit from *Y* program?			
Parents	How is my child doing? Is she or he making progress? How does his or her work and/or learning compare to others?			
Administrators	How effective is our program? For which students is it most effective? Least effective? How well are teachers doing?			
Policy makers	How well are schools meeting public expectations?			
Taxpayers	How well is our money being spent?			

Source: Adapted from Brenner, D., Pearson, P. D., & Rief, L. (2007). Thinking Through Assessment. In K. Beers, R. E. Probst, & L. Rief, *Adolescent Literacy: Turning Promise Into Practice* (p. 262). Portsmouth, NH: Heinemann.

The district needs to set clear expectations that reading assessment data will be used along with other data on student performance to ensure that students get the appropriate level of instructional support. This expectation means that reading assessment data must be collected and be accessible to teachers and administrators who are making placement and instructional decisions. The district needs to make sure that helpful data get to the people who need it. Where feasible, technology can be very helpful both in terms of test administration and the quick reporting of results. For teachers and administrators to make good use of the data that are available, the district may need to provide professional development on how to access the data and how to read and interpret the reports.

District leaders are wise to support the use of a variety of data sources to assess student performance, both in literacy and in content knowledge. It is important that the district

- reports results in a timely manner,
- presents information about progress that the district is making toward literacy improvement goals, and
- communicates data-based decisions about programming and resource allocation.

DEVELOP AND IMPLEMENT A DISTRICT LITERACY ACTION PLAN

An effective district literacy action plan coordinates and supports school-based literacy action plans. A district literacy action plan is best developed collaboratively by a district literacy team, which has representation from across the district and from school and district leaders, teacher leaders and literacy coaches, reading specialists, library media specialists, and others who will play important roles in carrying out the district literacy initiative. If the district is assembling a district literacy team for the first time, you may want to refer to Stage 1 and Stage 4 of the literacy leadership process for ideas on how to organize the team for action.

The district can use Literacy Action Rubric 6 as the basis for developing a literacy action plan by following the guidelines described in the next section of this chapter. If the district is just kicking off a literacy improvement effort, you may want to review the approaches described in Stage 1 and Stage 4 of the literacy leadership process and select those that may help launch the district initiative. For example, the district may want to host a literacy conference or develop a districtwide brand statement for the literacy initiative to generate awareness of the planned effort (see Chapter 4).

Use Literacy Action Rubric 6 to Assess Current Status

You and your district administrative or literacy team can assess the district's current practice, using the five components of Rubric 6. The steps for using the literacy action rubrics as a self-assessment tool prior to developing an action plan are described in Chapter 2. If you have not completed the school literacy action planning process, you may wish to read that chapter before continuing on to the next steps. The District Rubric can be found at the end of this chapter. We recommend that the following steps be followed sequentially:

1. Team members individually assess the district on each indicator of each component of the rubric by placing a check mark on the implementation level that they think best describes the current practice of the district. Individuals should average their ratings of indicators within each component, noting particularly high or low ratings. Team members should be prepared to describe specifically the evidence considered when rating each indicator.

2. The meeting facilitator constructs a chart and records the response of each member on each of the components. This results in a set of check marks that collectively represent the group's assessment of the district's implementation on each component. (You can refer to Chapter 2 for examples of how school-based teams completed this step with other literacy action rubrics.)

3. The team then engages in a discussion to reach consensus on the rating of each component. This may mean returning to and discussing the reasons why individual members rated implementation at a particular level, using evidence and examples to support an individual rating. The group decides on a consensus rating for each component and marks the consensus rating with a colored dot. The exact placement of the colored dot is not as important as seeing trends, recognizing strengths, and understanding the needs of the district. The discussion is essential because it helps the literacy team or other district administrators gain a collective understanding of the current status of literacy support of school-based initiatives in the district. This is a time to listen to and better understand the multiple perspectives the team brings to the process.

DEVELOP DISTRICT LITERACY ACTION GOALS

Once you have developed consensus on the level of implementation of district support for school-based literacy initiatives, you can use the language of Level 4 from Rubric 6 to help the team construct clear, meaningful measureable improvement goals. Since all five components are essential to district support of school-based literacy initiatives, you may wish to write one goal for each component of the rubric. As you construct goal statements, be certain to follow these guidelines:

- Develop goals that you can meet if there were a collaborative effort to do so.
- Develop goals that, if met, would make a positive difference for students.
- Develop a limited number of goals that will direct your literacy improvement efforts over the next year.
- Develop goals that are measurable and toward which the team can track progress.
- Write the goal statements in clear specific language that is jargon free and can be understood by everyone.

The district may want to attach specific percentages or numerical gains in areas such as student test scores, teacher participation in professional development, materials use, or availability of technology. Or the district may want to state the goals in language that shows what it has taken responsibility for carrying out. Either way, make sure that specific data that indicate the reason for selecting a specific goal are connected to presentations of that goal. For example, a goal to put effective interventions in place for more students might be generated because the data show 50% of students are scoring below the 40th percentile on the benchmark test. One sample set of district goals is listed in the following box. It is also helpful to discuss what measures of success would be. In other words, one year from now, if this were a priority, how much progress is reasonable to make on this goal?

Sample: Gate Park School District (GPSD) Literacy Action Goals
1. The GPSD literacy initiative will be evident through the display of a brand statement, districtwide collaboration, classroom activities, student products, and community awareness. Rationale: Although we have many district improvement initiatives focused on literacy, these are not widely known about or focused on. 2. GPSD will identify students who are at risk of falling behind or dropping out of school and provide the interventions and support they need to succeed. Rationale: Data indicate that the district needs to do a better job of effectively identifying students in need of additional support and ensuring that programs to support struggling readers are in place across the district. 3. GPSD will offer professional development for all administrators, literacy team leaders, and literacy coaches in Grades 4 through 10 concerning data collection and analysis, working with a literacy team, and monitoring tools such as walk-throughs. Rationale: Although there is a system of assessments in place, the data are not being used effectively to inform instruction or monitor program effectiveness, and there are only a few school-based literacy teams at this time.

Discuss the district literacy action goals stated above and determine which ones the team feels are good goals and which are too vague. How would you revise goals to be more specific or measurable? What makes a good goal?

Develop an Implementation Map for Each Literacy Action Goal

You can review Chapter 3 for the process of developing school-based implementation maps for each of the school's literacy action goals. When developing the district literacy plan, the process is the same. For each districtwide literacy action goal, you will identify the following parts to the implementation map shown in Figure 7.1.

Action Step	Timeline (Target Date)	Lead Person(s)	Resources Needed	Specifics of Implementation	Measure(s) of Success

Figure 7.1 Parts of the Implementation Map

It is helpful to have the whole team working on the implementation map for each goal statement, guaranteeing the entire team's input. If you have a large team, you might consider completing only one implementation map for the first goal statement as a team. After that, you can break the team into subgroups, with each subgroup completing an implementation map for one of the remaining goal statements. Then have the subgroups present their completed maps so the entire team can provide feedback and make additional suggestions. Figure 7.2 shows an example of a completed implementation map.

Literacy Action Goal Statement 3: GPSD will offer professional development for all administrators, literacy team leaders, and literacy coaches in Grades 4 through 10 in data collection and analysis, working with a literacy team and monitoring tools such as walk-throughs.					
Action Step	**Timeline (Target Date)**	**Lead Person(s)**	**Resources Needed**	**Specifics of Implementation**	**F Measure(s) of Success**
The district will provide a three-day workshop for literacy teams including principals and literacy coaches with three objectives: 1. To align school literacy action plans with the district literacy action plan 2. To review protocols on working with a literacy leadership team 3. To review collection, analysis, and dissemination procedures for working with data to inform decision making	Summer	Assistant Superintendent for Instruction Director of Reading	• Space to meet • Stipends • Materials and supplies • Copies of literacy action plans • Food for lunch each day	• The Director of Reading and Assistant Superintendent for Instruction will plan and facilitate the workshop. • Remind principals to bring their school data and implantation maps. • Professional development office will handle registration and credit toward recertification.	• Each school's literacy action plan is aligned with the district literacy action plan. • Every team leaves with specific next steps about how to improve data use in their school. • Evaluations show that the workshop increased teams' capacity to lead the literacy improvement efforts in their school.
The district provides monthly professional development for school-based literacy coaches to support their work.	Year-round	Director of Reading	• Time • Space to meet • Materials and supplies • Books and resources	• Survey professional development needs and assess literacy expertise in the district. • Schedule monthly meetings with district literacy coaches to determine ongoing professional development needs.	• Topics for monthly meetings are based on professional development survey results. • In-district literacy expertise was used during the monthly sessions whenever possible. • Pre- and post-surveys show that literacy knowledge and confidence in the position of coach increased for at least 90% of the literacy coaches.
The district will provide four workshops for school-based administrators throughout the year to develop expertise on walk-throughs to monitor implementation of their literacy action plans.	Year-round	Assistant Superintendent for Instruction	• Space to meet • Time • Outside consultant(s) • Materials and supplies	• Secure outside consultant to provide literacy walk-through training and implementation monitoring tools and leadership strategies. • Schedule four meetings.	• Evaluations show that administrators increased their knowledge and proficiency with being literacy leaders. • Evidence shows that administrators are conducting literacy walk-throughs and reporting results to the faculty.

Figure 7.2 Sample District Implementation Map

Publish the District Literacy Action Plan

A formal literacy action plan communicates to all stakeholders that literacy improvement is a priority in the district. Some of the components you may wish to incorporate in this plan include the following:

- Your district mission statement and how the plan connects to the literacy action plan
- The process the schools engaged in to develop their literacy action plans (if applicable)
- The process the district engaged in to develop districtwide improvement goals and implementation maps
- The role, function, and membership on the district literacy leadership team
- The goals and implementation maps
- A summary of the major activities planned for the upcoming year that are associated with the literacy goals

Throughout the year, the district literacy team will engage in Stage 4 of the literacy leadership process—overseeing the literacy initiative, monitoring implementation, and progressing toward goals. At the end of the year, the district team will use the steps in Stage 5 of the literacy leadership process to review progress toward goals, revise and update the plan accordingly, and plan for how to sustain momentum as the work continues. District leaders may want to review Chapters 4 and 5 to select approaches for how the team will carry out these tasks.

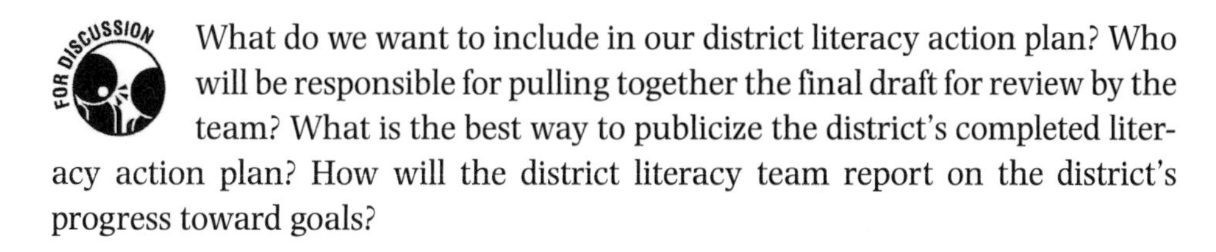

What do we want to include in our district literacy action plan? Who will be responsible for pulling together the final draft for review by the team? What is the best way to publicize the district's completed literacy action plan? How will the district literacy team report on the district's progress toward goals?

USE THE FIVE ACTION POINTS OF THE *TAKING ACTION LITERACY LEADERSHIP MODEL*

In our extensive work with schools, we have found that school-based literacy initiatives are far more successful when they have district support and are aligned with district resources and priorities. Strong district support for school-based efforts can be especially important when there is a high level of transition in personnel. In addition, districts that coordinate literacy efforts across schools can enable smoother transitions for students as they move from school to school and can maximize the allocation of resources in support of literacy development.

The five action points of the *Taking Action Literacy Leadership Model* describe roles and responsibilities that school leaders can undertake to improve student literacy and learning. When viewed from a district perspective, these action points include supporting school-based efforts to do the following: build the literacy leadership capacity in the school, use data to make decisions, support teachers to improve instruction, allocate resources to enhance literacy and learning at the school level, and implement and monitor the school's literacy action plan. The chart that follows offers some suggestions of how small, medium, and large districts we have worked with have actively supported school-based literacy initiatives using these five action points. Many of these can become action steps in a district literacy action plan. The team should review the district plan to be certain that these types of support are being provided to schools charged with improving literacy and learning.

<table>
<tr><td>

</td><td>
<ul>
<li>Provide stipends for school-based literacy team members and/or substitute teachers so that the team can meet during the school day.</li>
<li>Send administrators and teacher leaders to literacy conferences.</li>
<li>Support teachers to observe and discuss demonstration lessons within schools and across schools.</li>
<li>Provide training for potential teacher leaders.</li>
</ul>
</td></tr>
<tr><td>

</td><td>
<ul>
<li>Deliver data in usable form to teachers and administrators.</li>
<li>Ensure that reading and writing assessment data are collected and disseminated in a timely manner.</li>
<li>Provide professional development in using data to improve instruction.</li>
<li>Support school-based data teams to analyze data related to program efficacy.</li>
</ul>
</td></tr>
<tr><td>

</td><td>
<ul>
<li>Assign a district literacy coach to a small group of schools to provide coordination across the district and support schools and teachers as they implement their plan. Responsibilities may include the following:
<ul>
<li>Working with the school literacy coach</li>
<li>Presenting school data and helping teachers and literacy leaders make inferences about instructional decisions</li>
<li>Providing professional development to whole school faculties</li>
</ul></li>
<li>Sponsor professional development for content area teachers.</li>
<li>Provide protocols and stipends for peer coaching and mentoring in schools throughout the district.</li>
<li>Host topic-centered meetings for teachers across schools.</li>
</ul>
</td></tr>
<tr><td>

</td><td>
<ul>
<li>Provide opportunities for leadership teams to collaborate and share ideas between and among schools.</li>
<li>Provide fiscal support for resources such as materials, books, and technology.</li>
<li>Allocate funds explicitly to support school and districtwide literacy initiatives.</li>
<li>Communicate with community and families about resource needs and opportunities to volunteer.</li>
<li>Reach out to community, grant organizations, and school business partners.</li>
<li>Align resources to strategic goals.</li>
</ul>
</td></tr>
<tr><td>

</td><td>
<ul>
<li>Set districtwide literacy improvement goals, and ask that all schools set school-based improvement goals that align with the district goals.</li>
<li>Support an annual action planning institute where school-based literacy teams come together to develop plans using the literacy action rubrics and the literacy leadership process and then annually review and update their plans based on what was accomplished during the school year.</li>
<li>Offer to review and provide feedback on school plans, noting where district resources can be used to support the action steps described in the plan.</li>
<li>Create a vehicle for schools to share their plans with one another.</li>
</ul>
</td></tr>
</table>

REVIEW THE DISTRICT PLAN TO ENSURE ALIGNMENT WITH STATE PLANNING AND ADVOCACY

As the achievement gap continues to widen among groups of students, state policy makers and business leaders are increasingly searching for ways to enhance adolescent literacy development so that all students gain the knowledge and skills for workforce and college readiness. Educators at the district level have the opportunity to form partnerships with state officials and to benefit from heightened attention to the issues and needs of adolescent literacy instruction. To this end, district personnel should be knowledgeable about the various policies for promoting K–12 literacy in their state, as well as about noteworthy approaches being implemented by several state and national organizations. As you explore these policies, you can review your district's literacy action plan to be sure that it reflects these agendas and takes advantage of the thinking on this issue that is being carried out on a state and national level. If there are initiatives in your state, aligning the language and intent of your district literacy action plan may make you eligible for funding or other resources available through state channels. If these efforts are not being undertaken in your state, you can take the lead in helping state-level policymakers understand why it is critical that they support district actions to address this important area.

In February 2009, the National Governor's Association (NGA) Center for Best Practices published an *Issue Brief* that listed five state-level policy strategies for improving adolescent literacy:

1. Build support for a state focus on adolescent literacy.
2. Raise literacy expectations across the curriculum.
3. Encourage and support school and district literacy plans.
4. Build educators' capacity to provide adolescent literacy instruction.
5. Measure progress in adolescent literacy at the school, district, and state levels.

Referencing these strategies when you seek outside funding and discussing how they connect to your district literacy action plan may be a wise move. This is part of an ongoing trend in which states are being encouraged to put together plans to improve student literacy and learning far beyond the early grades.

Some states have formed task forces to address the issue of adolescent literacy and have allocated funds to support schools and districts that implement the state's goals. For this reason, if your state has an adolescent literacy plan, it seems prudent to align your school's goals and actions with the state plan.

Statewide plans have been developed or are in development in many states such as New Hampshire, Massachusetts, Wisconsin, Kentucky, New Jersey, and Delaware. In many cases, money for planning grants and teacher professional development has been tied to the state plan. In other states, Title IID funds have been specifically earmarked to support teacher professional development in the area of content literacy.

One state, Wisconsin (Wisconsin Department of Public Instruction, 2008), formed a task force of 25 members, including teachers, library media specialists, school and district administrators, and parents and community members from across the state. The charge of the task force was to do the following:

- Review state and local policies and initiatives that support adolescent literacy.
- Identify research-based resources related to effective practices that promote literacy development, raise performance, and close the achievement gap.
- Develop an adolescent literacy plan for the state of Wisconsin.

The task force developed five core components of the state adolescent literacy plan and established phases of implementation (see www.dpi.wi.gov/adolescentliteracy.html). The five implementation phases indicate the far-reaching nature of the plan and are described in the plan as follows:

- *Leadership and Collaboration:* Creating literacy teams and plans for organizing and implementing an effective approach to adolescent literacy.
- *Academic Standards:* Examining Wisconsin Model Academic Standards through the lens of adolescent literacy.
- *Instruction, Assessment, and Intervention:* Establishing systems of support and examining their effectiveness.
- *Professional Learning and Resources:* Developing professional learning opportunities, Web resources, and initiatives that enhance literacy and learning for educators.
- *Literacy Leaders and Personnel:* Clarifying roles of specific literacy educators and supporting literacy instruction in teacher education programs.

To ensure that adolescents are truly prepared to meet the literacy demands of 21st-century careers and citizenship, states and districts must get involved to collaboratively support school-based literacy improvement efforts. If politicians, educators, community members, and parents work together, it is much more likely that additional resources will be allocated to assist upper elementary, middle, and high school students improve their abilities as readers, writers, and thinkers.

Literacy Action Rubric 6

District Support of School-Based Literacy Improvement Efforts

Desired Outcome		Level 1 *Little or No Evidence of Implementation*	Level 2 *Evidence of Emerging Implementation*	Level 3 *Evidence of Consistent Implementation*	Level 4 *Evidence of Exemplary Implementation*
The district actively supports school-based literacy improvement efforts.	A Literacy as a Priority	Any support for literacy improvement for students in Grades 4 through 12 is dependent on school-based decisions.	Literacy improvement for students in Grades 4 through 12 has been identified as a district area of focus.	The district communicates the importance of student literacy improvement in Grades 4 through 12, including targeted support for struggling readers and writers.	The district actively promotes the importance of student literacy improvement in Grades 4 through 12, including targeted support for struggling readers and writers.
		Improving student literacy in Grades 4 through 12 has not been identified as a district priority.	Improving student literacy in Grades 4 through 12 is included in the district strategic plan.	A district literacy plan is in place, implemented, and updated annually.	A district literacy plan is published, implemented, regularly reviewed, and updated annually.
		No district team focuses on literacy improvement for students in Grades 4 through 12.	A district team annually reviews student reading and writing assessment data to determine progress toward district goals.	A district literacy team that includes district and school-based educators meets regularly to review and monitor progress toward literacy improvement goals.	A district literacy team that includes district and school-based educators, parents and community members, and students meets regularly to review and monitor progress toward literacy improvement goals.
		No district administrator is assigned to oversee literacy improvement in Grades 4 through 12.	A district level administrator is in charge of reading interventions being implemented in schools.	A district level administrator is responsible for implementation of the district literacy action plan.	A district level administrator coordinates with other district content specialists and is responsible for implementation of the district literacy action plan.
		No hiring preference is given to administrators or content areas teachers with a literacy background.	Literacy background is seen as a positive factor when hiring English/language arts teachers but is not a strong factor in hiring administrators or other content area teachers.	Hiring preference is given to administrators and content area teachers with <u>at least some</u> literacy background.	Hiring preference is given to administrators and content area teachers with a <u>strong</u> literacy background.

(Continued)

(Continued)

Desired Outcome		Level 1 *Little or No Evidence of Implementation*	Level 2 *Evidence of Emerging Implementation*	Level 3 *Evidence of Consistent Implementation*	Level 4 *Evidence of Exemplary Implementation*
	B Professional Development	The district does not provide literacy leadership professional development.	The district provides very limited literacy leadership professional development for literacy coaches.	The district provides some literacy leadership professional development for school administrators, literacy coaches, and teacher leaders.	The district provides ongoing literacy leadership professional development for school administrators, literacy coaches, and teacher leaders.
		The district does not provide content literacy professional development for teachers.	The district provides occasional content literacy professional development for teachers.	The district expects that all content area teachers will participate in some literacy professional development.	The district expects that all content area teachers will participate in ongoing literacy professional development.
		The district does not provide training and professional development for intervention and special education teachers and teachers of English language learners.	The district provides very limited training and professional development for intervention and special education teachers and teachers of English language learners.	The district provides some training and professional development for intervention and special education teachers and teachers of English language learners.	The district provides ongoing training and professional development for intervention and special education teachers and teachers of English language learners.
		The district does not provide new teachers with support to implement the integration of literacy and content learning.	The district provides new teachers with very limited support to implement the integration of literacy and content learning.	The district provides new teachers with some support and mentoring to implement the integration of literacy and content learning.	The district provides new teachers with sufficient support and mentoring to implement the integration of literacy and content learning.
	C Fiscal Support	The district does not allocate funds for personnel (e.g., district administrator(s) charged with literacy improvement, literacy coaches, reading specialists).	The district allocates very limited funds for personnel (e.g., district administrator(s) charged with literacy improvement, literacy coaches, reading specialists).	The district allocates some funds for personnel (e.g., district administrator(s) charged with literacy improvement, literacy coaches, reading specialists).	The district allocates sufficient funds for personnel (e.g., district administrator(s) charged with literacy improvement, literacy coaches, reading specialists).
		The district does not allocate funds for resources (e.g., books and materials, site licenses, technology, reading and writing assessments, interventions) to support literacy improvement in Grades 4 through 12.	The district allocates very limited funds for resources, (e.g., books and materials, site licenses, technology, reading and writing assessments, interventions) to support literacy improvement in Grades 4 through 12.	The district allocates some funds for resources, (e.g., books and materials, site licenses, technology, reading and writing assessments, interventions) to support literacy improvement in Grades 4 through 12.	The district allocates sufficient funds for resources (e.g., books and materials, site licenses, technology, reading and writing assessments, interventions) to support literacy improvement in Grades 4 through 12.

Desired Outcome		Level 1 *Little or No Evidence of Implementation*	Level 2 *Evidence of Emerging Implementation*	Level 3 *Evidence of Consistent Implementation*	Level 4 *Evidence of Exemplary Implementation*
		The district does not seek additional grant and foundation monies and community-based funding to support literacy improvement in Grades 4 through 12.	The district seldom seeks and obtains additional grant and foundation monies and community-based funding to support literacy improvement in Grades 4 through 12.	The district sometimes seeks and obtains additional grant and foundation monies and community-based funding to support literacy improvement in Grades 4 through 12.	The district regularly seeks and obtains additional grant and foundation monies and community-based funding to support literacy improvement in Grades 4 through 12.
	D Policies and Procedures	The district does not expect that literacy support strategies will be used with students in Grades 4 through 12.	The district recommends that certain literacy support strategies to be used with students in Grades 4 through 12.	The district specifies literacy support strategies to be used consistently with students in Grades 4 through 12.	The district curriculum includes a scope and sequence for literacy development in Grades 4 through 12 that aligns with district and state content standards.
		The district does not support flexibility in school-based scheduling.	The district does not interfere with school scheduling that permits more students to have access to rigorous course content and strong literacy support.	The district supports school-based scheduling options that increase the likelihood that students have access to rigorous course content and strong literacy support.	The district supports school-based scheduling that ensures that all students have access to rigorous course content and strong literacy support.
		The district does not support those school administrators who function as strong literacy leaders.	The district supports those school administrators who function as strong literacy leaders.	The district expects most school administrators to function as strong literacy leaders.	The district expects all school administrators to function as strong literacy leaders.

(Continued)

(Continued)

Desired Outcome		Level 1 *Little or No Evidence of Implementation*	Level 2 *Evidence of Emerging Implementation*	Level 3 *Evidence of Consistent Implementation*	Level 4 *Evidence of Exemplary Implementation*
		Teacher evaluation processes do not include the expectation that all teachers integrate literacy support into content instruction.	Teacher evaluation processes include the expectation that all teachers sometimes integrate literacy support into content instruction.	Teacher evaluation processes include the expectation that all teachers occasionally integrate literacy support into content instruction.	Teacher evaluation processes include the expectation that all teachers consistently integrate literacy support into content area instruction.
		The district has no policy for including parents and community members in literacy events.	The district policy includes an expectation to invite parents and community members in the literacy events.	The district deliberately includes parents and community members in the literacy improvement effort.	The district works with parents and community members as partners in the literacy improvement effort.
	E Data Use	The district does not assure that schools administer reading and writing assessments in addition to state testing in Grades 4 through 10.	The district assures that schools administer reading and writing assessments in addition to state testing only in Grades 4 through 5.	The district assures that schools administer reading and writing assessments in addition to state testing only in Grades 4 through 8.	The district assures that schools administer reading and writing assessments in addition to state testing in Grades 4 through 10.
		The district does not provide data to schools in a timely manner.	The district provides data to schools once a year.	The district provides data to schools twice a year.	The district provides quality data in user friendly formats to schools in a timely manner.
		The district does not expect data use to drive decision making about placement and classroom instruction.	The district rarely expects data use in a placement decisions and classroom instruction.	The district often expects data use in placement decisions and classroom instruction.	The district expects data use to drive decision making about placement and classroom instruction.
		The district does not collect and analyze data about program effectiveness and student growth as readers and writers in Grades 4 through 10.	The district only collects and analyzes data about program effectiveness and student growth as readers and writers in Grades 4 and 5.	The district only collects and analyzes data about program effectiveness and student growth as readers and writers in Grades 4 and 8.	The district collects and analyzes data about program effectiveness and student growth as readers and writers in Grades 4 through10.

Copyright © 2010 by Judith L. Irvin. All rights reserved. Reprinted from *Taking the Lead on Adolescent Literacy: Action Steps for Schoolwide Success*, by Judith Irvin, Julie Meltzer, Nancy Dean, and Martha Jan Mickler. Thousand Oaks, CA: Corwin, www.corwin.com. Reproduction authorized only for the local school site or nonprofit organization that has purchased this book.

Resource A

School Vignettes

ELEMENTARY SCHOOL VIGNETTE

You arrive at Ridgewood Elementary at the appointed time and enter a friendly foyer with plants and lots of children's artwork on display. On an easel is a "Poem of the Day." Three students, obviously in different grade levels, stand reading the poem by Jack Prelutsky. As they go off down the hall you hear, "That's pretty good—I like that one!"

You arrive in the office and are quickly met by the principal, who bubbles with enthusiasm about the school's welcoming and culture of acceptance for each child (and their families) who attends the school. As you travel through the fourth-grade wing, you expect to notice the infamous "fourth-grade slump." Instead (to your pleasant surprise), you notice that students appear not to be slumped about learning and literacy at all. You see students in small groups reading a variety of leveled texts and using reciprocal teaching to make sure that everyone understands the major concepts of the topic. In one classroom, you notice that students are reading aloud in pairs and then summarizing for one another before reading on. You see teachers walking around, listening, questioning, and taking notes. "All of our teachers use a paired reading strategy," the principal says. "It is great for improving fluency, comprehension, and summarizing. It has really gotten some of our struggling readers up to speed."

In other classrooms, you observe guided reading groups, independent reading, small group, and partner work. Each classroom has a library, and there are lists of books read by students and their ratings of the books against various criteria: interesting, well written, good ending, and so on. In one classroom, the teacher is using the projection unit to model and explain how the students are going to do the summaries and the translation of their science fiction or fantasy books into picture books for younger students. In another, the teacher has a piece of writing up on the document projector, and she is marking it up with a pen as students point out descriptive phrases.

The library is a bright and airy space with books, magazines, and other print materials attractively displayed, and colorful posters describing the importance of reading, writing, and thinking. Sets of computers are on tables in one-half of the room. The librarian is using a projection unit to model how to tell whether a Web site is a good source for information, and a class of fifth graders is checking the Web site they chose for their research to see if they have been "duped" by false information. A steady flow of students come in and out to check out books and work on projects. Some giggling and talking can be heard but no real "fooling around." Parent volunteers circulate to help students find what they need.

Evidence of literacy and technology is everywhere. Students in the art classroom are using a graphics design program to develop logos, while others in the computer classroom are using Kidspiration to map out their science fiction stories, In the math lab, fourth graders are using Lego Logo to create short computer animations. All struggling students have access to computers using leveled programs to improve fluency, comprehension, and writing skills.

In the hallway you see *I-Search* projects on a variety of topics, autobiographies with self-portraits, and persuasive essays for and against instituting daylight savings time earlier in the year. You are impressed with the level of the writing and mention that to the principal. He shakes his head, "We've come a long way. We're not there yet, but the kids are the ones that drive it. The scores are slowly going up. We have worked hard as a staff to learn how to teach them better, and it is really paying off." You thank the principal for the tour and leave the building. Images of students reading, writing, and thinking stick in your mind for days.

MIDDLE SCHOOL VIGNETTE

Enter Hope Middle School and you immediately notice the mission of the school prominently displayed: *Every Student: Read to Succeed.* Two students show up in the entry to greet you and introduce themselves as Cassie and Brett. They inform you that they are both seventh graders and will serve as your tour guides. They first lead you to the media center, and you notice that the room is full of students reading, researching, using the computers, and working together on projects. At the computer stations, the media and technology specialists, along with a seventh-grade social studies teacher, are helping students at computers use digital resources to plan for an upcoming debate on the issue of global warming. You immediately notice that all students are working collaboratively to search specific Internet sites for information to use in the debate. Cassie tells you that students throughout the school are honing their digital literacy skills, both in the media center and in their classrooms. "Lots of kids today are pretty savvy with the computer and Internet and have lots of opportunity to use their skills in their assignments and classroom activities," she says. Brett then remarks that one of the most popular activities is called *Controversy Circles,* in which students and community visitors read the same article and do a discussion web about the important issues. Brett explains, "Sometimes the visitors are people who work in the school or people from different businesses. And the topics are sometimes really interesting, like about gun control and medical ethics and dilemmas, like if it is good to have economic development if it causes pollution and stuff like that."

Leaving the media center, you and your tour guides visit the sixth-grade wing and walk into a science class. Students are working in pairs doing research on chemical solutions and planning demonstrations that illustrate key concepts related to salinity and saturation. In the science classroom next door, students are reading intently on computers and coding the articles they are reading using digital highlighting. The teacher explains they are reading about chemical reactions to determine if the information confirms or contradicts the experiment they just did. In a third science classroom, students are working in small groups to create chapters for a lab manual. In one sixth-grade English/language arts classroom, students are doing a nonfiction study, and everyone in the room is reading, writing, or conferencing with a peer or with the teacher. In another, some students are creating reader's theatre scripts based on various science fiction books found in the classroom library, while others are working in literature circles on a set of texts based on a theme from their social studies classes.

You then visit several more subject-area classrooms. In Ms. Jackson's math class, you notice that students are using a graphic organizer to solve word problems. Students of Mr. Jefferson are engaged in a paired reading of the chapter in the textbook, questioning, summarizing, and clarifying as needed. In social studies classes, students are writing *A Day in the Life* papers for Greek or Roman times, preparing for talk show interviews of famous Greeks and Romans, and completing compare and contrast charts around cultural aspects of today's Greece versus ancient Greece.

As you wander to the eighth-grade wing, you are impressed with the abundance of literacy projects on the walls of the hallways. Student work is prominently displayed on every available wall space. You notice that eighth-grade students are as actively involved as their younger peers. Some students are reading and classifying letters from soldiers from different eras. Others are working on an interdisciplinary unit on roller coaster design and using reciprocal teaching to understand a variety of texts on the topic. Still others are designing their own poetry anthologies, analyzing the pond water they collected then entering the data into a database that an environmental agency has created, and deciding how to write up the experiments they just completed.

As you head back to the office, you pass the family resource room in which a class is being held on strategies for passing the General Education Development (GED) test. Further down the hall is a conference room where a group of teachers is having an intense discussion about student performance data and how they will use specific literacy support strategies to address students' needs. Cassie explains that one of the teachers is the literacy coach who helps teachers teach better.

Once back at the office, you thank Cassie and Brett for their time and insights. The principal joins you in his office after his schedule of classroom walk-throughs and asks for your impressions. You point out that in every class you noticed that teachers were modeling or teaching literacy-support strategies and that students were practicing them both individually or in small groups. What astounded you was the high level of student engagement, collaboration, critical thinking, and discussion as well as the amount of reading and writing you saw. You mention that in many schools you don't think you would have seen this much reading, writing, presentation, and discussion in a week, much less a day! The principal smiles and says that three years ago, you wouldn't have seen this much at Hope Middle School either. "At first, both teachers and students resisted. Students were asked to work harder, and teachers had to learn how to integrate literacy into their subject areas. I arranged for the literacy coach to attend each team meeting once a month for several months, and once they got to know what she had to offer, the teachers realized she was a real resource to them. They also learned that I was serious about this literacy effort as well. Each teacher has an Individual Professional Development Plan, and I make sure it contains work on literacy improvement. Now, literacy is the way we do business. Everyone contributes to a culture of literacy throughout our school. It took clear expectations, lots of professional development and coaching, and strong leadership, but I think we are getting there. Our achievement scores are slowly improving, and everyone has really taken it on as a collective responsibility." Reflecting on what you have observed at Hope Middle School, you can't help but agree.

HIGH SCHOOL VIGNETTE

As you enter the front corridor of Lakeview High School, you immediately notice that literacy is featured throughout the school. Watching the morning announcements on the television just outside the family welcome center, you learn that the speech and drama clubs are meeting during fifth period and that the literary magazine and newspaper editors are presenting their ideas to the English faculty meeting during lunch. You see student art work and science projects prominently displayed in the area as well. You also notice that all of the signs are in English and Spanish since more than 40% of Lakeview students speak Spanish at home.

You are greeted by LaTasha and Alberto, your student guides, who represent a group of students who have made rapid gains in their grades during the semester and have been chosen to be tour guides for visitors. Your first stop is the history wing where you find students who are reading, writing, and discussing as they work on the computer alone or in pairs. One student explains, "We are working on our research project on the economic costs of malnutrition, and we have to come up with solutions that are economically sound. We have a lot of content to cover, so we are doing a jigsaw to distribute the work load." Other students are comparing their answers on last night's anticipation guide with the information from a Renaissance text.

You move on to the English wing where you find an equally diverse array of activities. Some students are working in small groups on a *Romeo and Juliet* Webquest requiring them to rewrite a scene in contemporary language and specific style. Others are doing reciprocal teaching with a section of *The Grapes of Wrath.* In another room, students are doing "book commercials" that students rate using a rubric. Samples of student writing are posted everywhere.

You wonder if math teachers are also providing students with inventive ways to integrate literacy in their subject area learning, and you are pleasantly surprised when you visit math classrooms. In one geometry class, students are reading and discussing a section of *Flatland.* In the Algebra I class, students are reading and coding the text in pairs; in another, they are working together to develop problems to be included on the test. Word walls are in every classroom; triple entry vocabulary journals are evident on many students' desks.

In the science wing, embedded literacy learning is evident. In one class, the small engine repair teacher and the physics teacher are co-teaching to help students build real-word connections between theory and application. In another, students are conducting research using stream pollution data collected in a near by stream. Students are working in groups to create summaries of articles related to aspects of habitat and biodiversity; working in pairs to fill out a semantic feature analysis on characteristics of diseases; working on their own to write persuasive essays about the pros and cons of genetically altered foods. Words, books, and discussions are everywhere. The voices are those of the students, not the teacher, and just about everyone seems to be on task.

LaTasha and Alberto point out several classes where one of the English language learner teachers coteaches with a content area teacher. You remember that you noticed that almost half of the classes you observed had two teachers.

LaTasha explains, "A lot of our special education teachers and literacy coaches coteach classes with subject area teachers so that all students can be successful learners." Alberto pipes up, "Yeah, students say they love classes with more than one teacher because there is more than just one person to go to for help; it mixes it up a little and makes it more interesting."

The emphasis on vocabulary, reading, and writing is apparent as you tour the unified arts and vocational classes. Students are reading and discussing articles, creating repair manuals, writing art critiques, completing nutrition logs, and writing work sample reports, much of which goes into a portfolio that is showcased at the end of the year in juried presentations.

Before returning to the principal's office, you visit the media and technology center that is organized around a flexible scheduling model. The media and technology specialists are available to all teachers for planning and integration of technology and multiliteracies. In one corner, you notice that a student is videoconferencing with his elementary reading buddy in the school down the street. Together they are reading and discussing *Frog and Toad.* Your guides explain that some kind of literacy community service is expected of all students throughout their four years at Lakeview High. Students can choose to read the newspaper to blind people, create books on tape for the elementary school students, tutor in the afterschool program, work on the school newspaper or literary magazine; translate and record school newsletters for parents who do not speak English or who do not read, and write letters for nursing home residents.

As you meet with the principal for debriefing, you learn what has transpired in the last few years that lead up to the high degree of literacy focus at Lakeview High. The principal says, "My main job has been to be out there leading the charge. Of course, I was lucky that I have two good literacy coaches and that my district and community members were supportive of the changes we wanted to make. We did a lot of discussion and visioning; we had a number of book discussion groups; we made a literacy plan that we monitor and revise; we did a lot of teacher professional development. We worked it out with the district so that teachers could get inservice points toward recertification. We had to get the intervention piece right too. That took a lot of finagling with the master calendar to free up time for students as well as for teacher collaboration and planning. At first, we merely offered a reading course for students scoring below level. We realized that the one course was not enough. We began our summer reading camp three years ago. That did a lot to provide additional support for students who scored in the lowest levels."

All in all, you conclude that Lakeview High School teachers, staff, and administrators have worked hard to build a culture of literacy for all of their students. Now you wonder how their success can be replicated at other schools.

Resource B

Tools to Use When Implementing the Five-Stage Process

LIST OF TOOLS

Tool 1: Student Performance Data Assessment Grid

Tool 2: Implementation Map Template

Tool 3: Potential Activities for Faculty Kickoff

Tool 4: Involving Students in the Literacy Initiative

Tool 5: Implementation Monitoring Template

Tool 6: Support Teachers Checklist

Tool 7: Use Data Checklist

Tool 8: Build Capacity Checklist

Tool 9: Allocate Resources Checklist

Tool 10: Progress Toward Goals Summary Chart

Tool 11: Implementation Review Chart

Tool 12: Literacy Leadership Team Assessment

Tool 13: Then, Now, Next Chart

Tool 14: Proactive Steps for Sustaining a Literacy Improvement Effort

Tool 15: Types and Uses of Data

Tool 16: Professional Development Needs Assessment

Tool 17: Roles of Support Personnel

Tool 18: Data Questions and Decisions

TOOL 1: STUDENT PERFORMANCE DATA ASSESSMENT GRID

Reading or Writing Assessment	Who Takes It?	When Was It Last Given?	Do You Have Multiple Years of Data?	What Does This Test Tell You About Students as Readers or Writers? (e.g., Is the score based on the reading of narrative text, expository text, or both?)

Copyright © 2010 by Judith L. Irvin. All rights reserved. Reprinted from *Taking the Lead on Adolescent Literacy: Action Steps for Schoolwide Success*, by Judith Irvin, Julie Meltzer, Nancy Dean, and Martha Jan Mickler. Thousand Oaks, CA: Corwin, www.corwin.com. Reproduction authorized only for the local school site or nonprofit organization that has purchased this book.

TOOL 2: IMPLEMENTATION MAP TEMPLATE

Literacy Action Goal Statement:					
Action Step	Timeline (Target Date)	Lead Person(s)	Resources Needed	Specifics of Implementation	Measure(s) of Success

Copyright © 2010 by Judith L. Irvin. All rights reserved. Reprinted from *Taking the Lead on Adolescent Literacy: Action Steps for Schoolwide Success*, by Judith Irvin, Julie Meltzer, Nancy Dean, and Martha Jan Mickler. Thousand Oaks, CA: Corwin, www.corwin.com. Reproduction authorized only for the local school site or nonprofit organization that has purchased this book.

TOOL 3: POTENTIAL ACTIVITIES FOR FACULTY KICKOFF

Tool 3: Potential Activities for Faculty Kickoff		
Stage 1	**Include in Kickoff**	**Do Not Include in Kickoff**
Introduce the literacy leadership team and its charge and responsibilities. Explain how members were chosen.		
Make a case for the importance of the initiative (e.g., present 21st-century literacy skills needed by students to make the case that all students need literacy support).		
Introduce the *Taking Action Literacy Leadership Model* to the faculty.		
Use the vignette activity to envision a literacy-rich school. (Stage 1, Step 2)		
Stage 2		
Present the school strengths map or repeat the activity with faculty. (Stage 1, Step 1)		
Present current data about students as readers and writers and discuss improvement goals.		
Introduce the rubrics or use one or more with departments, grade-level teams, or professional learning groups to self-assess.		
Present the literacy action goals that the team developed and get feedback.		
Stage 3		
Present the formal literacy action plan and get feedback from the faculty.		
Communicate the types of professional development opportunities planned for teachers and administrators.		
Ask faculty what professional development they need and how they would like the professional development delivered (whole faculty, by departments or teams, during faculty meetings, on workshop days or during common planning time).		
Ensure that everyone understands his or her role and the expectations for implementation of content area literacy support.		
Clarify the structures, policies, and schedule that will be put into place to support the work.		
Provide time for teachers to examine and discuss beliefs about literacy and learning.		
Present the implementation calendar and solicit feedback.		
Stage 4		
Introduce the Brand Statement or describe how this will be developed. Get feedback or suggestions from entire school community.		
Describe how the implementation maps will be rolled out and how the team will monitor implementation and progress toward goals during the school year.		
Introduce a common set of specific instructional strategies (If selected by the team) that enhance content area literacy and learning.		

Copyright © 2010 by Judith L. Irvin. All rights reserved. Reprinted from *Taking the Lead on Adolescent Literacy: Action Steps for Schoolwide Success*, by Judith Irvin, Julie Meltzer, Nancy Dean, and Martha Jan Mickler. Thousand Oaks, CA: Corwin, www.corwin.com. Reproduction authorized only for the local school site or nonprofit organization that has purchased this book.

TOOL 4: INVOLVING STUDENTS IN THE LITERACY INITIATIVE

Tool 4: Involving Students in the Literacy Initiative		
	Needed	Not Needed
Sponsor a student contest to develop a poster and/or logo to publicize the brand statement.		
Form a student literacy team.		
Have students discuss what assists them to be better readers, writers, and thinkers and report back to the literacy leadership team.		
Ask one or more student groups to complete one of the rubrics to assess their school and build a student-centered goal to share with the literacy leadership team.		
Have student focus groups give feedback about the literacy initiative and how it can be more relevant to students.		
Have the student literacy team organize literacy-related activities such as poetry slams, readings, and book clubs.		
Have the student literacy team publicize the literacy initiative through announcements, the school newspaper, and community media.		
Survey students on their perceptions of specific aspects of school environment, culture, and policy.		
Nominate students to serve as student representatives to the literacy leadership team.		
Other:		
Other:		
Other:		
Other:		

Copyright © 2010 by Judith L. Irvin. All rights reserved. Reprinted from *Taking the Lead on Adolescent Literacy: Action Steps for Schoolwide Success*, by Judith Irvin, Julie Meltzer, Nancy Dean, and Martha Jan Mickler. Thousand Oaks, CA: Corwin, www.corwin.com. Reproduction authorized only for the local school site or nonprofit organization that has purchased this book.

TOOL 5: IMPLEMENTATION MONITORING TEMPLATE

Tool 5: Implementation Monitoring Template			
Literacy Action Goal Statement:			
Date of Meeting:			
Attendees:			
Action Step	**Where Are We Now?**	**Are We on Track? (Yes/No/Somewhat)**	**Actions the Team Needs to Take (Based on the Action Points of the Model)**

Copyright © 2010 by Judith L. Irvin. All rights reserved. Reprinted from *Taking the Lead on Adolescent Literacy: Action Steps for Schoolwide Success*, by Judith Irvin, Julie Meltzer, Nancy Dean, and Martha Jan Mickler. Thousand Oaks, CA: Corwin, www.corwin.com. Reproduction authorized only for the local school site or nonprofit organization that has purchased this book.

TOOL 6: SUPPORT TEACHERS CHECKLIST

Tool 6: Support Teachers Checklist			
	Yes	**No**	**If no, team members can do the following:**
Teachers are receiving professional development that includes teaching and modeling of literacy strategies aligned to goals and action steps.			Meet with the professional development committee and discuss the professional development required to implement the literacy action plan successfully. Decide together how to make this support available to teachers.
Faculty members are satisfied with the quality of the teacher professional development that has taken place.			Determine what participants perceive as impediments to high-quality professional development. Use that perception data to adjust future professional development activities.
Professional development is being tied to the authentic issues that teachers face in their classrooms.			Survey teachers to determine what they consider to be the most pressing issues for students as readers, writers, and thinkers. Find time for teachers across various content areas to share concerns and insights and tie professional development to these areas of challenge.
School administrators are attending and reinforcing essential messages from the professional development.			Meet with the principal and revisit the plan, clarifying the roles and responsibilities of the principal associated with each goal and set of action steps. Develop a process for moving forward with more active engagement by the principal.
School administrators and/or the literacy coach follow up professional development with classroom observations and coaching to make sure teachers are implementing suggested activities.			Ask the team leader to meet with the administrators and/or literacy coach to set up a schedule of follow-up classroom visits.
Participation in planned teacher professional development is high.			Meet with teachers who are not attending professional development. Work toward finding solutions based on feedback from those teachers.
Professional development is provided live or through video models when introducing new instructional strategies.			Meet with the library media specialist to determine if video and DVD resources are available through interlibrary loans. Create a hot-linked list of examples available on the Internet for teachers to have as a reference point.
Coaching and mentoring are available to team members and participating teachers.			Meet with the administrator responsible for curriculum and instruction to discuss opportunities for co-planning with a coach or peer. Seek insights from department chairs about literacy-savvy content teachers who would be willing to mentor team members and participating teachers.
Evidence suggests that professional development is positively impacting classroom practice.			Ask literacy leaders to do classroom observations and discuss which teachers would benefit from targeted support to improve classroom practice.
Teachers and support personnel are being provided opportunities for collaborating, brainstorming, and sharing strategies.			Examine the master schedule to determine where time can be allocated during the school day for opportunities to collaborate. Establish an electronic collaboration tool so that teachers and staff can conduct collective action research and communicate with experts.
Professional development is taking advantage of teachers' professional expertise.			Meet with department chairs and team leaders to assess which teachers have literacy expertise and recruit them to be peer presenters.
Literacy team members open their doors, demonstrating effective literacy practices in their own content areas.			Bring in an outside consultant to demonstrate instructional strategies related to your literacy action plan (e.g., a specific strategy, differentiated instruction). Coordinate opportunities for classroom exchanges and co-teaching, to shift the culture from one of isolation to one of shared responsibility for student learning.

Copyright © 2010 by Judith L. Irvin. All rights reserved. Reprinted from *Taking the Lead on Adolescent Literacy: Action Steps for Schoolwide Success*, by Judith Irvin, Julie Meltzer, Nancy Dean, and Martha Jan Mickler. Thousand Oaks, CA: Corwin, www.corwin.com. Reproduction authorized only for the local school site or nonprofit organization that has purchased this book.

TOOL 7: USE DATA CHECKLIST

Tool 7: Use Data Checklist			
Indicator	**Yes**	**No**	**If no, team members can do the following:**
We are collecting the data we said we would collect.			Revisit who is responsible for collecting the data and determine what support is needed.
We are analyzing and drawing conclusions from the data we have collected.			Determine what is preventing the data from being analyzed. Is it a matter of time for the team to meet? Is it a lack of a process for data analysis?
We have the data we need to answer our questions about implementation.			Determine what additional data are needed and how these can be collected.
The data suggest that we are on track with implementation.			Identify goals or action steps where more data are needed to determine if implementation is on track.

Copyright © 2010 by Judith L. Irvin. All rights reserved. Reprinted from *Taking the Lead on Adolescent Literacy: Action Steps for Schoolwide Success*, by Judith Irvin, Julie Meltzer, Nancy Dean, and Martha Jan Mickler. Thousand Oaks, CA: Corwin, www.corwin.com. Reproduction authorized only for the local school site or nonprofit organization that has purchased this book.

TOOL 8: BUILD CAPACITY CHECKLIST

Tool 8: Build Capacity Checklist			
Indicator	**Yes**	**No**	**If no, team members can do the following:**
The Faculty as a Whole			
The faculty as a whole is becoming more knowledgeable about literacy.			Dedicate part of every faculty meeting to discussing the progress and accomplishments of the literacy initiative. Invite team members to make presentations at faculty and parent meetings. Publicize the work of the team on the school's Web site and publications.
Members of the faculty are serving as resources to others through providing demonstration classes and sharing resources.			Publicly acknowledge faculty who are serving as resources and mentors. Ask teacher leaders to recommend colleagues with whom they could collaborate and support as future presenters and mentors. Provide time for teacher pairs to develop presentations and instructional routines for classroom demonstrations.
Content area teachers are buying into the goals and action steps of the implementation maps.			Determine which teachers are on board and which are not. Continue to work with the teachers who are enthusiastic and willing to integrate literacy support with content learning. Continue to offer support and professional development to all teachers.
The literacy action plan is understood by most of the teachers outside of the literacy team.			Periodically, ask to have some time at a faculty meeting or at department or team meetings to reintroduce the plan and report on progress thus far. Make sure that faculty members are invited to suggest additional ways to help make the literacy initiative successful.
Administrators and Literacy Coaches			
Administrators and literacy coaches are meeting regularly with designated team members to support progress toward goals.			Ask the principal to free up administrators to meet with the literacy team. Be sure that administrators and literacy coaches are notified in plenty of time to put team meetings on their calendars. Send out minutes of the meeting to keep the work of the team on their minds.
Media and Technology Specialists			
The media and technology specialists provide time and support for the action steps of the implementation maps.			Include the media and technology specialists in the events and activities led by the literacy leadership team. Send reports and minutes of the meetings if specialists are not attending team meetings. Ask the specialists to identify teachers who are experienced in multiple literacies and ask them for suggestions for integrating media and technology with literacy instruction.
Department Chairs and/or Team Leaders			
Department chairs and team leaders are providing adequate support for the literacy action plan.			Discuss the plan with department chairs and team leaders. Solicit ideas for how department and/or team leaders can support and advocate for quality implementation of the map. Allow time during department meetings so that additional questions and concerns can be aired.
Parents and Community Members			
Parents and community members are aware and supportive of many events and activities of the literacy action plan.			Publish the activities of the literacy leadership team and participating teachers in the newsletter and/or on the Web site. Invite parents and community members to activities sponsored by the team. Include a parent and/or community representative on the literacy team.

Copyright © 2010 by Judith L. Irvin. All rights reserved. Reprinted from *Taking the Lead on Adolescent Literacy: Action Steps for Schoolwide Success*, by Judith Irvin, Julie Meltzer, Nancy Dean, and Martha Jan Mickler. Thousand Oaks, CA: Corwin, www.corwin.com. Reproduction authorized only for the local school site or nonprofit organization that has purchased this book.

TOOL 9: ALLOCATE RESOURCES CHECKLIST

Tool 9: Allocate Resources Checklist			
Indicator	**Yes**	**No**	**If no, team members can do the following:**
Resources described in the implementation maps are available as anticipated.			Schedule time with the principal to confirm that these resources were reasonable to expect and to discuss why they may or may not be available. Schedule meetings with those who control specific resources (e.g., technology, time, space) and discuss why the resource is needed and how it connects to the plan's goals and successful outcomes. Report the results of each meeting to the principal and discuss options.
Resources are being used effectively to support the action steps outlined in the implementation maps.			Revisit the resources identified for each action step. Determine if the resource is critical to successful implementation. If so, meet with the principal or team administrative leader to determine alternatives for supporting the action step.
District leaders are providing adequate support for implementation.			Ask for a meeting with key district leaders to communicate the plan, what has been accomplished, why this work is important, and what types of support would be helpful to the plan's goals and action steps. Discuss how the literacy action goals are aligned with the district's goals and ask district leaders what other resources they have that would be helpful in supporting the work.
The literacy action plan is aligned with and connected to the School Improvement Plan so that resources can be shared.			Meet with school administrators and discuss how the literacy action plan connects to other instructional improvement initiatives at the school. Then, discuss how the literacy improvement initiative can be used to connect to other initiatives. The results of this discussion can be shared with the entire faculty so everyone can understand the connections. Ask the administrator to publicly state ongoing support for the plan and expectations that everyone will work collaboratively to fully implement the plan.

Copyright © 2010 by Judith L. Irvin. All rights reserved. Reprinted from *Taking the Lead on Adolescent Literacy: Action Steps for Schoolwide Success*, by Judith Irvin, Julie Meltzer, Nancy Dean, and Martha Jan Mickler. Thousand Oaks, CA: Corwin, www.corwin.com. Reproduction authorized only for the local school site or nonprofit organization that has purchased this book.

TOOL 10: PROGRESS TOWARD GOALS SUMMARY CHART

Tool 10: Progress Toward Goals Summary Chart
Literacy Action Goal:
What data do we have that will tell us if we have met this goal? (check all that apply) _____ Analysis of teacher-designed assignments _____ Literacy action rubrics _____ Teacher feedback (focus groups or survey data) _____ Student feedback (focus groups or survey data) _____ Literacy walk-through data _____ Student performance data _____ Other (be specific) ______________________ Summarize what the data and evidence reveal relative to meeting the goal. Did we meet the goal? Yes/No What did we do that directly supported success? Did we fall short of the goal? Yes/No Do we need to revise the goal for next year? Yes/No What revisions would make a strong goal for next year?

Copyright © 2010 by Judith L. Irvin. All rights reserved. Reprinted from *Taking the Lead on Adolescent Literacy: Action Steps for Schoolwide Success*, by Judith Irvin, Julie Meltzer, Nancy Dean, and Martha Jan Mickler. Thousand Oaks, CA: Corwin, www.corwin.com. Reproduction authorized only for the local school site or nonprofit organization that has purchased this book.

TOOL 11: IMPLEMENTATION REVIEW CHART

Tool 11: Implementation Review Chart		
Literacy Action Goal: **Was the goal met? Yes/ No/ Partially** **Evidence that we met the goal:**		
Action Steps	**Was the Action Step Accomplished?**	
	Progress	Continued Needs
	Progress	Continued Needs
	Progress	Continued Needs
	Progress	Continued Needs
	Progress	Continued Needs
	Progress	Continued Needs
	Progress	Continued Needs
	Progress	Continued Needs

Copyright © 2010 by Judith L. Irvin. All rights reserved. Reprinted from *Taking the Lead on Adolescent Literacy: Action Steps for Schoolwide Success*, by Judith Irvin, Julie Meltzer, Nancy Dean, and Martha Jan Mickler. Thousand Oaks, CA: Corwin, www.corwin.com. Reproduction authorized only for the local school site or nonprofit organization that has purchased this book.

TOOL 12: LITERACY LEADERSHIP TEAM ASSESSMENT

Tool 12: Literacy Leadership Team Assessment			
The team is working well to make good decisions.	**Yes**	**No**	If not, discuss the extent to which the team is (or is not) doing the following: • Supporting and including a variety of viewpoints and perspectives • Soliciting contributions from all team members • Establishing an environment of inclusion and safety • Working to reconcile disagreements and reduce tension by using consensus-building • Exploring and validating differences and suggesting areas of consensus
Team members are working to expand or deepen their knowledge about literacy.	**Yes**	**No**	If not, analyze what is preventing members from increasing their professional knowledge. Consider the following: • Need for professional development • Need for adequate time to network, read, and reflect • How to reduce excessive demands on members' time • How to address lack of perceived support and recognition for efforts from colleagues and administrators • How to seek out resources to target and address these problems
The team is taking a leadership role in planning and supporting teacher professional development.	**Yes**	**No**	If not, determine which members have expertise and are comfortable with making faculty presentations or conducting classroom demonstrations. Pair up experienced team members with novice teachers and provide time to develop leadership knowledge and skills.
The team is being effective in getting others on board with the initiative.	**Yes**	**No**	If not, ask each team member to share the team's activities with their colleagues—either individually or in a department or team-level meeting.
The team is being effective in supporting others' efforts to contribute to improved student literacy and learning.	**Yes**	**No**	If not, discuss which faculty members are attempting to implement some of the steps in the literacy action plan. Publicly acknowledge the efforts of all faculty and staff to support the initiative.
The team leader or facilitator ensures that all members have an equal voice in discussion and decision making.	**Yes**	**No**	If not, have one team member collect informal data on the amount of time that all members contribute to the discussion. Present that data to the team for discussion about the need for sharing the voice of discussion.

Copyright © 2010 by Judith L. Irvin. All rights reserved. Reprinted from *Taking the Lead on Adolescent Literacy: Action Steps for Schoolwide Success*, by Judith Irvin, Julie Meltzer, Nancy Dean, and Martha Jan Mickler. Thousand Oaks, CA: Corwin, www.corwin.com. Reproduction authorized only for the local school site or nonprofit organization that has purchased this book.

TOOL 13: THEN, NOW, NEXT CHART

Tool 13: Then, Now, Next Chart			
	Then . . .	**Now . . .**	**Next . . .**
What students were, are, or will be doing			
What teachers were, are, or will be doing			
What the school environment was, is, or will be like			

Copyright © 2010 by Judith L. Irvin. All rights reserved. Reprinted from *Taking the Lead on Adolescent Literacy: Action Steps for Schoolwide Success*, by Judith Irvin, Julie Meltzer, Nancy Dean, and Martha Jan Mickler. Thousand Oaks, CA: Corwin, www.corwin.com. Reproduction authorized only for the local school site or nonprofit organization that has purchased this book.

TOOL 14: PROACTIVE STEPS FOR SUSTAINING A LITERACY IMPROVEMENT EFFORT

Tool 14: Proactive Steps for Sustaining Literacy Leadership and Improvement			
1 = No evidence of planning 2 = Some evidence of planning 3 = Fully planned for			
When the Principal Leaves . . .			
There is a strong literacy leadership team that works with the principal to implement and monitor progress on the literacy initiative.	1	2	3
A strong vision and action plan is communicated to all stakeholders.	1	2	3
Policies and procedures for using reading assessment data are in place.	1	2	3
Expectations for content area reading and writing instruction are clear.	1	2	3
Use student performance results and other data are used to publicly tell the story of the literacy improvement effort so that results are clearly attached to the literacy work.	1	2	3
When the Literacy Coach Leaves . . .			
There is a clear job description for the position of literacy coach.	1	2	3
The literacy coach is expected to be an essential member of a strong literacy leadership team.	1	2	3
The literacy coach is expected to meet regularly with the principal so the principal is informed, can act, and be seen as co-leader of the literacy improvement effort.	1	2	3
Literacy leaders take responsibility for many specific processes such as content area classroom support, library/media center promotion, and student book talks.	1	2	3
When Key Teacher Leaders Leave . . .			
Expectations of teachers in leadership positions are clearly defined in terms of their roles as literacy leaders.	1	2	3
Leadership selection is based on establishing a commitment to literacy improvement as a selection criterion.	1	2	3
The principal, coach, and other leaders provide explicit support for mentoring new leaders in their roles.	1	2	3
When District Leadership Changes . . .			
School leaders communicate to district leadership how new mandates are being addressed and implemented in their school.	1	2	3

(Continued)

(Continued)

School leaders provide evidence that the school's literacy improvement effort is aligned with district priorities.	1	2	3
School leaders communicate a clear vision and action plan that is actively supported by the community.	1	2	3
When There Is High Teacher Turnover . . .			
Teacher induction includes a literacy mentor and coaching support.	1	2	3
New teachers have access to content area literacy materials and professional resources.	1	2	3
Teachers have clear understanding about the amount and types of students' reading and writing, as well as reading and writing instruction expected in each of the courses to which a teacher is assigned.	1	2	3
Teachers have access to quality and ongoing professional development.	1	2	3
Teachers are involved and participate from the beginning in the use of reading and writing assessment data to drive instruction.	1	2	3
Attention and feedback from administration is focused on the quality of content area literacy development.	1	2	3

Source: Adapted from Irvin, J. L., Meltzer, J., Mickler, M. J., Phillips, M. P., & Dean, N. (2009). *Meeting the Challenge of Adolescent Literacy: Practical Ideas for Literacy Leaders.* Newark, DE: International Reading Association, pp. 218–219.

TOOL 15: TYPES AND USES OF DATA

Tool 15: Types and Uses of Data		
Type of Data	**Possible Uses**	**How Do You Currently Use This Data at Your School?**
Standardized assessments	To conduct item analyses; to screen students for placement; to evaluate program efficacy	
Leveled reading assessments	To determine where additional support and challenge might be needed; to determine if additional diagnostic tests are needed; to order parallel reading materials	
Diagnostic reading tests	To determine what types of interventions would be most helpful for specific students	
School or district writing prompts	To determine individual performance for instructional purposes; to evaluate program efficacy	
Course and/or grade-level assessments that require reading and writing	To look across assignments and discuss if students are demonstrating necessary proficiency and where additional explicit instruction, modeling, and guided practice might be needed; to calibrate expectations across classes; to monitor student progress; to differentiate instruction	
Student survey data	To understand reading and writing experiences and instruction from the students' points of view	
Collaborative examination of student work	To calibrate expectations across classes; to brainstorm how to provide additional support	

Source: Adapted from Irvin, J. L., Meltzer, J., & Dukes, M. S. (2007). *Taking Action on Adolescent Literacy: An Implementation Guide for School Leaders.* Alexandria, VA: Association for Supervision and Curriculum Development, pp. 167–169.

TOOL 16: PROFESSIONAL DEVELOPMENT NEEDS ASSESSMENT

Tool 16: Professional Development Needs Assessment	
We would like your input for our literacy professional development this year. Please rank in order the following literacy professional development needs, with *1* being *least important* to you and *9* being *most important* to you.	
Area of Literacy Professional Development	**Rank Order**
How to teach and use literacy strategies to improve content reading	
How to teach students to summarize and analyze text	
How to teach content area vocabulary	
How to increase student motivation to read and write	
How to implement interventions for struggling students	
How to use data to inform instruction	
How to create a literacy-rich environment in the classroom	
How to differentiate literacy instruction	
How to teach writing in my content area	
Other areas that you would like to learn more about include the following: **Elements that best support my implementation of instructional strategies into my classroom** Use the following ranking system: * **(not helpful)** ** **(sometimes helpful)** *** **(very helpful)** Specific content area examples Time to talk with colleagues about possible applications Time to plan with colleagues Access to written descriptions and templates Observing in other classrooms Strategies modeled by the consultant One-to-one coaching support to implement Time to share and discuss with colleagues' attempts at implementation Getting feedback from others	

Source: Adapted from Irvin, J. L., Meltzer, J., Mickler, M. J., Phillips, M. P., & Dean, N. (2009). *Meeting the Challenge of Adolescent Literacy: Practical Ideas for Literacy Leaders.* Newark, DE: International Reading Association, p. 201.

TOOL 17: ROLES OF SUPPORT PERSONNEL

Tool 17: Roles of Support Personnel		
Role	**Role in Literacy Support**	**District Support of This Role**
School-based literacy coaches		
District-based reading specialists		
Content area teacher leaders		
Special education teachers or teachers of English language learners with a background in reading		
Library media specialists		
Technology specialists		

Copyright © 2010 by Judith L. Irvin. All rights reserved. Reprinted from *Taking the Lead on Adolescent Literacy: Action Steps for Schoolwide Success*, by Judith Irvin, Julie Meltzer, Nancy Dean, and Martha Jan Mickler. Thousand Oaks, CA: Corwin, www.corwin.com. Reproduction authorized only for the local school site or nonprofit organization that has purchased this book.

TOOL 18: DATA QUESTIONS AND DECISIONS

Tool 18: Data Questions and Decisions				
Stakeholder	**Questions and/or Decisions**	**Reading and/or Writing Assessments We Give**	**How We Communicate Results**	**How We Use the Data Internally**
Students	How am I doing? What should I do next?			
Teachers	Have my students met my learning goals? How effective was my instruction? Should Student A take *X* class? Would Student B benefit from *Y* program?			
Parents	How is my child doing? Is she or he making progress? How does his or her work and/or learning compare to others?			
Administrators	How effective is our program? For which students is it most effective? Least effective? How well are teachers doing?			
Policy makers	How well are schools meeting public expectations?			
Taxpayers	How well is our money being spent?			

Source: Adapted from Brenner, D., Pearson, P. D., & Rief, L. (2007). Thinking Through Assessment. In K. Beers, R. E. Probst, & L. Rief (Eds.), *Adolescent Literacy: Turning Promise Into Practice.* Portsmouth, NH: Heinemann, p. 262.

Resource C

Examples of Each Rubric Component in Action

These examples are intended to give you an idea of how each component of the six rubrics is implemented at an *exemplary* (or Level 4) level. (Remember that some components are intentionally repeated across the rubrics.) If you are not familiar with each strategy or practice mentioned in the examples, there is no need to spend time researching; you can still get the gist of the example. Remember that these practices are examples only and are not meant to be prescriptive. As you go through each rubric, you should read the example appropriate for your level and then assess your school's implementation of the component.

LITERACY ACTION RUBRIC 1: STUDENT MOTIVATION, ENGAGEMENT, AND ACHIEVEMENT

Component	Indicators
A. Relevance	• Students can see connections between work in school and their lives and the world at large. • Assignments are meaningful and have an audience beyond the teacher.

- **Upper Elementary:** Students discuss the issue of bird migration as both a threat to the health and safety of humans and as a necessity for the birds to fly the routes they have always taken. Students then read two articles about bird migration, noting the conflicts between the natural migration routes, airplanes, wind farm proponents, and cities. They mark the points that they agree and disagree with as they read. The teacher uses video and maps to teach about migration flyways. Students then complete a Webquest about how bird migration affects local communities and the different ways they handle the situation. After completing the Webquest—which requires the students to work in pairs and engage in substantive reading, writing, discussion, and analysis—they work in groups of four to develop a Web site showcasing what they have learned and providing their best advice about what their community should do.
- **Middle School:** Seventh-grade students read a local newspaper story about possible contaminants in the local water supply and design an investigation to see if there are unacceptable levels of contaminants in the school drinking water. They create two column notes as they read an initial set of articles provided by their teacher. They then research further to select a small set of articles for others to read about the issue. Students get test kits from a local nonprofit watershed protection organization and contact a lab at a local company who agrees to do the tests at a low cost. The students develop presentations in small groups. After getting additional suggestions from their peers, they make a successful presentation to the PTA and obtain funds to pay for the tests. Using the data-collection protocols outlined in the test kits, the students carefully collect samples and send them to the lab. When the results come, they put together an informational Web site and a brochure letting people know the findings and what actions they can take to ensure their drinking water is safe.

(Continued)

(Continued)

<table>
<tr><th>Component</th><th>Indicators</th></tr>
<tr><td colspan="2">• High School: The ninth-grade English teachers inform their students that reading tutors are needed for several struggling second and third graders at the elementary schools closest to the high school. The guidance department organizes a reading tutor corps and volunteers agree to meet their assigned reading buddies three times per week for nine weeks. After initial training period of two weeks, the students work with their buddies in reading and writing, supervised by a trained reading teacher. The high school students are diligent, and the elementary students make good gains as readers, which is celebrated at the end-of-the-year party.</td></tr>
<tr><td>B. Choice</td><td>• Students have choices about how they will complete an assignment.
• Students have choices about what they read, write, and/or investigate.
• Students have choices in how they will demonstrate learning.</td></tr>
<tr><td colspan="2">• Upper Elementary: Fifth-grade students read The Westing Game together, noting in their journals all of the elements that make this a mystery as well as tracking the behaviors and clues associated with their assigned character. To continue to build on the mystery unit, the teacher previews several mystery books at different reading levels. Students then choose the book they want to read and participate in literature circles with others who are reading the same book. Each group selects a culminating book activity to present to the class from a list of options provided by the teacher.

• Middle School: Eighth-grade students study the Civil War and choose the perspective of a character through which to comment on each of the events being studied (Union soldier, Confederate soldier, abolitionist). As part of the unit, students watch video clips, read primary sources, and take virtual fieldtrips to historical sites. They study different events leading up to and through the war. Students choose which three events their character would have a strong opinion about and compose commentary as a podcast or on a blog that the whole class can listen to or read at specific points throughout the unit.

• High School: Tenth-grade students are given a choice of which career cluster to explore. Technical reading, critical reading of journal articles, and technical writing are stressed in the English classes associated with engineering, environmental sciences, health sciences, and building trades; world literature, media analysis, and persuasive and analytical writing are emphasized in classes related to the hospitality, marketing, and international relations clusters. Because the reading material and writing formats are directly related to areas of interest, engagement with reading and writing is high.</td></tr>
<tr><td>C. Collaborative Learning</td><td>• Students work collaboratively in pairs or small groups when reading or creating text.
• Group assignments are clear with explicit roles, purpose, and expectations.</td></tr>
<tr><td colspan="2">• Upper Elementary: Students work in small groups to read word problems, map the problems onto a five-step graphic organizer, and then work to solve the problems. The teacher models the use of the organizer and walks around to help groups that are getting stuck. At the end of the class, students write on an exit slip how the graphic organizer did or did not help with problem solving and how the group worked together.

• Middle School: After being introduced to essential vocabulary, students break into their Reciprocal Teaching groups, assign roles, and collaboratively reread a chapter in their science book, asking and answering questions, making</td></tr>
</table>

Component	Indicators
predictions, clarifying for one another where necessary, and collectively summarizing at the end of the chapter. When they are finished with the chapter, they collaboratively complete a sequencing graphic organizer so that the steps of the cycle are clear for everyone in the group. • **High School:** In groups of four, students read an article about alternative energy and discuss the issues using a discussion protocol. Each student then takes a stand and declares which approach to the energy problem is the strongest avenue for the country to take. Students form groups of three and work together to develop a thesis statement, do further research to collect evidence, and then create compelling PowerPoint presentations advocating for the approach they chose. Students are motivated to produce quality work because these presentations will be submitted to the citywide environmental forum and viewed by all who attend.	
D. Use of Technology	• Students use technology to research and evaluate content, collect and analyze data, and communicate and collaborate with others. • Students use technology to research, write, and present.
• **Upper Elementary:** Fifth-grade students are learning about media and persuasion and are completing a unit on an analysis of advertising. To demonstrate that they understand core concepts in the unit, students in groups of three create podcast advertisements with audio, music, and video for a product. All of the advertisements are evaluated by all of the teams using a rubric that the class created that specified how language, format, and image are used to persuade consumers to buy. The two getting the highest ratings will be shown at the next schoolwide assembly. • **Middle School:** Eighth-grade students are working on comparison and contrast essays based on reading a fiction and nonfiction piece about the same historical incident. Every student posts his or her work on the class blog for feedback from three other students who post substantive feedback based on a protocol that the teacher reviewed with the class. Students then revise their work based on the feedback they receive. When the final drafts are posted, students are assigned to groups to read all of the pieces in their group and to vote on the best one or two pieces. Then the whole class reads these essays and nominates three to five to be recognized on the Wall of Fame. • **High School:** Eleventh-grade students work in trios to research online an aspect of World War I for a community-wide Veterans Day assembly. After learning about hoax Web sites and how to evaluate the truthfulness of online information, students select their topic from a list and develop a line of inquiry regarding the topic. Then they find three articles about the topic they are exploring and rigorously evaluate each one against criteria for valid informational Web sites. They develop their thesis statement and create a short multimedia presentation making their case, using evidence they have found, and setting the work to appropriate music and pictures. These virtual exhibits are projected at the opening of the Veterans Day ceremony.	
E. Goal Setting	• Students are supported to set and work toward goals related to improving their performance as a reader, writer, or learner.
• **Upper Elementary:** As a class, fourth-grade students discuss and evaluate themselves against a chart showing what active versus passive readers do when confronted with challenging text. Then they decide as a class what they will work on this year to become more proficient readers. They decide to collectively read 100 recommended books, to use graphic organizers and other strategies when they read, and to help one another stay focused when discussing text.	

(Continued)

(Continued)

Component	Indicators
• **Middle School:** Students are screened using both a fluency (correct words per minute) and a comprehension measure and are given their scores on both, including how each score compares to the national norm. If students feel that they did not do their best, they can retake the test to better reflect their reading ability. Students then set a reading improvement goal and participate in small group book clubs that read and discuss books focusing on different themes or genres. Students can periodically recheck their proficiency to chart their progress in meeting their goal. • **High School:** Ninth- and tenth-grade students take a formal reading test at the beginning of each academic year and are urged to do their best because the data will help them plan for their future. The test provides a Lexile range so they can get a sense of their current strength as a reader across genres. They also fill out a career interest form online. After they complete the form, they get an estimated Lexile level for the level of the reading materials expected of new employees in three fields that align with their interests. Advisors meet with all students to discuss their Lexile scores and how they compare with the fields they might be interested in pursuing and develop a growth plan with a target growth score. Then, they meet each quarter to check how they are strengthening or maintaining their proficiency as a reader. At the end of the year, students retake the test and note if they made progress toward their goal and why this might or might not have been the case.	
F. Teacher Expectations	• Teachers hold and communicate the expectation that students will succeed academically. • Use of modeling and guided practice opportunities to scaffold students to higher levels of success.
• **Upper Elementary:** Fourth- and fifth-grade teachers get together at the beginning of each school year and draft a brief list of literacy skills and habits all students should master by the end of the year. Teachers explain and prominently display this list to students, referring to it frequently throughout the year. Teachers also explain the behaviors of successful students and help students behave in a way that guarantees success. Teachers model these behaviors, and students are given opportunities to role-play and practice the behaviors as they make them their own. • **Middle School:** The seventh-grade social studies teachers demonstrate a belief in all students' abilities by using a Socratic seminar system in which all students contribute to the discussion of issues and topics. Students follow a discussion protocol that requires them to use the text to support a response and to be able to restate the position of others in the group. The teacher models ways of positively contributing to discussions and guides students toward appropriate responses when they falter, as full participation in the educational community becomes the norm. • **High School:** Biology teachers are doing a unit on photosynthesis. They are certain that all students can master the material but know that some students will have more difficulty than others with the content. Therefore, teachers approach the unit from several different directions. They first find out what students know about photosynthesis and record this on a large chart. They then explain the process using words, pictures, and video. Finally, they divide the class into centers: reading, illustrations, and explanations. In the reading center, students choose a text from a selection of short articles written at different reading levels. They must read one article and write a one-sentence summary. In the illustration center, students work in pairs to look at charts of photosynthesis and label the steps. In the explanation center, students choose to either write or draw an explanation of photosynthesis. As students work in centers, teachers walk from group to group, guiding and encouraging students.	

Component	Indicators
G. Classroom Instruction	• Instruction includes a plan for active involvement in reading, writing, and vocabulary development. • Teachers use instructional strategies to strengthen content learning and support literacy development. • Students independently use literacy strategies.

- **Upper Elementary:** Fourth graders have been introduced to all of the elements of Reciprocal Teaching (RT) and use this strategy when they read nonfiction text. Students take turns predicting, clarifying, questioning, and summarizing. All classrooms have Interactive Word Walls where the words pertain to current units of study and vocabulary are reinforced through word games and word sorts.
- **Middle School:** All seventh-grade teams have introduced students to a set of graphic organizers they can use to analyze their reading and plan their writing. In the fall, teachers model how and when to use each organizer and give students multiple assignments requiring that they use each. After using the organizer, students discussed how the organizer helped them complete the assigned task. During the second half of the year, students are encouraged to choose which graphic organizer they want to use to help them complete a reading or writing assignment. A brief discussion ensues after each assignment is completed as to which graphic organizers students used and if they thought they had made a good choice.
- **High School:** Across the six sections of biology and chemistry, students use specific discussion protocols for every reading assignment. When given an assigned reading, students quickly get into groups and begin the task of working through the text. Students also use systematic note taking to organize their notes when reading or listening and vocabulary journals to keep track of vocabulary. They use a peer revision and editing protocol when writing lab reports prior to turning papers in for a final grade.

Component	Indicators
H. Feedback and Grading Practices	• Specific feedback is given on student performance. • Teachers use rubrics and models. • Grading practices support revising work.

- **Upper Elementary:** When fifth-grade students write, they always share what they write with two peers. The teacher provides targeted areas for comment such as voice, organization, or idea development, depending on the assignment. The two peer reviewers make suggestions relative to the specific area, and the author revises based on that area before working with a peer editor using an editing checklist.
- **Middle School:** Middle school students know that they must continue working on an assignment until they achieve a specified level on the associated rubric. Students get feedback and assistance so that they can pass a class because they completed all of the essential assignments. Students receive no grade penalty for a late key assignment that has been successfully revised or reworked. They are expected, however, to continue other assignments so that they do not get behind. The result is often that students work harder in the first place and pay more attention to the rubric earlier in the process so they do not have to keep redoing assignments.
- **High School:** Ninth-grade English students conference in groups of four to brainstorm ideas and then again before passing in their major papers. At the second meeting, the students read each others' papers and use the schoolwide rubric to rate each paper on each dimension of the rubric: content, organization, logic, and presentation. Then each reviewer provides feedback on what the author could do to make the paper one ranking higher on each dimension where they have not ranked it at the highest level. The author takes this specific feedback and works on the paper again before turning it in.

(Continued)

(Continued)

Component	Indicators
I. Recognition of Student Work	• Student work is prominently displayed. • Academic achievement is publicly recognized.

- **Upper Elementary:** Fourth-grade teachers reserve one large bulletin board for posting exemplary student work. They clearly explain the rubric designed to help students understand the criteria for displaying student work. One section of the bulletin board includes teacher-selected exemplary features of the work highlighted. Another section of the bulletin board is selected by a team of students who create the rubric, select the work, and post the work. This team's responsibility is rotated monthly so each student has a chance to select student work for display. Another section of the room has students' reading charts posted. Students who meet their reading goals are celebrated weekly with a visit from the principal. The teacher also calls home to celebrate literacy accomplishments with families.
- **Middle School:** Each middle school team has a special bulletin board in the hallway of the school. Language arts teachers post exemplary written compositions, book reviews, and poems; math teachers post exceptional tests, concept maps, and homework; social studies teachers post student-produced geography maps, concept maps, and essays; science teachers post well-written lab results, diagrams, and concept papers. The bulletin boards are changed monthly. In addition, teachers sponsor a Wall of Fame, highlighting students who have met their reading and vocabulary mastery goals. The Wall of Fame is updated monthly, and parents are invited to view their students' work.
- **High School:** The school has installed display cabinets for each department to use to display student work. Each department has a student committee that helps the teachers select work for display, based on a departmental rubric. The teachers and students meet monthly to decide on student work to display, and the display is arranged by students in the cabinets monthly. Parents are informed when their students are honored in the display so that they can come to the school and see the work, and students who are featured in the display cases are honored on the morning announcements.

LITERACY ACTION RUBRIC 2: LITERACY ACROSS THE CONTENT AREAS

Component	Indicators
A. Classroom Instruction	• Instruction includes a plan for active involvement in reading, writing, and vocabulary development. • Teachers use instructional strategies to strengthen content learning and support literacy development. • Students independently use literacy strategies.

- **Upper Elementary:** Fourth graders have been introduced to all of the elements of Reciprocal Teaching (RT) and use this strategy when they read nonfiction text. Students take turns predicting, clarifying, questioning, and summarizing. All classrooms have Interactive Word Walls where the words pertain to current units of study and vocabulary are reinforced through word games and word sorts.
- **Middle School:** All seventh-grade teams have introduced students to a set of graphic organizers they can use to analyze their reading and plan their writing. In the fall, teachers model how and when to use each organizer and give students multiple assignments, requiring that they use each. After using the organizer, students discussed how the organizer helped them complete the assigned task. During the second half of the year, students are encouraged to choose which graphic organizer they want to use to help them complete a reading or writing assignment. A brief discussion ensues after each assignment is completed as to which graphic organizers students used and if they thought they had made a good choice.

<table>
<tr><th>Component</th><th>Indicators</th></tr>
<tr><td colspan="2">• High School: Across the six sections of biology and chemistry, students use specific discussion protocols for every reading assignment. When given an assigned reading, students quickly get into groups and begin the task of working through the text. Students also use systematic note taking to organize their notes when reading or listening and vocabulary journals to keep track of vocabulary. They use a peer revision and editing protocol when writing lab reports prior to turning papers in for a final grade.</td></tr>
<tr><td>B. Curriculum Alignment</td><td>• Content area courses include development of literacy.
• Course content and literacy build by grade level.
• Students have access to rigorous content and strong literacy support.</td></tr>
<tr><td colspan="2">• Upper Elementary: A grade-level team gets together and reviews the fifth-grade curriculum for all content areas and identifies the types and amounts of text that students will be supported to read and write in each content area. They meet weekly to develop common rubrics, discuss how they are modeling for students, and to share ideas about how to increase the amount of reading and writing in all classes.
• Middle School: A middle school teaching team identifies five power strategies that they will use regularly: text coding, QAR (Question-Answer Relationship), use of graphic organizers, two-column note taking and RAFTS (Role, Audience, Format, Topic). For each strategy, the team identifies who will explicitly teach and model each strategy and how they will all provide reinforcement and practice opportunities. They pledge to have students use each strategy 12 to 15 times in their core classes throughout the year. Team meetings with the literacy coach focus on how strategy instruction and use is going and how they can make the use of the strategies as powerful as possible.
• High School: A high school decides that as part of its annual course catalog, it will publish course descriptions, along with the literacy habits and skills that will be focused upon in each course. Professional learning community meetings over the course of the following year will include checking in with each teacher as to how she or he has included a focus on these every month in every class taught.</td></tr>
<tr><td>C. Differentiation</td><td>• Teachers use flexible grouping.
• Teachers use different materials to accommodate different interests and skill levels.
• Teachers use specific strategies to support various learning needs.</td></tr>
<tr><td colspan="2">• Upper Elementary: Fifth-grade teachers work with one small group of students on activating prior knowledge about bees while a second group uses Reciprocal Teaching with an assigned article on the social hierarchy of a bee hive and a third group, broken into six pairs, is engaged in paired reading and summarizing of a short story about beekeeping.
• Middle School: Seventh-grade English language arts teachers do a quick book commercial for each of the memoirs students can select to read. As part of the commercial, the teacher mentions what makes each choice interesting as well as the relative difficulty of the text. Students preview their choice and read to test the difficulty using a teacher-developed test on the first three pages. Students are placed into literature circles based on their final choices.
• High School: The eleventh-grade American history teachers know that their textbook is written at the college level and is too hard for many of their students to read and understand. To make the text more accessible to students, they preteach vocabulary. They have collected a set of articles and videos related to each chapter, and they provide time at the beginning of each unit for students to explore these in small groups and develop collaborative charts based on these resources. Teachers then use Think Alouds to model the reading of the textbook. The small groups convene throughout the unit to add to and modify their charts.</td></tr>
</table>

(Continued)

(Continued)

Component	Indicators
D. Feedback and Grading Practices	• Specific feedback is given on student performance. • Teachers use Rubrics and models. • Grading practices support revising work.

- **Upper Elementary**: When fifth-grade students write, they always share what they write with two peers. The teacher provides targeted areas for comment such as voice, organization, or idea development, depending on the assignment. The two peer reviewers make suggestions relative to the specific area, and the author revises based on that area before working with a peer editor using an editing checklist.
- **Middle School:** Middle school students know that they must continue working on an assignment until they achieve a specified level on the associated rubric. Students get feedback and assistance so that they can pass a class because they completed all of the essential assignments. Students receive no grade penalty for a late key assignment that has been successfully revised or reworked. They are expected, however, to continue other assignments so that they do not get behind. The result is often that students work harder in the first place and pay more attention to the rubric earlier in the process so they do not have to keep redoing assignments.
- **High School:** Ninth-grade English students conference in groups of four to brainstorm ideas and then conference again before passing in their major papers. At the second meeting, the students read each others' papers and use the schoolwide rubric to rate each paper on each dimension of the rubric: content, organization, logic, and presentation. Then each reviewer provides feedback on what the author could do to make the paper one ranking higher on each dimension where they have not ranked it at the highest level. The author takes this specific feedback and works on the paper again before turning it in.

Component	Indicators
E. Assignments	• Assignments have a meaningful purpose. • Assignments include high-order thinking. • Students have various ways to demonstrate learning. • Assignments use technology.

- **Upper Elementary:** Fourth-grade students are responsible for creating podcasts on three books they read during the year. Students describe what they liked and did not like about the book, provide a summary of the plot without giving away the ending, discuss the character they most identified with or would like to meet and why, and describe what type of reader would like the book. When students cannot find a book to read during sustained silent reading time, the teacher suggests they listen to the podcast reviews of books. After listening to a podcast, students can rate the helpfulness of the podcast in assisting them to find a book and can post comments if they read the book as to whether they agree or not with the original podcast and why.
- **Middle School:** For a year-end review project, eighth graders create a pre-algebra handbook for students in Kenya who cannot afford math textbooks. They examine what they like and do not like about math textbooks and compile a criteria list for a quality handbook. The class divides up what they see as the most important topics, and each work group votes for five topics to focus on. Students work in small groups to develop the text and graphics they need to communicate key concepts about their topics. Each group reviews the work of two other groups to provide feedback and ensure quality control. Workgroups then revise and edit based on the feedback they receive. The class asks three math teachers to review and check all content in the handbook before sending the handbook to their peers in Kenya.
- **High School:** Tenth graders in pairs prepare multimedia presentations comparing and contrasting their perspectives on the uses of science and technology with the responses of three community elders they previously interviewed, demonstrating their understanding of the interactions between science, technology, and society. The presentation rubric requires them to show intergenerational similarities and differences and discuss the causes and effects of these similarities and differences. The presentations need to showcase comments about at least four technologies and must incorporate images, charts, and quotes. The presentations will be shown at two area senior centers where students will ask for feedback on their work before posting the work on the Web.

Component	Indicators
F. Research and Use of Text	• Students read a variety of text. • Regular research with synthesis of multiple sources is used. • Students have multiple opportunities to present findings.

- **Upper Elementary:** In a fifth-grade classroom, students are studying the colonial era in American History. Students choose from several historical novels, conduct Internet research on the time period, and read from the textbook. They compare and contrast the information in each source and use what they have learned to make up a fictional character and write "A Day in the Life of..." paper. Papers are compiled into a class book, and copies can be made for everyone in the class.
- **Middle School:** In an eighth-grade classroom, students are studying the Civil War and are reading and discussing packets of letters from soldiers to their loved ones. Using clues in the letters, students are figuring out and making a case for when in the war the letter was written, based on whether if it was written by someone on the Union or Confederate side someone wealthy or poor, and as much else as can be inferred from the letter. Next, students work in pairs to research a specific battle, using printed and electronic resources, and present the implications of the outcome of the battle for the war. They will also write "A Letter From a Soldier" in that battle. Students then create podcasts juxtaposing the real and the student-written letters and ask listeners to vote on which are the authentic letters.
- **High School:** In a high school health classroom, students working in small groups choose a lifestyle habit that is contributing to the huge healthcare costs in this country based on the reading of several articles provided by the teacher (e.g., smoking, sugar content of soft drinks, not exercising). Students then read two scientific studies on the topic, two articles in the popular press, and information on two reputable Web sites on the subject. They then create an informational brochure that persuades people to change their lifestyle habits to be healthier. The brochures are reviewed by the other groups for accuracy and persuasiveness and then published and distributed to the nurse's office, science classes, and the cafeteria as well as dropped off at convenience stores around town.

LITERACY ACTION RUBRIC 3: LITERACY INTERVENTIONS

Component	Indicators
A. Reading Assessment	• Ready access to current assessment data is available. • Students with scores two-years behind are tested further. • Reading assessment data are collected at least three times a year for intervention planning.

- **Upper Elementary:** All students are screened at least once a year to monitor their progress in reading. Benchmarks or growth rates (or a combination of the two) are used to identify children at low, moderate, or high risk for reading difficulties. Students who are at risk of reading problems or those who are performing two or more years below grade level are further assessed using the Developmental Reading Inventory as well as informal assessments to plan for appropriate interventions. All teachers receive professional development on methods for collecting and interpreting student data on reading efficiently and reliably.
- **Middle School:** Students' assessment and intervention data are sent from elementary school to the middle school. Student records and portfolios are also sent to the receiving school. All teachers receive professional development on methods for collecting and interpreting student data on reading efficiently and reliably. The school's intervention specialist regularly monitors the progress of designated students and provides further assessment data as warranted.

(Continued)

(Continued)

<table>
<tr><th>Component</th><th>Indicators</th></tr>
<tr><td colspan="2">• High School: Students' assessment and intervention data are sent from the middle to the high school. All teachers receive professional development on methods for collecting and interpreting student data on reading efficiently and reliably. The school's intervention specialist monitors the progress of students placed in exceptional student services and meets with department heads to plan course interventions.</td></tr>
<tr><td>B. Use of Data</td><td>• Multiple kinds of data are used for student assignment to interventions.
• Intervention classes include regular progress monitoring.
• Data are used to guide instruction.</td></tr>
<tr><td colspan="2">• Upper Elementary: Students who are at risk are tested using both formal and informal reading and writing assessments, such as running records and informal reading inventories. Teachers regularly access a variety of student test data to plan for instruction based on the students' current reading level. Such data include checklists and rubrics, student/teacher conferences, interviews, reading/writing logs, and student exhibitions. Teachers provide extra tutoring and instruction that provides students with multiple opportunities to show what they have learned as well as what they still need to learn.
• Middle School: All students are tested at least twice a year using an electronic reading inventory that assesses reading levels. Teachers participate in professional development that is focused on using student assessment data to effectively guide, inform, and influence classroom planning and instruction. Student placement decisions for intervention classes are based on reading levels, state reading tests, as well as informal reading inventories. Student progress is monitored weekly by instruction that is performance-based. Developed data-driven decision rules are used to provide differentiated instruction to students at varied reading proficiency levels for part of the day. Teachers and students use electronic portfolios that provide data about student literacy development so that proficiency and growth in applying reading, writing, presentation, and thinking skills can be assessed over time. Students use daily planners to record assignments and grades as well as monitor their progress toward personally set goals.
• High School: The school's intervention specialist uses a district level reading assessment for placement in intervention classes. Mathematical equations compare the data points to determine appropriate reading placement. The data are also used to confirm or change placement recommendations and to monitor progress. Teachers and students use electronic portfolios that provide data about student-literacy development so that proficiency and growth in applying reading, writing, presentation, and thinking skills can be assessed over time. Data-driven decisions are used to provide differentiated instruction to students at varied reading proficiency levels for part of the day. Teachers participate in professional development that is focused on using student assessment data to effectively guide, inform, and influence classroom planning and instruction. Students regularly use a planner to set goals and to record assignments, grades, and test scores.</td></tr>
<tr><td>C. Types of Interventions</td><td>• Multiple types of interventions are provided.
• Placement procedures and exit criteria are in place and applied.
• Struggling readers and writers receive differentiated instruction in content classes.</td></tr>
<tr><td colspan="2">• Upper Elementary: Students who score below the benchmark score on universal screenings are provided intensive, systematic instruction in small groups. Typically, these groups meet between three and five times a week, for 20 to 40 minutes. Students also attend tutoring and small-group instruction after school in which they work on projects and the creative arts. Teachers have been trained to embed literacy strategies in science and social studies instruction and have access to leveled reading materials. The school's intervention specialist monitors the progress of designated students in order to adjust their placement when warranted.</td></tr>
</table>

<table>
<tr><th>Component</th><th>Indicators</th></tr>
<tr><td colspan="2">

- **Middle School:** A schoolwide reading class for all students is offered for one period a day in which students have access to differentiated instruction and to leveled texts. Science and social studies teachers are trained to embed literacy strategies in their content area. Teachers use flexible grouping and leveled tasks for small group instruction. They also use grouping practices that enable different student groups to participate in different activities. Students work with partners or in small groups to collaborate on assignments and tasks. The school offers a variety of computerized literacy-intervention programs that provide individual and small group differentiated learning opportunities that appeal to students' interest in computer technology. The school's intervention specialist monitors student progress and uses a criterion-reference rubric to adjust student placement when warranted.
- **High School:** Underperforming students are placed in a class that integrates language arts and reading with a content class, such as social studies or science. Teachers provide instruction that help students successfully learn from a variety of materials, genres, and author styles. The master schedule includes a number of reading classes in various elective slots so that underperforming students have opportunities to improve their literacy development. Teachers use flexible grouping and leveled tasks for small group instruction. They also use grouping practices that enable different student groups to participate in different activities. The school offers students opportunities to participate in computerized literacy-intervention programs to develop self-directed learning habits through computerized literacy instruction that provides feedback to students about their performance and growth. The school's intervention specialist monitors student progress and uses a criterion-reference rubric to adjust student placement when warranted.

</td></tr>
<tr><td>D. Staffing</td><td>

- Intervention classes are staffed by certified reading specialists.
- Teachers of English language learners and special education teachers have a strong background in literacy.
- A certified reading specialist consults with content and intervention teachers.

</td></tr>
<tr><td colspan="2">

- **Upper Elementary:** All intervention teachers are certified literacy specialists or are in the process of becoming certified. Special education teachers and teachers of English language learners serve as consultants to classroom teachers and work as partners in classroom instruction. The district provides services from a district literacy coach who visits the school on a weekly basis to consult with teachers.
- **Middle School:** Special education and ELL teachers serve on teaching teams to help plan instruction and select materials. The district places a certified literacy specialist in the school who plans demonstration lessons and provides coaching and feedback to all teachers of underperforming students. The specialist works collaboratively with teachers to set professional goals for developing, extending, and improving effective research-based instructional skills, strategies, and practices.
- **High School:** Special education and ELL teachers serve on teaching teams to help plan instruction and select materials. The district places a certified literacy specialist in the school who plans demonstration lessons and provides coaching and feedback to all teachers of underperforming students. The specialist works collaboratively with teachers to set professional goals for developing, extending, and improving effective research-based instructional skills, strategies, and practices.

</td></tr>
</table>

(Continued)

(Continued)

Component	Indicators
E. Implementation of Interventions	• Intervention programs are implemented as intended. • Instructional approaches reflect a match to student needs. • Appropriate materials and technology are used by intervention teachers.

- **Upper Elementary:** Teachers create learner-centered intervention classrooms where students have control over their learning and have choices. Students have access to leveled books and materials. Teachers use the intervention program's data management component to ensure that the program is implemented as designed.
- **Middle School:** Teachers use the intervention program's data management component to ensure that the program is implemented as designed. Teachers create classroom opportunities to embed and link content learning and literacy through virtual courses and delivery systems, communication tools, artificial intelligence tools, and word processors for developing content knowledge and writing. Teachers and students create Web pages that provide current windows into classrooms by posting student writing, homework assignments, lecture notes, and collaborative projects. Teacher-monitored e-mail, blogs, and chat rooms provide the means for regularly communicating between educators and students.
- **High School:** Teachers use the intervention program's data management component to ensure that the program is implemented as designed. Teachers and students use threaded discussion groups to facilitate text study through electronic discussions that provide thoughtful conversational control, joint construction of meaning, and connections to students' lives and world. Students exchange messages about a single text or common topic based on student choice or teacher assignment of particular text. Teachers and students create Web pages that provide current windows into classrooms by posting student writing, homework assignments, lecture notes, and collaborative projects. E-mail, blogs, and chat rooms provide the means for regularly communicating between educators and students.

Component	Indicators
F. Teacher Collaboration	• Content and intervention teachers meet regularly to coordinate assignments and discuss student needs.

- **Upper Elementary:** The school provides teachers with time during the day to meet with grade-level colleagues to coordinate materials and instruction for designated students. Intervention teachers use the services of the school's literacy coach to set professional goals for developing, extending, and improving effective research-based instructional skills, strategies, and practices.
- **Middle School:** The master schedule provides time for content and intervention teachers to meet weekly with each other as well as with the library media specialist to coordinate materials and instruction. The school provides an area in the faculty lounge for information about best intervention practices and for teachers who seek specific information or materials. Inservice days include time for content and intervention teachers to discuss issues when they don't share common planning time during the school day.
- **High School:** The master schedule provides time for content and intervention teachers to meet monthly with each other as well as with the library media specialist to coordinate materials and instruction. Content and intervention teachers collaborate across grade levels to ensure an alignment of course content and outcomes throughout departments.

LITERACY ACTION RUBRIC 4: LITERACY-RICH SCHOOL ENVIRONMENT, POLICIES, AND CULTURE

Component	Indicators
A. Vision	• An articulated, shared vision for improved literacy is publicly displayed. • Evidence of a focus on literacy in classrooms and throughout the community is evident. • Resources support literacy improvement.
• **Upper Elementary:** The school's literacy brand statement is publicly displayed with a large banner at the school's entrance and in all classrooms. In addition, the school's literacy brand, goals, and action plan are posted on the school's Web site, translated into the main language groups represented in the school, and distributed through parent newsletters. The literacy team meets monthly to discuss progress toward meeting the goals of the action plan, and grade-level teams meet weekly to discuss applications of the literacy plan. All classrooms and hallways have literacy strategy posters, vocabulary work, student writing, and book talk posters displayed prominently. • **Middle School:** A student-designed and painted mural that captures the school's literacy brand is displayed prominently in the front office. In addition, the school's literacy brand, goals, and action plan are posted on the school's Web site, translated into the main language groups represented in the school, and distributed through parent newsletters. The literacy team meets monthly to discuss progress toward meeting the goals of the action plan, and grade-level teams meet weekly to discuss applications of the literacy plan. All classrooms and hallways have literacy-strategy posters, vocabulary work, student writing, and book talk posters displayed prominently. Teachers have posters on their doors highlighting what they are reading. Student leaders give book talks on the morning announcements. • **High School:** A student-designed and painted mural that captures the school's literacy brand is displayed prominently in the front hallway. In addition, the school's literacy brand, goals, and action plan are posted on the school's Web site, translated into the main language groups represented in the school, and distributed through parent newsletters. The literacy team meets monthly to discuss progress toward meeting the goals of the action plan, and content area departments meet regularly to discuss applications of the literacy plan. All classrooms and hallways have literacy strategy posters, vocabulary work, and student work displayed prominently. A student literacy team organizes and sponsors literacy-related activities such as book drives, literacy tutoring, and read-ins.	
B. Teacher Expectations	• Teachers hold and communicate the expectation that students will succeed academically. • Use of modeling and guided practice opportunities to scaffold students to higher levels of success.
• **Upper Elementary:** Fourth- and fifth-grade teachers get together at the beginning of each school year and draft a brief list of literacy skills and habits all students should master by the end of the year. Teachers explain and prominently display this list to students, referring to it frequently throughout the year. Teachers also explain the behaviors of successful students and help students behave in a way that ensures success. Teachers model these behaviors, and students are given opportunities to role-play and practice the behaviors as they make them their own. • **Middle School:** The seventh-grade social studies teachers demonstrate a belief in all students' abilities by using a Socratic seminar system in which all students contribute to the discussion of issues and topics. Students follow a discussion protocol that requires them to use the text to support a response and to be able to restate the position of	

(Continued)

(Continued)

Component	Indicators
others in the group. The teacher models ways of positively contributing to discussions and guides students toward appropriate responses when they falter, as full participation in the educational community becomes the norm. • **High School:** Biology teachers are doing a unit on photosynthesis. They are certain that all students can master the material but know that some students will have more difficulty than others with the content. Therefore, teachers approach the unit from several different directions. They first find out what students know about photosynthesis and record this on a large chart. They then explain the process using words, pictures, and video. Finally, they divide the class into centers: reading, illustrations, and explanations. In the reading center, students choose a text from a selection of short articles written at different reading levels. They must read one article and write a one-sentence summary. In the illustration center, students work in pairs to look at charts of photosynthesis and label the steps. In the explanation center, students choose to either write or draw an explanation of photosynthesis. As students work in centers, teachers walk from group to group, guiding and encouraging students.	
C. Time to Read and Write	• Multiple opportunities to read, write, and discuss content during the school day are available for students.
• **Upper Elementary:** The fifth-grade teacher begins each day with a discussion of the home reading from the night before. Students are given a clear discussion protocol and practice both listening and speaking in accordance with the protocol. Later in the day, the teacher reminds students of the discussion protocol as they discuss their social studies reading assignment in small groups. Students then reflect on the concepts of their social studies assignment in a two-way journal with a partner. • **Middle School:** The eighth-grade team has decided to do a cross-disciplinary unit on the Civil War, with social studies covering the history, language arts covering the literature, science covering the diseases, and math covering mortality rates and graphing. To encourage reading, writing, and discussion and to reinforce the idea that the unit is across disciplines, students write to a team-designed prompt at the beginning of every class and share their writing with a partner. At the end of every class, students must write a quick explanation of how the content in this class relates to the content in the other core classes. Students then exchange their explanations with a partner and write a response to the first commentary. • **High School:** The geometry teacher regularly uses the schoolwide strategies agreed upon by the faculty: column notes, quick writes, and one-sentence summary frames. Students have a notebook dedicated to literacy strategies in math. When students read a problem, they use column notes, explaining the task in the left column and writing their questions in the right column. After they work with a partner to solve the problem, they complete a one-minute power write on what they must remember in order to solve the problem and share their reflections with another partner pair in the class. At the end of class, students write a one-sentence summary frame capturing what they learned in the class.	
D. Recognition of Student Work	• Student work is prominently displayed. • Academic achievement is publicly recognized.
• **Upper Elementary:** Fourth-grade teachers reserve one large bulletin board for posting exemplary student work. They clearly explain the rubric designed to help students understand the criteria for displaying student work. One section of the bulletin board includes teacher-selected exemplary features of the work highlighted. Another section of the bulletin board is selected by a team of students who create the rubric, select the work, and post the work. The team responsibility is rotated monthly so each student has a chance to select student work for display. Another section of the room has student-reading charts posted. Students who meet their reading goals are celebrated weekly with a visit from the principal. The teacher also calls home to celebrate literacy accomplishments with families.	

<table>
<tr><th>Component</th><th>Indicators</th></tr>
<tr><td colspan="2">• Middle School: Each middle school team has a special bulletin board in the hallway of the school. Language arts teachers post exemplary sample written compositions, book reviews, and poems; math teachers post exceptional tests, concept maps, and homework; social studies teachers post student-produced geography maps, concept maps, and essays; and science teachers post well-written lab results, diagrams, and concept papers. The bulletin boards are changed monthly. In addition, teachers sponsor a Wall of Fame, highlighting students who have met their reading and vocabulary mastery goals. The Wall of Fame is updated monthly, and parents are invited to view their students' work.
• High School: The school has installed display cabinets for each department to use to display student work. Each department has a student committee that helps the teachers select work for display, based on a departmental rubric. The teachers and students meet monthly to decide on student work to display, and the display is arranged by students in the cabinets monthly. Parents are informed when their students are honored in the display so that they can come to the school and see the work, and students who are featured in the display cases are honored on the morning announcements.</td></tr>
<tr><td>E. Teacher Participation</td><td>• Teachers participate in literacy professional development.
• Teachers share of resources and strategies.
• Teachers consult with others to examine and use data to improve instruction.</td></tr>
<tr><td colspan="2">• Upper Elementary: The school professional development plan provides opportunities once a month for teachers to deepen their learning about literacy. These opportunities include book studies, literacy team-led strategy training, and literacy consultant-led training. All teachers participate in these trainings. In addition, grade-level teams meet biweekly with the school literacy specialist to discuss students' literacy achievement and design ways to improve classroom instruction.
• Middle School: The school has a day set aside for literacy professional development once every two months. The mornings are set aside for literacy team-led strategy training or literacy consultant-led training. In the afternoons, teams meet to plan applications of the training. In addition, all teachers visit a colleague's classroom to watch demonstration literacy lessons once each semester. They then debrief the visits through team meetings. Since the school gathers progress-monitoring literacy data three times a year, teams meet with the school literacy specialist after each assessment to analyze the data and develop classroom instruction to improve literacy learning.
• High School: Each spring, the principal of the high school gives teachers a survey asking them the way they learn best in professional development. This year, the faculty voted overwhelmingly to use planning period meetings and department meetings rather than day-long professional development. As a result, the literacy specialist schedules monthly planning period meetings with all faculty members to discuss the use of literacy support strategies in the content areas. Department meetings provide time for specific content area applications of the work from planning period meetings. In addition, all teachers visit a colleague's classroom to watch demonstration literacy lessons once each semester. They then debrief the visits through department meetings.</td></tr>
<tr><td>F. Master Schedule</td><td>• Allow time for literacy interventions.
• Common planning time for teachers to work on literacy and learning is provided.
• Time for literacy-related professional development is allocated.</td></tr>
<tr><td colspan="2">• Upper Elementary: The fifth-grade teacher uses the school's scheduled, two-hour reading block to build the skills of all of students. Students proficient in reading are in Reciprocal Teaching groups, reading and discussing articles they select from the class article library. Students who need some additional support in reading are working in pairs, reading and practicing summarization with a novel at their independent level that they have selected from the class library. Students who need substantial support and guidance in reading are working with the teacher.</td></tr>
</table>

(Continued)

(Continued)

<table>
<tr><th>Component</th><th>Indicators</th></tr>
<tr><td colspan="2">
<ul>
<li>Middle School: The seventh-grade team has common planning time daily. The team meets weekly during common planning to collaborate with special education teachers and the team-assigned guidance counselor about improving literacy and learning for their students. They discuss students who are not meeting academic expectations and plan adjustments to the academic program to meet their needs. During one meeting, they look at progress monitoring data and decide to investigate the use of new summarizing strategies since students in reading intervention classes have scored lower on this skill.</li>
<li>High School: The high school schedule is designed with literacy in mind. Students who do not meet state reading standards are scheduled into reading intervention classes taught by certified reading teachers. Students who meet state standards but need additional support are scheduled into content area classes taught by teachers who have been trained in the use of literacy support strategies in the content area. All teachers participate in monthly literacy professional development on one of the weekly, built-in early release days reserved for professional development. These professional development days include training in literacy support strategies and departmental discussions of applications of the training in the content areas.</li>
</ul>
</td></tr>
<tr><td>G. Clubs and Activities</td><td>
<ul>
<li>Literacy-related clubs and extracurricular activities are available.</li>
<li>Authentic literacy experiences are available.</li>
</ul>
</td></tr>
<tr><td colspan="2">
<ul>
<li>Upper Elementary: The fifth-grade teacher sponsors a student-written literary e-journal after school. Students write and edit stories, poems, and cartoons, using a variety of technology to produce the e-journal. The e-journal has become so popular that about a third of her class stays after school each Thursday to participate.</li>
<li>Middle School: The school sponsors a Literacy Community Day twice a year. On these days, teachers choose an activity to sponsor and students sign up to participate. Activities include reading to nursing home residents, reading to young children, structured conversations with younger English language learners, writing letters to the editor of a local newspaper, debates with invited community moderators, reading or writing tutoring, recording books for the blind, creating a school literacy wiki or blog, and working with the media specialist to create recommended books for middle school students.</li>
<li>High School: The school provides a full range of literacy-related clubs and activities: debate, drama, newspaper, and yearbook. These clubs and activities attract a large number of students each year with 25 to 30 students in each activity. In addition, the school sponsors a poetry slam each year, which attracts over 50 participants. As part of the reading intervention program, the school has a class in which struggling high school readers are taught to teach reading to elementary students. This class not only addresses the reading skills of both tutors and tutees, but it also gives the high school students life skills and the confidence they need to read successfully in a real world setting.</li>
</ul>
</td></tr>
<tr><td>H. Library Media Center</td><td>
<ul>
<li>Students and teachers consistently use the library media center.</li>
<li>Reading level information is available to teachers.</li>
<li>Certified and qualified personnel staff the media center.</li>
<li>The library media center sponsors literacy activities.</li>
</ul>
</td></tr>
<tr><td colspan="2">
<ul>
<li>Upper Elementary: Fourth-grade teachers take their class to the media center twice weekly so the students can work on the independent research projects they complete every six weeks. The media specialist is a former reading teacher with a strong background in educational technology. Students learn how to find and evaluate the information they need to independently access the text. Students use the computer stations in the media center to find information and to design the multimedia presentations of their work.</li>
</ul>
</td></tr>
</table>

Component	Indicators

- **Middle School:** All of the print material in the media center is leveled, and students understand the leveling system. When students visit the media center, they know which texts they can read at their independent level. This helps students choose books for the silent sustained reading they do daily. Students also get ideas for independent reading from the bulletin boards and featured books center in the media center.
- **High School:** The high school media specialist holds a family book talk at the beginning of the school year. The book talks started with limited success with only 10 parents attending the first session with their children. By the winter holiday, the book talk became an important part of the school's literacy effort. Small groups of parents and students use a discussion protocol to discuss *In the Time of the Butterflies* by Julia Alvarez. Since many in the school community are Dominican, parents have profound insights to share with their children. Students gain a new understanding of their parents as well as the book.

LITERACY ACTION RUBRIC 5: PARENT AND COMMUNITY INVOLVEMENT

Component	Indicators
A. Involvement	• Families actively support the school's focus on literacy development. • Family members and community leaders serve on committees or volunteer and participate in school-based literacy events. • Community members support many students' engagement in literacy-rich experiences in civic, business, and organizational settings.

- **Upper Elementary:** Fourth- and fifth-grade students interview residents of a nursing home asking about their lives as 9 to 11 year olds. They then write poems that they read for their parents at family night. A large group of parents turn out for the poetry reading featuring the intergenerational themes. Refreshments are served by the school literacy parent volunteers.
- **Middle School:** The eighth-grade social studies classes hold an "Abraham Lincoln Celebration Day" after studying famous Americans. Students set up their stations on leadership, his presidency, his role in the Civil War, and his early years. Several parents attend each PowerPoint presentation and ask questions about each stage of Lincoln's life. An introduction to the evening's activities is made by the chair of the Parent Literacy Advocacy Committee that organizes parents to assist with book drives, poetry jams, and work in the community that involves literacy performances.
- **High School:** A career night is held for parents and students; community members present various career opportunities and discuss the literacy demands for preparing for and performing each of these careers. Students and parents ask questions and discuss ways to prepare for these careers. The career night is organized by the Parent Literacy Advocacy Committee and announcements are made for the upcoming essay sharing event and the parent/student community read discussion.

(Continued)

(Continued)

Component	Indicators
B. **Communication**	• The school communicates with all stakeholders about literacy activities. • Communication with non-English speaking family members includes multiple forms of native language outreach about literacy activities.
• **Upper Elementary:** The school's Web site features the fifth-grade biographies of local community members each month. After reading several biographies, students discuss the components of a powerful biography. They then interview several community leaders and write a biography of each which they published in both Hmong and English. A feature of the Web site is a video of the community member and a place to post questions to be answered by students. • **Middle School:** The school's telephone message system provides information in three languages represented in the school. The Web site and parent newsletters featuring literacy activities are available in each language as well. The local newspaper has a column written by a middle school student describing a literacy activity each month. • **High School:** The journalism class maintains the "From the Student Perspective" column in the local newspaper that features Op Ed (Opinion Editorial) pieces by students. These articles are reproduced in newsletters for parents and on the Web site and translated into several languages. A discussion forum featuring these articles is held four times a year, and translators are available for non-native English speakers.	
C. Collaborative Support	• Most families discuss their child's progress as a reader and writer with teachers. • All families are provided with assistance to help their child improve as readers and writers. • All students communicate with parents and teachers about their progress as readers and writers.
• **Upper Elementary:** When parents come to talk to teachers about their child's progress, they review test scores. Resources available within the school district are discussed if additional literacy development is necessary. Students give their parents a presentation of their literacy development over the year using several sample assignments as examples. • **Middle School:** Students typically lead the parent conferences that feature the Literacy and Learning ePortfolio they compile for the end of year conference. Students describe any special assistance they receive in reading and writing development and parents have an opportunity to discuss their child's progress as readers and writers and any assistance they may wish to receive. • **High School:** All students reflect on their literacy development by reviewing test scores, reading and writing assignments, and teacher feedback. They write a reflective paper on their growth as readers and writers along with implications for their career goals. Students present their reflections to their parents at a midterm parent-student-teacher conference. If additional support is required, options are discussed.	

LITERACY ACTION RUBRIC 6: DISTRICT SUPPORT OF SCHOOL-BASED LITERACY IMPROVEMENT EFFORTS

<table>
<tr><th>Component</th><th>Indicators</th></tr>
<tr><td>A. Literacy as a Priority</td><td>• The district promotes the importance of student literacy improvement.
• A district literacy plan is published, implemented, regularly reviewed.
• A district literacy team meets quarterly to review and monitor progress toward literacy improvement goals.
• A district-level administrator is responsible for implementation of the district literacy action plan.
• Hiring preference is given to administrators and content area teachers with a strong literacy background.</td></tr>
<tr><td colspan="2">• The district forms literacy teams in each of the schools in the district and begins the discussion of how to improve literacy in elementary, middle, and high schools. Two representatives from each school join a districtwide literacy team. In addition, two parents and community members are added to the team as well as two student representatives. The district office is represented by the district's special education coordinator. The K–12 Director of Language and Literacy convenes this team and runs the meetings. This team is responsible for the following:
o Reviewing data for all students and tracking growth of student groups
o Coordinating and reviewing literacy interventions across all schools
o Identifying common elements in the school-based literacy action plans and discusses ways that support the professional development and resources needs of schools
o Developing and updating a districtwide literacy action plan that aligns with each school's literacy action plan, the district curriculum standards, and the district's strategic plan
o Promoting a focus on literacy throughout the district and the community
• The personnel department of the district actively seeks new hires at both the district and school levels with a strong commitment to and experience in literacy. They work closely with the local university to identify students who excel in the courses that teach students how to support literacy.</td></tr>
<tr><td>B. Professional Development</td><td>• The district provides ongoing literacy leadership professional development for school administrators, literacy coaches, and teacher leaders.
• The district provides ongoing literacy professional development and expects that all content area teachers will participate.
• The district provides ongoing literacy training and professional development for intervention, special education, and teachers of English language learners.
• The district provides new teachers with sufficient support and mentoring to integrate literacy with content learning.</td></tr>
</table>

(Continued)

(Continued)

<table>
<tr><th>Component</th><th>Indicators</th></tr>
<tr><td colspan="2">

- The district invests heavily in professional development for school and district administrators to improve their ability to function as instructional leaders. Improving student achievement is seen as their primary responsibility. Administrators, literacy coaches, and teacher leaders attend literacy conferences and report back what they learned and what they recommend to others.
- Administrators participate in literacy professional development and extend the discussions by departments and team back at the school site. These professional development opportunities occur regularly as the content teachers adopt new literacy support strategies and deepen their literacy understanding and work with students.
- Teachers who work with literacy interventions programs, special education, and ELL teachers receive specific professional development on how to implement the programs with fidelity, how to integrate technology into the instructional program, and how to meet the needs of students who struggle with reading and writing.
- When new teachers are hired, they are assigned mentors who work with them to integrate literacy support into their content area teaching and make sure they have the appropriate books to read on literacy across the content areas. The literacy coach spends a lot of time in their classroom helping them understand how to support literacy.

</td></tr>
<tr><td>C. Fiscal Support</td><td>

- The district allocates sufficient funds for personnel related to literacy.
- The district allocates sufficient funds for resources to support literacy improvement. The district regularly seeks and obtains additional grant and foundation monies to support literacy improvement.

</td></tr>
<tr><td colspan="2">

- Tough decisions are made with dwindling resources within the district. Since literacy development and improvement is a primary focus in the district, the superintendent meets with the district literacy team to discuss the nonnegotiables for keeping the literacy improvement efforts alive and moving forward. The committee suggests that the personnel charged with coordinating literacy must be protected from budget cuts. The literacy coaches discuss ways to build capacity within their schools to spread the coaching model.
- Reading specialists assess the resources needed for the new literacy intervention programs. They conclude that site licenses for technology literacy support are essential. They agree as a team to review print resources to maximize use across the schools. A subcommittee of the district literacy team investigates grant funding opportunities to provide needed professional development in the district as well as the purchase of additional materials to supplement the classroom libraries with leveled books in the content areas.

</td></tr>
<tr><td>D. Policy and Procedures</td><td>

- The district requires schools to select and use literacy support strategies with students.
- The district requires schools to develop school-based scheduling that ensures that all students have access to rigorous course content and strong literacy support.
- The district expects all school administrators to function as strong literacy leaders.
- Teacher evaluation processes include the expectation that all teachers consistently integrate literacy support into content area instruction.
- The district works with parents and community members as close partners in the literacy improvement effort.

</td></tr>
</table>

<table>
<tr><th>Component</th><th>Indicators</th></tr>
<tr><td colspan="2">
<ul>
<li>The district literacy team begins planning professional development and monitoring and accountability measures for each school. Teachers are expected to participate in professional development and implement literacy support within each content area. A sequence of literacy support is developed within each content area (building complexity and demands of lab reports in science, increasing rigor of persuasive essays in English/language arts). Teachers throughout the district participate in discussions and give feedback on the curriculum alignment of literacy habits and skills within each content area. Administrators, literacy coaches, and teachers hold lively discussions about what literacy support looks like in each content area.</li>
<li>Administrators receive professional development in the use of literacy-focused walk-throughs and classroom observation forms so they can monitor the implementation of literacy support throughout the school. A teacher evaluation protocol is created in collaboration with central administration, teachers, and administrators that includes providing literacy support during content teaching. During the summer, administrators and literacy coaches work closely to examine the data on reading and writing achievement and determine the needs of specific students.</li>
<li>The superintendent and designated others in the district office regularly meet with parents and community leaders to involve them in the literacy initiative. Parent liaisons are assigned to each school so that they can help to advertise and support each school's literacy activities.</li>
</ul>
</td></tr>
<tr><td>E. Data Use</td><td>
<ul>
<li>The district requires that schools administer reading and writing assessments each year in addition to state testing.</li>
<li>The district provides quality data to schools in a timely manner.</li>
<li>The district expects data use to drive decision making about placement and classroom instruction.</li>
<li>The district analyzes and uses data to make decisions about program effectiveness and resource allocation to support student growth as readers and writers.</li>
</ul>
</td></tr>
<tr><td colspan="2">
<ul>
<li>The district purchases a districtwide electronic reading assessment to supplement the state-mandated reading and writing tests. The district assessment is administered twice a year for students on grade level and three times a year for students performing two or more years below grade level. Teachers and administrators receive student results in a user-friendly format that provides information for program and intervention planning.</li>
<li>The district maintains an office of research and accountability that oversees data collection and dissemination to schools. Office staff provide consulting services to school intervention specialists so that programming decisions are aligned with data analysis.</li>
<li>The district provides funds for a data specialist at each school who is responsible for maintaining student records and providing teachers with current student information. The data specialist meets regularly with the assistant principal for curriculum and instruction to troubleshoot problems when data are needed and are not available.</li>
</ul>
</td></tr>
</table>

Resource D

Riverton High School Case Study[1]

Amid consternation and some resistance, the newly formed literacy team at Riverton High School decided to launch a full-scale effort to improve literacy among students. They analyzed data, examined student work, determined students' needs, set professional development agendas, and supported teachers as they tried out new ways of teaching and learning. With guidance from a districtwide literacy initiative, the literacy team conducted weekly professional development sessions with Riverton faculty.

During the first two years, teachers in all content areas gradually began to see the benefit of using strategies such as graphic organizers, KWL (What do I KNOW? What do I WANT to know? What did I LEARN?), and Cornell Note-Taking System in their instruction. Administrators and department chairs responsible for coaching and mentoring teachers attended the professional development sessions and, as the principal Ann Russell said, "We knew what to look for when we observed in classrooms that week because we all heard the same thing during our Monday session." The reading specialist, department chairs, and literacy team members supported teachers in implementing the strategies. Roger, a math teacher and literacy team member, reflected on the progress by saying that teachers moved from a "TTSP (this too shall pass)" attitude to a "This is the way we do things around here" attitude.

After four years of weekly professional development and a slow but steady improvement in test scores, the literacy team decided to concentrate on the Question-Answer-Relationship (QAR) strategy. Teachers across the content areas taught students to use their knowledge of a subject along with information from the text to answer questions. Peter, a science teacher, took QAR to the next level in his classroom and created Science Newsmagazine Assignment Paper (SNAP) to assist students in reading current news magazines on science topics and to urge students to read increasingly complex texts. He reported, "Students are enjoying texts (such as *Scientific American*) that they never thought they could read or would want to read." The Literacy Team felt that the schoolwide implementation of QAR and four years of focusing on literacy and learning was central to the consistent gains in reading scores.

Since the beginning of the focus on literacy at Riverton High, Ms. Russell has hired 130 new teachers. She has worked diligently to make certain that new teachers experience a solid support network at the school. Currently, Ms. Russell, her administrative team, the reading specialist, department heads, and literacy team members have been vigilant about ensuring that literacy is incorporated in every class and that they maintain a strong support network for Riverton's teachers. Ms. Russell stated, "It has taken a long time for literacy to be part of our culture, but it has paid off."

RIVERTON HIGH SCHOOL'S LITERACY IMPROVEMENT EFFORT

Similar to other high schools in the district, Riverton serves a large, diverse population of Hispanic, African American, Asian, and white students. Of these, almost 90% of the students are low income and 9% of students are English language learners. From the beginning, Ms. Russell saw the district's literacy initiative as an opportunity for something meaningful to teachers and students and not just a "one-shot thing." She sought to make "the district literacy initiative our own." For Ms. Russell and the literacy team, the successful whole-school focus on literacy has rested on several different but related steps. To begin with, it was imperative that teachers be involved in the design and implementation of the model. In the five years of the initiative, the reading task force at Riverton grew to include fourteen teachers. Of these, two teachers had participated for the full five years. At the end of the five years, 20% of the faculty had participated for at least one year on the literacy team. To support teachers in their work, the school administrators were educated about literacy in the different content areas so that they could work along with teachers in integrating literacy throughout the curriculum.

As a school with a history of well-respected magnet programs, Ms. Russell and the literacy team sought to preserve the integrity of programs and subject matter identities while integrating the focus on literacy. They viewed both as crucial to motivating teachers and students. They did not see the literacy initiative as superseding or replacing the existing curriculum but rather as strategies teachers could use to enhance their content area instruction. Ms. Russell and the literacy team also structured professional development so that all teachers could participate in the literacy initiative, either in the design stage or as a participant.

After three years, to avoid complacency, the literacy team embarked on a self-analysis of the status of literacy learning at Riverton High School. They used a self-analysis process to re-evaluate and redesign their literacy action plan. Through reflection and analysis, they set new goals for literacy, solicited feedback from department chairs, and shared the plan with colleagues. With the initial guidance of district literacy initiative and support by their principal, this group of educators changed the culture at Riverton High School to one that focused on literacy.

Understanding Stages of Teaming

Before Ms. Russell embarked on the literacy initiative, she learned about the various stages of teaming and how those stages affect teaming outcomes. She used Bruce Tuckman's *Team Development Model*[2] as a framework that provides valuable insights about the various stages in the literacy teaming process. These stages shed light on what team members will experience during the teaming process over time. As she began to understand the dynamics of teaming, she was able to provide support when the team was dysfunctional and even combative. In the following pages, we explain the five stages: Forming, Storming, Norming, Performing, and Adjourning, and relate the stages to the work of the literacy team.

The Forming Stage

The initial stage is the forming stage, which involves the search for team members and the organization of the team. The leadership of the team is usually offered to a teacher or administrator other than the principal. This individual should have a reading background and experience and be viewed by colleagues with respect. Since the forming stage consists of high dependence on the leader, this person should be someone who willingly accepts the task, and who has some input into the selection of team members and materials. The forming stage is in the hands of the team leader who directs the process, brings in materials, helps to establish team roles, and seeks to gather input from team members who at this stage are cooperative, albeit somewhat apprehensive and uncertain about what lies ahead. Team members may be unclear about their roles and will often have lots of questions about the team's purpose, objectives, individual roles and responsibilities. This stage may last for as little as one semester and for as long as an entire school year. We have found that this stage can be effectively traversed when team members participate in a summer literacy institute that focuses on literacy knowledge building and teamwork preparation.

The Riverton High School Literacy Team was formed in the spring by the principal who chose the reading coordinator as team leader. Other team members represented the departments of English/language arts, science, social studies, and math. Team members attended a two-week literacy summer inservice sponsored by the district to build foundational knowledge about literacy and to begin the work of designing a literacy plan. The team also made plans for providing departmental colleagues with information and strategies for integrating literacy into their content areas. Everyone was cooperative, though a bit nervous, and wondered just how he or she was going to pursue this new responsibility.

The Storming Stage

The storming stage can catch team members and the leader by surprise and create a great deal of anxiety unless they are aware that this is part of the team-development process. It is an unsettling phase during which questions arise, disagreements occur, members may opt out, and leadership is challenged. Some common problems for the literacy team may center on meeting times and dates, materials, inservice topics, and personality differences. Rough as this stage may be, it is necessary to allow members to take on stronger and more decisive roles and the team leader to address the challenges that arise and adjust management style to weather out the storm. Compromise appears to be the key during this phase. It is at this juncture that the leadership role shifts from that of director to that of coach and counselor. It is vital during the storming phase that the team remains focused on their mission as literacy planners.

The storming stage has the potential to repeat itself whenever a new member is added to the team. Unpleasant as this phase might be, the problem-solving process ensures that the team will emerge as a stronger unit, capable of working collaboratively on literacy plan design.

The pace of the Riverton Literacy Team that first year was hectic. By late October dissention began to erupt. Meeting time was the contentious issue. One teacher led the opposition to morning meetings and went from member to member collecting support for afternoon meetings. The leader was the last to hear about this discussion. By the time the leader got the news, the principal also had the news that all was not well with the team. The disgruntled teacher threatened to resign from the team. The leader also thought about leaving the team. Before the problem could be resolved, it had to be aired openly at a team meeting and all parties had to reach consensus. The team concluded that meetings were best held in the morning as some members had to pick up young children so late day meetings were also a problem. Team member also agreed that issues needed to be discussed at meetings rather than outside of the meeting room. In retrospect, members agreed that if they had known about and anticipated this state, they may have avoided the level of frustration that almost paralyzed the team.

A second big "storm" occurred three years later with the addition of a dynamic teacher who wanted to be a member of the team. There was dissention on the team about whether or not to enlist this volunteer. The leader thought it was a mistake to discourage someone's interest. The problems intensified as the new member broadcast that the reason for joining was to "shake things up." This person did so by building support among the newest team members. The veterans were annoyed and came to the leader with reports about who said what to whom and about whom when. The result was a head-to-head meeting between the leader and the new teacher. The leader gave an ultimatum that the teacher either support and respect the team or leave it. The tempest broke as the new member apologized and went on to become a hard-working, cooperative member of the group.

The Norming Stage

The norming stage can be called "the calm after the storm." Team roles have been clarified and responsibilities are accepted. Team members now assume a share in decision-making. Big decisions are made through consensus while smaller decisions may be delegated to individuals or small teams within the larger group. Discussion at meetings flows freely. The team has fun and even enjoys some degree of socializing. The leader has earned more respect, even as team members have begun to share leadership duties. As team members become confident in their roles, the leader relies on them and enables them to participate more fully in all aspects of the team. Literacy team members grow in esteem as their roles strengthen. The leader serves as facilitator, having evolved from both director and coach. Team commitment and unity are evident. When disagreements occur, they can be resolved by collaboration and attention to structures and process needed to accommodate a resolution of differences.

During the fall, the team began working together in a much more collaborative way. Members themselves set up a team pact for behavior guidelines. Although disagreements arose from time to time, team members were able to asses the source and amicably resolve the differences. It was not uncommon to hear supportive comments at meetings such as "Good idea" and "You are so great when it comes to. . . ."

It was during the norming phase that the Riverton Literacy Team first learned about the Tuckman model. A district supervisor presented the model before the holidays and team spirits were significantly buoyed by the news that the storming stage was normal. The team was asked to place themselves in one of the four stages. Three chose the norming stage and two selected the performing stage. Although team members didn't agree, they all knew that the storming phase was over. This was truly a turning point in cooperation and enthusiasm.

The Performing Stage

The performing phase is the phase during which team members can be relied upon to perform their tasks with or without leadership. Team members fill in for one another in absences and/or emergencies. There is mutual respect for one another's work and ideas. When problems arise or disagreements occur, team members work them out among themselves. The team becomes a high performing unit that takes pride in their successes and develops troubleshooting strategies to deal with negative issues. Trust is built to the level that team members share problems they are having with instruction or communication with departmental members and the team offers suggestions to solve the issues. A high level of camaraderie exists. The team members are concerned for one another as they develop pride in their work. The team expects the leader to bring in new ideas and projects for them to discuss, but they no longer need instruction and assistance. They are now self-motivated enough to seek out information on their own. The leader now delegates and oversees the team. This phase represents a fully functioning team in which members experience a great deal of professional satisfaction that extends to their performance in the classroom. Frequently, their enthusiasm is evidenced by increased involvement in professional organizations and inservice presentations at workshops around the community or even the country.

The Riverton Literacy Team evolved into an admirable partnership. The team applied for inservice provider status during the following year and were able to grant recertification credits to teachers who attend their workshops. The team expanded to include several members of the core departments, a counselor, a media specialist, and special education teachers. The goal was to have a representative from each department. Many members of the team joined professional organizations including the International Reading Association (IRA). As IRA members, they wrote proposals and presented workshops at annual conventions.

The Adjourning Stage

The adjourning stage entails the termination of roles, the completion of tasks, and the reduction of dependency. This stage occurs naturally when team members decide to leave the team for a variety of reasons. They may retire, relocate, or accept a new position. This stage has been described as mourning, given the loss that is often felt by team members. This stage can produce stress, especially when the team breakup is unplanned.

In this stage, the culture and climate of the team undergo shifts in relationships and responsibilities that can either enhance or inhibit the teaming process. On the positive side, team members who move on to accept positions of leadership as department chairpersons or part of the administrative team will take their experience with literacy strategies and teamwork and use it in their areas of greater influence. In this case, their literacy team experience was time well spent. On the other hand, those remaining on the team will want to welcome new members and prepare once again to go through Tuckman's "Forming, Storming, Norming, and Performing" stages until they reach the level of confidence and proficiency of a high performing staff development team. The cycle can be both continuous and rewarding when the Tuckman stages are accommodated.

The Riverton Literacy Team experiences adjournment in some form each year. The first year the math teacher moved to another state and the social studies, teacher decided to leave the team. The second year, the team held constant with replacements for the two vacancies and a volunteer from world languages. The third year, the math teacher had to be talked into staying. The fourth year the science teacher left to become department chairperson, the social studies teacher left for graduate school, and the world languages teacher and the special education teacher both retired. The fifth year, the team grew in size to fourteen members, which was good because at the end of the year, the leader retired, the math teacher made good the vow to leave the team, one of the English teachers left to become the department chairperson, and a science teacher left to chair the assessment team. The literacy team itself, however, has not adjourned. It continues with a new leader and some new, enthusiastic members to once again evolve into a high performance team of staff developers.

NOTES

1. Although Riverton is a fictitious name, this vignette is based on the real story of a high school in an urban Midwestern city. We thank Dr. Stacey Rutledge at Florida State University for assistance with this case study.
2. Tuckman, B. (1965). Developmental sequence in small groups. *Psychological Bulletin, 63*, 384–399.

Resource E

Matrix of Resources Available in Taking Action on Adolescent Literacy *and* Meeting the Challenge of Adolescent Literacy

Taking the Lead on Adolescent Literacy is the third book produced with support of the Carnegie Corporation of New York. In *Taking Action on Adolescent Literacy*, we describe each component of the *Taking Action Literacy Leadership Model*. In *Meeting the Challenge of Adolescent Literacy*, we discuss and suggest solutions to 16 critical issues facing educators as they seek to improve adolescent literacy. In the following matrix, we suggest related resources that are available in the two previous books that may be helpful as you work through the five-stage literacy leadership process.

Taking the Lead on Adolescent Literacy		
Stage 1: Get Ready		
***Taking the Lead on Adolescent Literacy*—Action Steps**	***Taking Action on Adolescent Literacy*—Related Resources**	***Meeting the Challenge of Adolescent Literacy*—Related Resources**
Step 1: Build an Effective Literacy Leadership Team	• Figure 5.4: Action Plan Goals for Building Leadership Capacity (p. 124) • Figure 8.2: Key Roles for the Literacy Team (p. 185)	• Establishing a Literacy Leadership Team (pp. 120–121) • Table 8: Issues to Discuss at the Beginning of a Literacy Improvement Effort (p. 121) • Tool 22: Teacher Literacy Leader Selection Tool (pp. 210–211)
Step 2: Create a Vision of a Literacy-Rich School	• Creating a Vision (pp. 10–16)	• A Cohesive School Vision and Literacy-Rich School Environment (pp. 55–56) • Discussing a Common Vision (p. 120)

Taking the Lead Action Steps	Taking Action on Adolescent Literacy Resources	Meeting the Challenge of Adolescent Literacy Resources
Step 3: Use Data to Establish the Need for Literacy Improvement	• Figure 3.1: Prototypes of Struggling Readers and Writers (pp. 81–82) • Figure 5.7: Four Steps for Conducting a Literacy Needs Assessment (p. 132) • Figure 7.2: Seven Data Sources about Students Reading & Writing Performance (pp. 167–169) • Appendix C: Literacy Assessment Review Tool (pp. 241–243)	• Tool 3: Guide for Using Standardized Test Data for Placement Decisions (p.38.) • Tool 5: Critical Questions to Answer when Students Do Not Read or Write on Grade Level (p. 186) • Tool 7: Data Analysis Tool (p.189) • Tool 18: Types of English Language Learners in Your School (p. 205)
	Stage 2: Assess	
Step 1: Identify School Strengths	• Creating a Vision (pp. 10–16))	
Step 2: Summarize Key Messages from Your School Data	• Figure 5.6: Additional Key Data for Developing Literacy Action Plans (p. 129) • Figure 7.2: Seven Data Sources about Students Reading & Writing Performance (pp. 167–169) • Figure 7.3: How Various Forms of Data can Inform Instruction (p. 172) • Figure 7.5: How to Use Data to Improve Literacy and Learning (p. 175)	• Tool 7: Data Analysis Tool (p. 189) • Tool 8: Contributing Factors Assessment Tool (p. 190)
Step 3: Assess Current School Implementation Using the Literacy Action Rubrics	• Figure 5.7: Four Steps for Conducting a Literacy Needs Assessment (p. 132) • Figure 5.8: How School Capacity Can Support Literacy Improvement (p. 135) • Understanding Current Teaching Practices that Support Literacy (pp. 135–137)	• Tool 11: Observations of Literacy Support in the Classroom (pp. 194–195) • Tool 12: Writing Next Dialogue Tool (p. 196)
Step 4: Draft Literacy Action Goals	• Figure 5.1: Action Plan Goals for Literacy Development Across Content Areas (p. 120) • Figure 5.2: Action Plan Goals that Target Struggling Readers and Writers (p. 121) • Figure 5.3: Action Plan Goals for School Policies, Structure, and Culture (pp. 122–123) • Figure 5.5: Action Plan for Supporting Teachers to Improve Instruction (pp. 125–126)	• Tool 6: Common Reading Comprehension Strategy Selection Tool (pp. 187–188)

(Continued)

(Continued)

Taking the Lead Action Steps	Taking Action on Adolescent Literacy Resources	Meeting the Challenge of Adolescent Literacy Resources
Stage 3: Plan		
Step 1: Develop an Implementation Map for Each Literacy Action Goal	• Figure 5.1: Action Plan Goals for Literacy Development Across Content Areas (p. 120) • Figure 5.2: Action Plan Goals that Target Struggling Readers and Writers (p. 121)	• Tool 20: Content Teacher Literacy Implementation Rubric (pp. 207–208) • Possible Actions for Literacy Leaders at the end of each chapter
Step 2: Solicit Feedback From the School Community	• Figure 8.4: Key Roles for Curriculum Coordinators (p. 190) • Figure 8.5: Key Roles for Reading Specialists (p. 191) • Figure 8.6: Key Roles for Library /Media Specialists (p. 192) • Figure 8.7: Key Roles for English as a Second Language/Special Education Teachers (p. 192) • Figure 8.8: Key Roles for Department Chairs or Team Leaders (p. 193)	• Tool 26: Parent-School Interaction Assessment Tool (p. 216). • Possible Actions for Literacy Leaders (pp.156–157)
Step 3: Revise Literacy Action Goal Statements and Implementation Maps	• Figure 5.1: Action Plan Goals for Literacy Development Across Content Areas (p. 120) • Figure 5.2: Action Plan Goals that Target Struggling Readers and Writers (p. 121) • Figure 5.3: Action Plan Goals for School Policies, Structure, and Culture (pp. 122–123)	• Tool 6: Common Reading Comprehension Strategy Selection Tool (pp. 187–188) • Tool 8: Contributing Factors Assessment Tool (p. 190) • Tool 14: Professional Development Needs Assessment (p. 201)
Step 4: Publish the Formal Literacy Action Plan	• Chapter 5: Develop and Implement a Schoolwide Literacy Action Plan (pp. 117–143)	
Stage 4: Implement		
Step 1: Organize for Action	• Figure 6.1: Possible Professional Development Formats (p. 151). • Table 6.2: Suggestions for Supporting New Faculty (p. 156). • Figure 9.2: Formats and Resource Support for Professional Development in Content Area Literacy (p. 212)	• The Importance of Branding (p. 121) • Creating a Buy-In Plan (p. 123) • Table 10: Strategies for Overcoming Common Scheduling Dilemmas (p. 133). • Tool 2: Planning Template for Literacy-Rich Content Area Assignments (pp. 181–182)

Taking the Lead Action Steps	Taking Action on Adolescent Literacy Resources	Meeting the Challenge of Adolescent Literacy Resources
	• Figure 9.3: Approaches to Professional Development for Content Area Literacy Support (p. 213) • Appendix C.1: Teacher Knowledge Inventory (p. 238)	• Tool 23: Literacy Team/Study Group Log (p. 212)
Step 2: Monitor and Troubleshoot Implementation	• Figure 5.9: Inquiry Cycle for Program Monitoring (p. 139) • Figure 5.10: Mistakes in Monitoring Progress and How to Remedy Them (p.141) • Figure 9.1: Addressing Time and Personnel Issues (p. 210) • Figure 9.4: Addressing Issues on Materials and Technology (p. 217) • Appendix C.2: Classroom Observation Guide (pp. 239–240).	• Tool 8: Contributing Factors Assessment Tool (p. 190) • Tool 11: Observations of Literacy Support in the Classroom (pp. 194–195) • Tool 12: Writing Next Dialogue Tool (p. 196) • Tool 13: Content Area Writing Tool (pp. 197–200) • Tool 16: Peer Coach Content Literacy Observation and Reflection Tool (p. 203) • Tool 17: Literacy Mentoring Request and Debriefing Tool (pp. 204) • Tool 19: Observation of Teacher Instruction of English Language Learners in Content Area Classrooms (p. 206) • Tool 20: Content Teacher Literacy Implementation Rubric (pp. 207–208)
Step 3: Monitor Progress toward Goals	• Figure 5.9: Inquiry Cycle for Program Monitoring (p. 139) • Figure 5.10: Mistakes in Monitoring Progress and How to Remedy Them (p. 141)	• Table 2: Examples of Literacy-Rich Content Assignments that Meet Three Criteria (pp. 20–21) • Table 6: Literacy Support in Five Instructional Modes (pp. 81–82) • Tool 2: Planning Template for Literacy-Rich Content Area Assignments (pp. 181–182) • Tool 4: Assignment Discussion Protocol (p. 185) • Tool 8: Contributing Factors Assessment Tool (p. 190) • Tool 15: Literacy Walk-Through Form (p. 202) • Tool 16: Peer Coach Content Literacy Observation and Reflection Tool (p. 203) • Tool 19: Observation of Teacher Instruction of English Language Learners in Content Area Classrooms (p. 206)

(Continued)

(Continued)

Taking the Lead Action Steps	Taking Action on Adolescent Literacy Resources	Meeting the Challenge of Adolescent Literacy Resources
Step 4: Sustain Momentum and Celebrate Accomplishments	• Chapter 4: Sustaining Literacy Development (pp. 97–114)	• Tool 27: Sustainability Assessment (p. 217)
	Stage 5: Sustain	
Step 1: Summarize Progress Toward Goals	• Figure 5.9: Inquiry Cycle for Program Monitoring (p. 139) • Figure 5.10: Mistakes in Monitoring Progress and How to Remedy Them (p.141)	• Table 2: Examples of Literacy-Rich Content Assignments that Meet Three Criteria (pp. 20–21) • Table 6: Literacy Support in Five Instructional Modes (pp. 81–82) • Tool 15: Literacy Walk-Through Form (p. 202) • Tool 16: Peer Coach Content Literacy Observation and Reflection Tool (p. 203)
Step 2: Revise Implementation Maps	• Figure 5.1: Action Plan Goals for Literacy Development Across Content Areas (p. 120) • Figure 5.2: Action Plan Goals that Target Struggling Readers and Writers (p. 121)	• Tool 5: Critical Questions to Answer When Most Students Do Not Read or Write on Grade Level (p. 186)
Step 3: Analyze Success as a Literacy Leadership Team	• Figure 8.1: Questions to Consider for Distributing Leadership for Literacy Improvement (p. 183) • Figure 8.2: Key Roles for the Literacy Team (p. 185)	
Step 4: Plan How to Sustain Momentum	• Figure 4.1: Content of Ongoing and Frequent Communication with Parents (p. 106) • District Support for School-Based Literacy Efforts: pp. 107–113) • Figure 5.8: How School Capacity Can Support Literacy Development (p. 135) • Figure 6.2: Suggestions for Supporting New Faculty (p. 156) • Figure 8.1: Questions to Consider for Distributing Leadership for Literacy Improvement (p. 183) • Figure 8.3: Key Roles for School Administrators (p. 189) • Figure 8.10: Responding to Teachers Who Resist Literacy Improvement Efforts (pp. 196–197)	• Tool 27: Sustainability Assessment (p. 217)

Resource F

Glossary of Terms

Term	Definition
academic literacy	The reading, writing, presentation, and critical thinking skills that students need to be successful in school
academic vocabulary	Words or phrases that are critical to understanding the concepts of content taught in schools
action step	Components of an implementation map that specify the actions that support the attainment of the established literacy action plan goal
aliteracy	The ability to read and write adequately but typically choosing not to read or write
alternative assessment	Assessment of literacy skills through alternative methods, such as systematic review of samples of student work or documented observation of students' reading behaviors
authentic literacy tasks	Literacy tasks that ask students to read and write for reasons that are meaningful to them or are for an audience beyond the teacher
brand statement	A name, logo, or slogan that captures the essence of an activity, product, or initiative
classroom observation	An observation of instruction for the purpose of mentoring or coaching the teacher to improve instruction
coaching	Helping students or teachers complete a difficult task by showing them how to complete it
collaborative routine	A method of instruction and learning in which students interact with each other to complete literacy assignments using a protocol or sequence of steps
column notes	A note-taking strategy that divides a page into columns for students to record and monitor their thinking; students' write main ideas and concepts in the left column and supporting details and information in the right column
common agreements	Instructional agreements among grade level, department, or team members that might include the types and amounts of reading and writing students will complete in each content area; grading policies; the use of common instructional approaches and strategies; and the use of common rubrics for assessment
concept maps	A graphic organizer designed to help visualize the relationship of ideas around a particular concept
content area teachers	Teachers of social studies, math, science, art, music, literature, or other subjects where a body of content is covered

(Continued)

(Continued)

Term	Definition
content area literacy support	The use of strategies, guided practice, and scaffolding of instruction to improve student literacy development while learning a body of content
consensus building	A decision-making process that develops mutually advantageous decisions and approaches that everyone can live with
criterion-referenced assessment	Assessment designed to measure student performance in reference to established performance or content standards related to reading and writing
curriculum alignment	When a district curriculum is aligned to district and/or state standards and benchmarks, and vertically and horizontally articulated across all levels
data overview	A report of established data to guide literacy leadership team decision making during the literacy action planning process
data summary chart	A graphic that summarizes the accomplishments and continued literacy improvement needs based on the data
demonstration classrooms	Classrooms in which teachers and administrators can observe and discuss a particular method of teaching or use of a literacy support strategy
Developmental Reading Inventory	A graded series of passages of increasing difficulty to determine students' strengths, weaknesses, and strategies in word identification and comprehension
diagnostic assessment	Assessment of the literacy skills of students in a variety of areas against a set of criteria in each area to determine the difference between students' demonstration of skills in that area and the expected skills for their grade and/or ability level
differentiated instruction	Teaching students at their own levels of instruction by allowing some students to work on their own and pulling others into a small group for explicit instruction or providing leveled texts for students
discussion protocol	A process through which participants examine an issue in a short article or excerpt from a book and then talk about it together.
distributed leadership	Shared leadership responsibilities based on areas of expertise and knowledge
English language learner (ELL)	Generally, the preferred term in educational literature and school systems for students who are not native speakers of English
English as a second language (ESL)	Usually associated with English language instruction but may be used interchangeably with ELL, as in "ESL student"
English for speakers of other languages (ESOL)	Another term for English language learner, as in "ESOL student"
exemplars	Examples of quality completion of a task
feedback	Comments, questions, or suggestions that teachers provide students to help them improve their work
fidelity of implementation	When programs are implemented as intended

Term	Definition
flexible grouping	A process where teachers make grouping decisions by considering the needs of both individuals and the group (Teachers organize students into various grouping patterns: whole class, large groups, small groups, triads, pairs, and/or students working individually.)
fluency	The ability to read with appropriate speed, expression, and accuracy
focus group	A small group of interacting individuals having some common interest or characteristics, brought together by a moderator, who uses the group and its interaction as a way to gain information about a specific or focused issue
formative assessment	The assessment of literacy skills as a part of instruction so that the results can inform what additional types of instruction—review, reteaching, additional guided practice, enrichment—may be helpful for individual or groups of students
graphic organizer	A graphic representation of concepts or ideas
group consensus chart	A graphic depicting collective understanding of what team members believe to be the current level of literacy support practices
grading practices	Policies and guidelines for assessing the quality of student work
implementation calendar	A list of events throughout the school year to support the school's literacy action plan
implementation map	A set of action steps designed to support progress toward attaining the goal(s) of the literacy action plan
implementation monitoring template	A preexisting form used by literacy leadership teams to monitor the details of implementation and record actions necessary to deepen or sustain the literacy initiative
individual education plans (IEP)	A written document that describes the educational program for a student placed in special education
informal reading inventories	An individually administered assessment designed to help a teacher determine a student's reading instructional needs
intervention courses	Courses or experiences that offer intensive literacy support for students performing below grade level in reading or writing
leveled texts	Texts that are categorized by different levels of reading difficulty
lexile score or framework	A text-leveling approach based on semantic difficulty and syntactic complexity and set on a scale that ranges from 200L for beginning readers to above 1700L for advanced texts
limited English proficient (LEP)	A term used to describe students who have not yet become proficient English speakers, readers, and writers
list-group-label	A learning strategy that combines brainstorming and categorization to help students organize concepts
literacy	The symbolic communication modes of reading, writing, listening, speaking, viewing, and representing one's thinking

(Continued)

(Continued)

Term	Definition
literacy achievement gap	A condition in schools where some groups of students are significantly underperforming compared to other groups of students (e.g., impoverished students, students from specific ethnic groups, boys or girls, non-native English speakers)
literacy action plan	A schoolwide or districtwide plan to improve literacy that includes data-driven goals, action steps, timelines, responsible persons, indicators of effectiveness, and resources needed
literacy coach	An educator who works primarily with other teachers to improve content literacy and learning
literacy interventions	Supplementary programs or courses that address identified or anticipated problems in literacy
literacy kickoff	A presentation or event that raises awareness and builds collective faculty and student buy-in to the literacy initiative
literacy leader	Any educator who assumes a leadership role in a literacy improvement effort such as a literacy coach, state, district, or school administrator, reading specialist, department chair, team leader, or literacy team member
literacy support strategy	An instructional strategy that supports weaker readers, writers, and speakers as they develop the skills and strategies that competent communicators use
literacy team or literacy leadership team	A team that is representative of the school community and works on schoolwide literacy improvement efforts
literacy walk-through	A walk through individual classrooms in a school to collect real-time data to determine the literacy instructional practices being used
literature circles	Small, temporary groups in which students read different books; meet on a regular, predictable schedule; and use written notes to guide their reading and discussion
modeling	Demonstration of how to complete literacy tasks for students or demonstrating a literacy-support strategy for a colleague
peer coaching and/or mentoring	A process during which two teachers attend each other's classes, later discuss what they saw, and help each other solve problems
percentile rank	A score that indicates where a student stands in comparison to others who take the test
performance-based assessment	An assessment based on a specific performance of a student
poetry slam or jam	A competition at which poets read or recite original work (or, more rarely, that of others); these performances are then judged on a numeric scale by previously selected members of an audience
professional development plan	A process for professional improvement that involves self-assessment, outside feedback, and action steps

Term	Definition
professional learning community	A supportive group of educators committed to continuous learning
protocols	Structures for examining educational practice or content learning in a democratic and orderly manner that allow teachers and students to voice their opinions, ideas, and concerns with one another, typically in pairs or small groups
question-answer relationship (QAR)	A learning strategy that helps students understand that the answers they seek are related to the type of question that is asked
quick writes	A three- to five-minute writing strategy that gives students the opportunity to reflect on their learning of a specific topic or issue
reading specialist	Teachers who are certified in reading or literacy and who teach intervention classes or oversee other teachers' work with struggling readers or writers
role, audience, format, topic (RAFT)	A process where students use what they learned from reading to create a product that shows their depth of understanding
reciprocal teaching	A learning routine that involves students in predicting, asking questions, clarifying confusing points, and summarizing
rubric	A scoring tool used to assess levels of performance or implementation based on a range of criteria rather than a single numerical score
scaffolding instruction	Building a support structure for students so that they can tackle increasingly complex tasks
school strengths concept map	A graphic that depicts the strengths of the school
strategic intervention class	A class for students who scored below an acceptable level on standardized reading tests
student performance data	Data that provide information about student academic achievement
summary frames	A series of statements with details omitted that emphasize the important elements within a text pattern; students complete the statement thereby producing a summary
summative assessment	Assessment of the literacy skills of students at a particular point in time, at the end of a unit of study or annually at the same time of year, to determine what reading and writing skills they demonstrate relative to their peers and their own past achievement
sustained silent reading (SSR)	A time set aside during the school day for students to read independently and apply the reading strategies they have learned
team facilitator	The individual who manages team meetings; this responsibility is often rotated among team members

(Continued)

(Continued)

Term	Definition
team leader	The individual responsible for organizing team meetings, communicating with leadership, and troubleshooting problems encountered by the team
team norms	Agreements about how documentation, communication, logistics, and responsibilities will be handled by the literacy leadership team
team teaching	A collaboration of two or more teachers that promotes the healthy exchange of ideas in an instructional setting defined by mutual respect
think alouds	A teaching strategy in which the teacher shares his or her thinking processes out loud so that students can observe the thinking processes of a strong reader or writer
Webquest	An inquiry-oriented activity in which some or all of the information that learners interact with comes from resources on the Internet
writing to learn activities	Short, impromptu or otherwise informal writing tasks that help students think through key concepts or ideas presented in a course;

References

Biancarosa, G. & Snow, C. E. (2004). *Reading next: A vision for action and research in middle and high school literacy*. Washington, D.C.: Alliance for Excellent Education.

Brenner, D., Pearson, P. D., & Rief, L. (2007). Thinking through assessment. In K. Beers, R. E. Probst & L. Rief, *Adolescent literacy: Turning promise into practice* (p. 262). Portsmouth, NH: Heineman.

Carnegie Council on Advancing Adolescent Literacy. (2010). *Time to act: An agenda for advancing adolescent literacy for college and career success*. New York, NY: Carnegie Corporation of New York. Pg: viii.

Fogarty, R., & Pete, B. (2007). *From staff room to classroom*. Thousand Oaks, CA: Corwin.

Irvin, J. L., Meltzer, J., & Dukes, M. S. (2007). *Taking action on adolescent literacy: An implementation guide for school leaders*. Alexandria, VA: Association for Supervision and Curriculum Development.

Irvin, J. L., Meltzer, J., Mickler, M. J., Phillips, M. P., & Dean, N. (2009). *Meeting the challenge of adolescent literacy: Practical ideas for literacy leaders*. Newark, DE: International Reading Association.

National Governor's Association Center for Best Practices. (2009). *Supporting adolescent literacy achievement*. Washington, DC: Author.

Tuckman, B. W. (1965). Developmental sequence in small groups. *Psychological Bulletin, 63*, 384–399.

Wisconsin Department of Public Instruction. (2008). *State superintendent's adolescent literacy plan*. Madison, WI: Author.

Index

The Corwin logo—a raven striding across an open book—represents the union of courage and learning. Corwin is committed to improving education for all learners by publishing books and other professional development resources for those serving the field of PreK–12 education. By providing practical, hands-on materials, Corwin continues to carry out the promise of its motto: **"Helping Educators Do Their Work Better."**

The mission of the International Reading Association is to promote reading by continuously advancing the quality of literacy instruction and research worldwide.